SIR JOHN TEMPLETON

SIR JOHN TEMPLETON

SUPPORTING SCIENTIFIC RESEARCH
FOR SPIRITUAL DISCOVERIES

Revised Edition

Robert L. Herrmann

TEMPLETON FOUNDATION PRESS
PHILADELPHIA AND LONDON

Templeton Foundation Press
Five Radnor Corporate Center, Suite 120
100 Matsonford Road
Radnor, Pennsylvania 19087
www.templetonpress.org

*Templeton Foundation Press helps intellectual leaders and others learn about science
research on aspects of realities, invisible and intangible. Spiritual realities include
unlimited love, accelerating creativity, worship, and the benefits of purpose in persons
and in the cosmos.*

Designed and typeset by Gopa & Ted2, Inc.
Printed by Data Reproductions

Library of Congress Cataloging-in-Publication Data

Herrmann, Robert L., 1928-
Sir John Templeton : supporting scientific research for spiritual discoveries
/ Robert L. Herrmann.— Rev. ed.
p. cm.
Includes bibliographical references and index.
ISBN 1-932031-68-5 (pbk. : alk. paper)
1. Templeton, John, 1912- 2. Capitalists and financiers—United States—
Biography. 3. Philanthropists--United States—Biography. 4. Christian biog-
raphy. 5. Templeton Foundation—History. 6. Humility—Religious
aspects—Christianity. I. Title.
HG172.T45H474 2004
332.6'092—dc22

2004005025

04 05 06 07 08 09 10   10 9 8 7 6 5 4 3 2 1
Printed in the United States of America

Contents

Preface

THIS BOOK CHRONICLES the life of a man of extraordinary vision. John Templeton set the pace on Wall Street with an astounding record of mutual fund achievement, and also startled his contemporaries with his keen insights about market forces and his optimism about the growth of the economy. But John Templeton has made the real goal of his life the elaboration of a new concept of spiritual progress. While recognizing and appreciating the great religious insights of the past, he envisions a new era of spiritual discovery that may rival the astounding physical discoveries of the past few centuries brought to us through science.

It was an honor to be asked to write John's biography, and the revised edition as well. In doing so, I have relied heavily on our twenty-year association. During this time we have written two books together, *The God Who Would Be Known* and *Is God the Only Reality?* and I have assisted him in the editing of a number of others. I was also privileged to be a charter member of the John Templeton Foundation board of trustees, along with Sir John, Lady Irene, their son Jack Templeton, and Scottish theologian Thomas Torrance.

In order to work on these biographies over the past several years, I have been fortunate enough to have had relief from some of my administrative duties with the three major Templeton Foundation projects I directed through Gordon College. Professors Jack Haas and Harold Heie have provided tremendous help with the Science and Religion Course Program and Patsy Ames has been indispensable as managing editor of *Progress in Theology*, the humility theology newsletter I edited for the Foundation for the past several years. I am also grateful for day-to-day support and wisdom provided by my administrative assistants, Rebecca Keefe and Kathleen Scarpa, my secretary Alyson Lindsay Longacre, and for careful and painstaking editorial assistance from Laura Barrett at Templeton Foundation Press. Above all I am grateful to my wife, Betty, whose critique, encouragement, and word-processing skills have made this book a reality.

Robert L. Herrmann

SIR JOHN TEMPLETON

Introduction

S IR JOHN MARKS TEMPLETON celebrated his eightieth birthday with
a great gathering of family and friends on November 29, 1992, at
the Union League of Philadelphia. I was privileged to be there and to give
the invocation, though I am not a "man of the cloth" but only a biochemist
who happens to be a Christian and coauthor with Sir John of two of his
many books. Writing the biography of a man with so many accomplishments is a truly daunting task, and whenever I was tempted to forget how
enormous the assignment, I just thought back to that joyous night in
Philadelphia. The list of attendees would easily pass for a random excerpt
from *Who's Who in America* and *Who's Who in the World*. The variety of accents
emphasized the global nature of Sir John's relationships: Jewel Templeton,
brother Harvey Templeton's effervescent wife with the delightful twang of
the Tennessee mountains; the British Sir Sigmund Sternberg from London;
Irish-born Rev. Wilbert Forker, administrator of the Templeton Prize for
Progress in Religion'; Mena Griffiths, Sir John's private secretary of twenty-
five years in Nassau, Bahamas; and Wyoming State Senator Gail Zimmerman, spouse of daughter Anne Templeton Zimmerman, to name a few.

Now that he's over ninety, it is the considered opinion of many of his
friends that Sir John remains one of the youngest, most forward-thinking,
incisive, and progressive investors of the twentieth century. That may seem
an odd description for a man who left the world of stocks and bonds in 1992,
selling his $25 billion group of Templeton Funds to Franklin Resources,
Inc., but the truth is that Sir John has another investment program under

way, one that he hopes will rival the staggering \$10 billion per week the world now invests in scientific research. It is an investment in the spiritual development of human beings. As Sir John expresses it, "The enormous impact of scientific discovery on our physical lives and on our beginnings of an understanding of our place in the universe can show us how to achieve rapid progress in obtaining spiritual information, including information about the Unlimited Creative Spirit, in which we live and move and have our being." The benefits, he believes, would be staggering. As he said in a lecture at Templeton College, Oxford University, "Unfortunately, too often people focus on the negatives and lose sight of the multitude of blessings that surround us and the limitless potential that exists for the future. The beneficial effects of religion on our attitudes, our motivations, our interactions with people, our goals, and our basic well-being can be of immeasurable value."

Sir John believes the limitless potential of religion needs to be unlocked. The traditional religions have brought us wonderful and powerful insights and a legacy in sacred art and music, but in recent centuries they have produced little that could be called progress in spiritual information. One solution, he believes, lies in the application of the scientific method, so familiar to us in this age, to the cause of progress in religion. The billions spent on medical research — largely concerned with our physical and mental well-being — have brought us many miraculous cures and greatly increased longevity. Deaths from diseases like tuberculosis, typhoid fever, diphtheria, syphilis, pneumonia, polio, and cholera are now only a tiny fraction of what they were fifty years ago. Infant mortality has dropped sharply and longevity has increased greatly. Indeed, it has been estimated that 65 percent of all the people who ever lived beyond age 65 are alive today.

Furthermore, the impact that scientific research has had on our health shows every promise of intensifying. It is estimated that 50 percent of all that is known in medicine has been discovered in just the last fifteen years and 90 percent since 1900.

By contrast, the traditional religions have been largely backward looking, and the newer mystical religious movements of our day are often superstitious and unscientific. What may be needed, John Templeton says, is a new dynamic, empirical, scientific approach to investigation of spiritual phenomena carried out by those trained in the scientific approach and aware of the complexities of scientific interpretation. Furthermore, many of the current discoveries in fields like physics, cosmology, molecular biology, and neural science strongly suggest questions of a philosophical and theological nature, pointing to a great potential in these areas for new spiritual understanding and research. The power of science has been awesome, but even science seems to point beyond itself to a deeper, spiritual meaning.

There is fascination and even a hint of irony in the fact that John Templeton has made progress in religion the great goal of his life. Even though he was raised in a home where religion was taken quite seriously, he often expressed the conviction that his gifts did not lie in the Christian ministry. Instead, because of a habit of thrift and the appreciation of a good investment — strong influences from both his parents — he trained in economics at Yale and law at Oxford and became a part of the then new field of investment counseling. Actually, Sir John chose investing in part with the idea that he might make a financial contribution to progress in Christian ministry. And, indeed, that intention has been realized on the grand scale for the benefit of a large number of church organizations, the most notable being Princeton Theological Seminary, where he served for many years as chairman of the board. As head of the financial committee, he helped double the school's endowment. And John Templeton is now claiming new ground in the field of philanthropy. His approach goes beyond the mere "do-goodism" of ordinary philanthropy to express a deep sense of stewardship, a commitment to use the rewards of his gift as an investor to promote the moral and spiritual progress of mankind. What better *ministry* could one have?

But we might ask if the goal of progress in religion is really attainable. Sir John's answer is to point again at the remarkable progress in so many areas of our lives. At a lecture in Oxford, he said that we live in a period of prosperity never seen before in world history. In America, the gross national product is thirty times what it was just fifty years ago. The average hourly wage of a factory worker has increased in real terms by over 65 percent. Today, America has more than 3.5 million families with assets over $1 million and worldwide there are over four hundred billionaires. He went on to say,

> If you look further back to when Adam Smith wrote his great book called *An Inquiry into the Nature and Causes of the Wealth of Nations*, you will see that 85 percent of the world's population had to work in agriculture just to produce enough food. Today, less than 4 percent work on farms in America and they produce great surpluses. Dire predictions that farming output would be unable to meet the needs of a rapidly expanding population failed to account for the incredible productivity gains that have occurred. In the last thirty years, improvements in crop varieties, pesticides, and fertilizers have helped *triple* agricultural productivity. This has saved the clearing of forests equal in area roughly to the size of North America, the additional acreage that would have been needed for increased food supply. New methods such as high yield and no-till farming hold promise for continued improvements around the world.
>
> Since the time of Adam Smith's writing, the yearly production of goods and services has increased *one hundredfold*. In fact, more than half the goods produced in history have been produced just in the last two hundred years. Before Adam Smith, there were fewer than one thousand corporations on earth. Today, corporations are being created at the rate of *two thousand* every business day in the U.S. Underlying this growth is the increasing acceptance of the importance of free trade and enterprise within and among nations. The trend toward greater free market economics accelerated in the early 1980s as the number of privatizations began to outpace nationalizations. Privatizations of state-owned enterprises around the world have soared from less than *$10 billion* in 1985 to more than *$300 billion* in 1992 as the failures of socialism have grown increasingly obvious and unbearable.

The trend toward greater capitalism unleashes tremendous potential for efficiency gains and greater wealth potential. So does the shift away from regulation and autarchy toward free trade. In real dollar terms, world exports today are more than *eleven times* what they were just forty years ago. Numerous institutions have arisen to protect the principles that have fostered this dramatic growth and to spread the preconditions necessary for ongoing free trade throughout the world. Consider this: Just sixty years ago, there was no General Agreement on Tariffs and Trade, no Organization for Economic Cooperation and Development, no United Nations, no World Bank, no Organization of American States, no International Monetary Fund, no European Economic Community, and no North American Free Trade Agreement.

The new International Monetary Fund revisions also indicate that the world output is in fact growing faster. Standards of living in some of the developing countries are rising 8 percent yearly on average. As income levels rise, so will consumer spending, creating new opportunities not only for local businesses but also for companies in industrialized countries, which will find massive new marketplaces opening up for their products. In India, for example, the middle class is estimated to be equal in size to more than the entire population of the United Kingdom and is growing at a rate of 20 percent a year.

Sir John also reminds us that technologically, we have seen incredible progress. Fiber optics allows for transmission of eight thousand conversations as compared with forty-eight on the old copper wire. In 1940 there were no VCRs, no computers, no photocopiers, no compact discs, no microprocessors, no man-made satellites, no fax machines, no modems, no answering machines, no Internet. More than half the books ever written were written since 1940 and more than twenty-five times as much is now spent on research and development. There are also four times as many scientists and engineers.

More than half the discoveries in natural science have been made since the beginning of the twentieth century. Authors John Naisbitt and Patricia Aburdene, writing in *Megatrends 2000*, told us that the amount of information available is doubling every two-and-a-half years. At that rate, there will be one thousand times as much information available in the next twenty-five years. In 1950, 17 percent of the American population worked in information-related occupations. In 1982 the number had risen to 65 percent. The significance of this continuing information explosion cannot be overemphasized. Sir John says:

> Perhaps the most significant implication this information revolution holds for the future stems from its seemingly infinite nature. Our economic prosperity is no longer primarily a function of *limited natural* resources but is becoming progressively more heavily dependent on the self-perpetuating, *limitless* body of knowledge. This bodes well for a continuation and acceleration of the underlying trend toward prosperity that has blessed mankind in this century. . . . The more we are able to take advantage of the information explosion around us, the more we are able to liberate our minds from routine tasks and cultivate high degrees of analytical thinking, the greater the prosperity with which we will be rewarded.

Momentous developments in the world economy and in technology lead Sir John to the conviction that we may be poised for a similar revolution in spiritual knowledge. Progress in additional new spiritual information is not only possible, but given these examples of advancement in our physical and intellectual lives, progress is the logical development for our spiritual nature as creatures of the Unlimited Creative Spirit.

The main barrier to our full flowering as spiritual beings, Sir John says, is human egotism. It has been our great sin as God's creatures to assume far more knowledge than we actually possess. Indeed, our successes in the worlds of economics and technology can easily give rise to a Promethean attitude, in which we are unteachable and self-satisfied. But the scientific approach, which has made all of this wondrous development possible, has, especially in the past generation, brought us to a place of acute awareness of how infinitesimal we are in the cosmic scheme of things. The end result, John Templeton says, should be a feeling of humility toward the Creator and an eagerness to learn. This awareness, this searching experience directed toward the God of the universe, he has called "humility theology."

So convinced is Sir John of the necessity for this humility toward God that he has built a major focus of his goal of progress in religion around this idea. He also organized what was originally called the Humility Theology Information Center within the Tennessee-based John Templeton Foundation, first organized in 1987, and brought together a distinguished group of scientists and theologians to form an advisory board. It is to this advisory board that Sir John looks for advice and for participation in programs he is developing to promote progress in religion. Descriptions of some of these programs will form some of the later chapters in this book. They include programs to stimulate the teaching of university courses in science and religion, worldwide lecture programs organized around the concept of humility theology, and prizes for articles on humility theology published in science and religion journals. Another exciting initiative involves high school students in Sir John's own Franklin County, Tennessee. Essay contests begun there several years ago offer prizes for essays on a student's own choice of moral or spiritual principles to live by. The Foundation is involved in a large expansion of this program to communities worldwide. Other programs include an in-depth study of spiritual factors in health and a program for medical schools to encourage the teaching of courses integrating medical science and religion.

The forerunner of these many new initiatives by the Foundation was the Templeton Prize for Progress in Religion, a program John Templeton began with his award to Mother Teresa of Calcutta in 1973. The prize has been awarded every year since then, the amount of the prize being always slightly larger than the various Nobel prizes, to signify Sir John's feeling that progress in religion is the most important goal of all.

All of these activities are a great source of personal joy and expectation for

John Templeton. One can sense his excitement and pleasure at meetings of the advisory board. He is clearly quite optimistic about these plans and about this group of advisors and staff members, which is not surprising given that optimism has been a hallmark of John Templeton since early childhood. This attitude developed partly because of a remarkable sense of self-assurance, and partly because of a belief that his mother, as a devoted follower of the Unity School of Christianity, had instilled in him very early in his life. She taught him that God wanted our material prosperity and provided for us an inner strength and wisdom, a kind of divine spark, which would enable us to prosper materially as a natural consequence of intelligent planning and spiritual preparation, especially as we seek to help and love everyone.

John Templeton has followed the principle of opening every board meeting of his Global Fund meetings — as well as any other meetings where he was in charge — with prayer, thanking God for multiple blessings and opportunities. I recall one special occasion, in 1984, when my wife and I attended the dedication of Templeton College in Oxford, England. The audience was a prestigious one, and those on the platform included the minister of education of the United Kingdom and the chancellor of Oxford University — complete with his starched Elizabethan collar — and various other school officials and dignitaries. At the end, Sir John made his address, dedicating the college to the memory of his parents and then concluding with an expression of deep thankfulness to God for the many blessings that had been poured out upon everyone attending, but especially for the blessing of his own parents and his associates in the development of the college. I recall the look of surprise on the faces of many of the academics as God was acknowledged, and I was proud that John had shown appreciation for the true source of Templeton College or any other institution put together with human hands but ultimately an expression of the Creator's love and generosity.

For John Templeton, optimism and gratitude go hand in hand. During an interview on the Canadian television program *Cross Currents*, he said of his philanthropy that he did not inherit his wealth, but that at the time of his marriage to Judith Folk, they began a pattern of saving in which they pledged half of their income to the church and investment. This led to a game of bargain hunting, budget control, and careful investment, which provided the foundation for his wealth. Coupled with this lifestyle of thrift and saving was a desire instilled in him from early childhood to help others, and he suggested that this willingness to be helpful and useful was actually a source of optimism, just as optimism was a basis for being helpful and useful. As he said, "The two go hand in hand." And then he added some thoughts about gratitude:

> Thanksgiving and gratitude will revolutionize your life. If you wake up every day and think of five new things that you are overwhelmingly grateful for, your day will go better, people will like you better, you'll be more successful. Try it! A girl said to me once, "I can't think of anything to *be* grateful for." So I said, "Just stop breathing for three minutes and you'll be very thankful you can breathe again."

Optimism and thankfulness have certainly characterized John Templeton's career, but they have always been accompanied by serious attention to in-depth study and thorough preparation. "Is it cost-effective?" is one of his favorite responses.

As we look to his many new investment programs for the encouragement of spiritual progress, we recall the stupendous results of his careful preparation and persevering optimism in the past. Those of us working with him in these new endeavors are learning the lessons that have been so productive for him throughout the past years. After all, who can question the effectiveness of the Templeton Growth Fund? An investment of $10,000 in the fund in November of 1954 was worth $3 million forty-three years later if dividends were reinvested. And, as Sir John points out, that was a gain in material benefits. Who can estimate the gain on an investment in the largely untapped spiritual potential of mankind? John Templeton believes it could dwarf even that global fund in its fruitfulness.

As a revised edition of *Sir John Templeton: Supporting Scientific Research for Spiritual Discoveries* is published, Sir John has celebrated his ninety-first birthday and is still going strong. He's had a few medical problems to cope with, the most notable being heart-valve surgery, but he still walks on his home veranda overlooking tropical gardens or in shoulder-deep water at the beach at Lyford Cay. And he's still at his desk every day, making the final decisions for the growing Templeton Foundation programs.

Likewise, his writing continues, with some half-dozen new books reflecting even sharper insights and enhanced breadth. His *Possibilities for Over One Hundredfold More Spiritual Information: The Humble Approach in Theology and Science* emphasizes Sir John's commitment to a major scientific effort to obtain solid empirical data about spiritual realities, particularly about, as he says, "those realities, neglected basic invisible realities such as love, purpose, creativity, intellect, thanksgiving, prayer, humility, praise, thrift, compassion, invention, truthfulness, giving, and worship."[2]

His expansive thinking is further reflected in *Wisdom from World Religions: Pathways toward Heaven on Earth*,[3] and in a searching volume *Why Are We Created? Increasing Our Understanding of Humanity's Purpose on Earth*, written with Rebekah Dunlap.[4]

In discussing his view of creativity, however, he is eager to reach beyond the human component and emphasize the much wider dimensions of the divine plan. He points out that thinking about this omniscient Creator raises numerous questions. He asks,

> Is our human consciousness only a tiny manifestation of a vast creative consciousness that is often referred to by a variety of names such as God, Allah, Spirit, Yahweh, Brahman, or the Creator? Has our human concept of this creative source been too small? Is our concept too centered on our human species? What is our relationship with this infinite divinity? Toward what ultimate purpose do we aspire? What evidences indicate that the invisible can be realized through ongoing creativity, change, and innovation? How can we learn to encourage progress and discovery in ways that tap the deep symphonies of divine creativity and involve us in God's purposes?

Perhaps future generations will use scientific methods to speed up the search. It seems the quest to find more answers to such unlimited questions may be rooted in the very deepest parts of the human soul.

Again, he asks, "What might we learn if we applied the same intensity of research energy to the pursuit of spiritual information that has been devoted to scientific inquiry? The world is presently in a state of unprecedented technical expertise, yet our knowledge of the vast spiritual realities has not progressed at the same pace." Sir John has pointed out that remarkable signals of transcendence have been placed in the heavens, on earth, and within ourselves. These signals, including sacred teachings from different world religions and scientific exploration from the study of the cosmos to the evolution of humans, all provide varieties of evidences of infinite divinity. He asks,

> Is it now time to channel our creative restlessness toward reaching into a grand cosmic design, recognizing that we are but tiny parts of divinity? Does this same universal design expand human imagination and invite our diligence to align with infinite creative intention? Is it now time to explore avenues for greater understanding of the question: Why are we created?

To pursue this last question, Sir John explores the impact of the spirit in our lives:

> What is the importance of recognizing that we may be tiny parts of creativity vastly beyond what humans can comprehend? Perhaps an effective starting point for our spiritual research would be a realization that the universe, and our participation in it, seems to be much more than a haphazard occurrence. Infinite invisible intelligence may be reflected by everything in the universe. Much evidence for deep meaning seems to be written into the laws and processes of nature. Could any activity be more relevant to our

lives than to research how we can help in the process of unlimited creativity? To regard with respect or reverence the divinity of the great mysteries that seem to be present everywhere?

Sir John hopes that these profound questions may find expression in the many new and expanding programs of the Templeton Foundation.

PART I

The Benefits of Investing
in Humility Theology Science

CHAPTER 1

An Investment in Scientific Research for More Spiritual Knowledge

I N THE VIEW of John Templeton, progress in spiritual information is not only possible, but may be a consequence of God's creative role in our evolutionary history. Ours is a fascinating pilgrimage, starting slowly with crude awakenings in our early ancestors, who sometimes buried their dead with food and implements for a next world, followed by the flourishing of druids and Mayans and Egyptians, who left to their gods their curious monuments and exquisite pyramids, then on to the great mystics of India and the Middle East who left us the Vedas, the Holy Bible, and the Qur'an as well as majestic cathedrals and temples. And now, it would seem that our fascination with the meaning of our existence is growing deeper and more powerful — a perhaps surprising phenomenon in a scientific age where some thought science would have explained away religion.

The prior periods of human evolutionary history emphasized our physical and intellectual development; brain size more than doubled in contrast to earlier species and we learned to walk upright and use our hands skillfully. The exquisitely painted caves of Europe are evidence of just how skilled our ancestors were! And the current rate of acceleration of our intellectual development is phenomenal. Technologically, as Sir John told us in his 1995 Templeton College lecture, our progress is astounding. In the past fifty years we have written as many books as were written in all of previous human history, and over half of the discoveries in the sciences have been made since 1900.

Sir John sees our rate of spiritual development as only now beginning to accelerate, just as there were periods of gradual growth followed by rapid physical and intellectual development over the course of our history as a species. However, the rapid changes currently occurring in the intellectual phase, especially in the sciences, have introduced for Sir John a radically new vision of our place in the cosmos and set the stage for a giant leap forward in our spiritual understanding, a second Renaissance.

Many of these recent discoveries in fields such as physics, cosmology, neural science, and evolutionary biology have been so mind-boggling that they have changed the very way we think of ourselves and of our place in the universe. Certainly they have brought many of the practitioners — the scientists themselves — to a state of wonderment and humility, and provoked their serious consideration of philosophical and theological questions.

In an earlier book, *The God Who Would Be Known*, Sir John and I talked about the spirituality of humankind.

> Humanity's fascination with a spiritual dimension, a hidden sphere of power, an underlying ordering principle that lies unseen behind everyday events as well as gigantic happenings, has grown and taken on new importance in the ensuing centuries. Science has given us knowledge of the fundamental structure of matter in terms of a plethora of subatomic particles, and knowledge of processes of biology in terms of molecular mechanisms. But each new explanation seems to open up deeper questions, as though we still see only the outline of things and explain our observations by means of models that only approximate the truth. Indeed, many in science now see the limitations of scientific description and do not presume that scientific descriptions are ultimate truth. For some there is the added conviction that the Creator is revealing himself through science, so that the results of science serve as signs pointing to a larger Reality.[1]

Among the scientific discoveries displaying this philosophic, searching character we would include the current evidence for the big bang, a gigantic explosion which appears to have generated our cosmos as well as both time and space some 15 billion years ago. The products of this grand synthesis, star systems of enormous proportions, number in the hundreds of billions. The numbers are so large that there is no simple analogy to help our minds take it in. Someone has said that the number of stars is roughly equivalent to all the grains of sand on all the beaches in the world! Timothy Ferris has addressed the question of size in his book, *Coming of Age in the Milky Way*. He says:

> And yet the more we know about the universe, the more we come to see how little we know. When the cosmos was thought to be but a tidy garden, with the sky its ceiling and the earth its floor and its history coextensive with that of the human family tree, it was still possible to imagine that we might one day comprehend it in both plan and detail. That illusion can no longer be sustained. We might eventually obtain some sort of bedrock understanding of cosmic structure, but we will never understand the universe in detail; it is just too big and varied for that. If we possessed an atlas of our galaxy that devoted but a single page to each star system in the Milky Way (so that the Sun and all its planets were crammed on one page), that atlas would run to more than ten million volumes of ten thousand pages each. It would take a library the size of Harvard's to house the atlas, and merely to flip through it, at the rate of a page per second, would require over ten thousand years. Add the details of planetary cartography, potential extraterrestrial biology, the subtleties of scientific principles involved, and the historical dimensions of change, and it becomes clear that we are never going to learn more than a tiny fraction of the story of our galaxy alone — and there are a hundred billion more galaxies. As the physician Lewis Thomas writes, "The greatest of all the accomplishments of twentieth-century science has been the discovery of human ignorance."[2]

This humbling realization is only one of the most recent occurrences. If we move from astronomy to physics, we are confronted with such things as the strange behavior of the elementary particles of matter, which sometimes display the character of particles and sometimes behave instead like waves. Then, too, there appears to be a built-in limitation in the accuracy of our observation of these elementary particles, a phenomenon Werner Heisenberg called the uncertainty principle. The upshot of this measurement limitation is that we cannot know simultaneously both the position and the momentum of such particles; if we know where the particle is, we don't know where it's going, and if we know where it's going, we don't know where it is!

Sir John anticipated much of what we see now as the significance of these and many other strange and wondrous observations from the sciences. In his earlier book, *The Humble Approach*, written in 1981, he spoke of this new revelation of God from the "vast unseen."

> Some people think supernatural events, such as miracles, are needed to prove God's existence. But natural processes and the laws of nature may be merely methods designed by God for His continuing creative purposes. When human scientists discover new laws, do they not merely discover a little more of God?
>
> Each of us every day is swimming in an ocean of unseen miracles. For example, each living cell is a miracle; and the human body is a vast colony of over a hundred billion cells. The miracle of this body includes both our ability to recognize it as well as our inability ever to exhaust the true significance of it. As Albert Einstein said, "The most incomprehensible thing about the universe is that it is comprehensible." That the universe exhibits order, not chaos, suggests the futility of trying to fathom the nature of matter without investigating the unseen spirit behind it. Each time new laws are discovered by scientists, however, we learn a little more about God and the ways He continually maintains and is building His creation.

A mythical observer from another universe, who might have witnessed the spectacular Big Bang when the universe was created about eighteen billion years ago, would have seen after the first year only a vast blackness within thin clouds of stars and other fragments flying apart. But we, who observe from the surface of our small planet earth, see a totally different picture. We see a drama of evolution and progress on the surface of our earth, which is truly amazing and miraculous. And this progress is speeding up faster and faster and faster. By an unbelievable miracle, billions of humans, each of whom is a colony of billions of atoms, have suddenly covered the face of the earth. Most amazing of all is the fact that the unseen minds of these humans are accumulating knowledge in explosive proportions — knowledge of themselves, of the universe, of their Creator. Could we ever make an observer from another universe believe that this unseen explosion of human knowledge really exists? Would we believe that these new invisible minds are themselves participating creators in the ongoing drama of evolutionary creation?[3]

These, then, are the kinds of scientific ideas and data that convince John Templeton that we are on the threshold of great discoveries of spiritual information. But he does not believe the leap forward will occur without a change in the hearts of the inquirers.

Sir John feels that a great barrier to our full flowering as spiritual beings is human egotism. Admittedly, there is much to be proud of, and our science and technology have brought us wondrous and often needful things, but we have forgotten the source. We assume far more knowledge and ability than we possess. We have forgotten Lewis Thomas's conclusion that this is the Age of Ignorance. And what we are *most* ignorant of is the Creator. It is humility toward the Creator that Sir John is concerned about!

In *The Humble Approach*, Sir John writes of a new approach to understanding more about God. His method consists of a broad, sweeping examination of our sources of theological knowledge from the various religions and from modern sources in the sciences, followed by proposals for research in spiritual progress. The essential ingredient for success, he says, is a humble approach.

> The word humility is used here to mean admission that God infinitely exceeds anything anyone has ever said of Him; and that He is infinitely beyond human comprehension and understanding. A prime purpose of this book is to help us become more humble and thereby reduce the stumbling blocks placed in our paths toward heaven by our own egos. If the word heaven means eternal peace and joy, then we can observe that some persons have more of it already than others. Have you observed that these are generally persons who have reduced their egos, those who desire to give rather than to get? The Holy Spirit seems to enter when invited and to dwell with those who try to surrender to Him their hearts and minds. "Behold, I stand at the door and knock; if any man hear my voice and open the door, I will come in to him and sup with him, and he with me" (Revelation 3:20). As men grow older and wiser, they often grow in humility.
>
> The humble approach has much in common with but is not the same as natural theology, process theology, or empirical theology, whose horizons are all too narrow. They often attempt to give a comprehensive or systematic picture of God in keeping with human observations. But the humble approach teaches that man can discover and comprehend only a few of the infinite aspects of God's nature, never enough to form a comprehensive theology. The humble approach may be a science still in its infancy, but it seeks to develop a way of knowing God appropriate to His greatness and our littleness. The humble approach is a search that looks forward, not backward, and that expects to grow and learn from its mistakes.
>
> All of nature reveals something of the Creator. That golden age of creation is reached as the Creator reveals Himself more and more to the minds of men. Man cannot learn all about God the

Creator by studying nature because nature is only a contingent and partial manifestation of God. Hence natural theology, which seeks to learn about God through nature, is limited. Recently a new concept of theology, called the theology of science, was born. It denotes the way in which natural scientists are meditating about the Creator based not only on their observations of the astronomic and subatomic domains, but also on investigations into living organisms and their evolution, and such invisible realities as the human mind.

Experimental theology can reveal only a very little about God. It begins with a few simple forms of inquiry, subject to little disagreement, and proceeds to probe more deeply in thousands of other ways. Spiritual realities are not quantifiable of course, but there may be aspects of spiritual life that can be demonstrated experimentally one by one, although there may be hundreds of failures for each success. This approach is similar to that of experimental medicine.

As with experimental theology, the humble approach implies that there is a growing body of knowledge and an evolving theology not limited to any one nation or cultural area. The truly humble should be so open-minded that they welcome religious views from any place in the universe that is peopled with intelligent life. Seekers following the humble approach are never so xenophobic that they reject ideas from other nations, religions, or eras. Because the humble approach to theology is ongoing and constantly evolving, it may never become obsolete.

To learn about God, a worldwide approach is much too small. Even a universe-wide approach is much too small. The "picture" 99 percent of people have of God is too small. Have you heard anyone say, "God is a part of my life"? Would it not be wiser to say of humanity that it is only an infinitesimal speck of all that has its being in and through God? Our own ego can make us think that we are the center rather than merely one tiny temporal outward manifestation of a vast universe of being, which subsists in the eternal and infinite reality that is God. Have you heard the words, "the realm of the Spirit"? Is there any other realm? Humanity on this little earth may be an aspect of all that is upheld by the Spirit, but the Spirit is not an "aspect" of humanity. To say that God is a "part" or an "aspect" of life is as blind as for a man, standing on a shore looking at a wave, to say, "The ocean is an aspect of that wave."[4]

Sir John anticipated much of what is happening and needs to take place today in the theological world, just as his investment strategies of the Templeton Investment Funds era showed a keen sense of analysis and a willingness to speculate responsibly but in the broadest international context. In the true spirit of humility, he calls for a strategy, which has served so well for the sciences but is so foreign in theology, of examining every possibility with a willingness to accept truth wherever it is found, and to continually test and reexamine what has been passed down and what has been accepted in the present.

Admittedly, this is a tall order for theology, which operates from the standpoint of revelation and knows little of the empirical methods of the sciences. In fact, major religions are only now coming out of a deliberate separation from the scientific world, led by some of theology's most eminent scholars. Theologian Ronald Cole-Turner has reminded us that the Church moved into a period of isolation from science and technology some fifty years ago through the leadership of theologians like Karl Barth and later Langdon Gilkey. Religion's rejection of science as a resource for theology contained one primary advantage: Religion was insulated from the misuse of science and from the disturbing theories of science that could be interpreted to explain away the uniqueness of human beings and human consciousness. The fallacy of this approach, which Gilkey has since admitted, is seen in the almost total isolation of religious values from our culture. Cole-Turner describes this failure and the desirability for a new engagement with science and technology:

The disadvantage is that this strategy alienates theology not only from science but from the natural world itself. If the scientific interpretation of nature has no implications for Christianity, then Christian interpretation of creation has no consequences for science's understanding of nature. Skeptics quickly asked whether Christianity had any consequences at all. Was it all nothing but a set of stories intended to motivate good behavior? Or was it an isolated language game, a way Christians talk in church but untranslatable into the common speech of the broader culture? Christianity was no longer taken seriously because it made no claim. It was simply God-talk, empty and irrelevant to life in the world.

Now, however, science and technology have permeated our whole conceptual universe, even redefining human consciousness. Our theology has been pushed off the conceptual map of contemporary thought, leaving science with its largely unchallenged reductionistic assumptions to define our existence. Our strategy of isolation must end, and our Christian convictions must be brought into an honest engagement with science and technology. Thus transformed, our theology can seek to transform this culture of science and technology. Then our theology and ethics might join with our science and technology in a new alliance to search for the future of humanity God intends.[5]

John Templeton is also eager for a "transformed theology," but with less emphasis on problem solving and more concern for a humble spirit and an open mind. Again in *The Humble Approach*, he says:

There are clear scriptural bases for advocating the need for an inquiring and open mind. According to St. Luke, Jesus said, "Ask, and it shall be given to you; seek, and you shall find; knock and the door shall be opened unto you. For everyone who asks, receives, and he who seeks, finds; and to him who knocks it shall be opened" (Luke 11:9–10). Maybe God reveals Himself where He finds an inquiring mind — an open mind.

In the Acts of the Apostles, St. Paul said, "The God who made the world and everything in it . . . made from one every nation of men . . . that they should seek God, in the hope that they might feel after Him and find Him. Yet He is not far from each of us, for 'In Him we live and move and have our being'; as even some of your poets have said, 'For we are indeed His offspring'" (Acts 17:24–28).

Christ came to reveal God to men. But because of the limitations of human minds and human language, maybe less than one-hundredth part has been handed down to us. It is easy for us to realize how ignorant and primitive were the Jews of two thousand years ago and the Hindus of three thousand years ago. We should be humble enough to admit that if they had only perhaps one-tenth of one percent of all knowledge, we may have only one percent, even though the little glimpses we do have are indeed awesome.

One following the humble approach thinks it possible that God may want to reveal Himself further than He has done to date in any major or minor religion. He may be ever ready to give us new revelation if we will but open our minds to seek and inquire, but first we must rid ourselves of that rigidity and intellectual arrogance that tells us we have all the answers already. Like natural scientists who already assume the humble approach in their studies, maybe we should recognize that the law of creation is a law of accelerating change. Human language has always been too inadequate and restricted to utter all truths once and for all. The human mind has never been ready to receive all knowledge.

Time, space, and energy are the limits of our lives as they are the limits of our knowledge. God, of course, is not bound in these ways. He is the Creator of the awesome vastness of His cosmos. He knows each person's most fleeting thought just as He knows the power of a quasar and the intricate complexity of a DNA molecule. His most marvelous and mysterious creation on earth is the human brain with its indwelling mind. With the use of our minds, we can participate in some small ways in the creation of matter and even life itself. It should be clear to us that even though we are seriously hampered by our human weaknesses, we are meant to share with God his readiness to reveal Himself to us. We have a duty of humility, the duty to be open-minded.[6]

This, then, is the foundation upon which John Templeton's spiritual investment program is proceeding. Since 1987, the ideas he has proposed have been formalized as major programs of the John Templeton Foundation with the words "humility theology" to signify the goal of a new attitude of humility toward the Creator God on the part of the theological community. Implied also is the importance of openness to the discoveries of current science; most recently, Sir John has suggested that our goal should be a new science in which additional spiritual knowledge is sought by the empirical and statistical methods of science. He has called this new goal "humility theology science."

CHAPTER 2

Research on Spiritual Characteristics

THE LAWS OF THE SPIRIT

S IR JOHN HAS HAD a strong interest in the study of what he calls spiritual laws — universal principles governing spiritual growth and development, which reflect God's purpose in bringing about change, process, and progress in His creation. It is, Sir John says in *The Humble Approach*, a research area of tremendous need and great opportunities.

> By "laws of the spirit" we mean universal principles of the unseen world that can be determined and tested by extensive examination of human behavior and other data. Partly for lack of clearly defined methodology and a body of research material, this field appears about as disorganized and controversial as the natural sciences were in the millenniums before Galileo. In the days of Moses or Muhammad, there was very little knowledge of the principles of physics, chemistry, or biology, and little appreciation among ordinary people of the progress and rich rewards that could be achieved through successful research in these fields.

> Just as people of earlier times were ignorant regarding the physical sciences, we today are ignorant about the principles of spiritual progress. In addition to having as yet little understanding or agreement as to what spiritual laws are, we do not seem to recognize that God's purpose is not some permanent status quo, but change, progress, and progress based upon the laws of the spirit.

The spiritual dimensions of the cosmos are dynamic, changing, ceaselessly interacting. Surely the time has come for us to concentrate our resources on the kind of investigations that will enable us to understand the patterns and laws governing spiritual growth and development. Ceaseless seeking may be a part of the growth of souls as well as minds. It may be possible through research that some agreement may be reached on laws of the spirit. This field of research may yet become as bounteously fruitful as the natural sciences were in the last four centuries. . . .

Of course, it is not very apparent at this moment in history exactly how each law of the spirit could be discovered, tested, and utilized. Nor can we predict what laws will be discovered by generations of scientists sifting data for evidence of the effects of the unseen. It would have been impossible five hundred years ago to predict anything of the laws of thermodynamics or nuclear physics, let alone to devise experiments to test and establish them as laws. The difficulties of bringing to light, of describing and testing the laws of the spirit, are not any less than those that faced chemists two hundred years ago.

Studying and teaching the laws of the spirit should benefit humanity in even greater measure than did, for example, the laws of chemistry. Matthew Arnold thought that the decreasing influence of the Bible in the nineteenth century could be reversed if the ideals and hopes and laws expressed in the poetic and allegorical language of the scriptures could be explored experimentally. He hoped that dogmatic theology could be succeeded by empirical theology or experimental theology. If people could understand religious principles in their own everyday language rather than in ancient metaphors, they might take them more seriously.

More benefits may result in the domains of the spirit if each individual were to draw up his or her own personal list of the laws governing spiritual matters. Of course, this would be easier if he or she first studied the books and articles of scientists engaged in investigating powerful laws of the spirit. However, only when we understand and claim as our own some actual laws of the spirit do we begin to build our own heaven. What could be more uplifting than for each human to write in his mind and heart, as well as on paper, the various laws by which he or she ought to live? Individuals could measure their spiritual growth every year as they revise and rewrite their own personal list of laws. How beneficial it would be if every school devoted a few minutes each day to help pupils study the laws of the spirit as they are brought to light and formulated by great scientists, so that each student could improve his or her own written list. The supreme moments in the life of each of us occur whenever we grasp a new inspiring truth and appropriate it so that it revitalizes our personality and becomes a part of our life.

When any field of research is begun, no one can possibly predict what may be discovered eventually. Astronomers before Copernicus could not have predicted or even imagined galaxies, or supernovas, or pulsars. Even so, no one can yet say what laws of the spirit will be formulated and proven eventually.[1]

Sir John goes on to give some examples of laws of the spirit that might be researched by experimental and statistical methods: "As a person thinks, so is that person. This example is generally agreed upon by all religions. Its benefit, if taught to young people, could be the basis for future generations to become much more disciplined in the control and management of their minds and lives."[2]

It is interesting that Sir John would suggest this law of the spirit first, because discipline is certainly the hallmark of his own life. As a child, growing up in the small town of Winchester, Tennessee, John was given extraordinary opportunity to develop characteristics of discipline, self-reliance, and enterprise. His father, Harvey Templeton, was a successful lawyer and businessman-investor who gave John an early introduction to thrift and planning. At the age of 4 John was raising beans in a part of his mother's large garden and selling them at the local country store for a handsome profit. At the age of 8 he had developed a very profitable venture selling fireworks to his schoolboy chums. No store in Winchester sold fireworks, so John found an outlet in Ohio that supplied them at a good price. At the appropriate time for fireworks — Christmas and Fourth of July — he would make a good profit and his friends would be happy to provide it!

John's mother also had a great impact on his character. Vella Handly Templeton was a well-educated woman for those days. She had attended grammar school and high school in Winchester, and then had gone on to study mathematics, Greek, and Latin for seven years at Winchester Normal College. At the age of thirty she married Harvey Templeton, and they settled into a comfortable home in Winchester. The Templetons were relatively well-to-do and yet followed a pattern of thrift that John has carried on throughout his life. John, his mother, and his brother Harvey had charge accounts at all the local stores but charged very little. His requests for money from his father were always granted, and he was given free rein in choosing his activities. Only very rarely did his parents give him any advice on ethics, religion, business, or school. This freedom of choice, with only gentle parental influence, was a tactic deliberately chosen by the elder Templetons; it came largely out of a philosophy of living that stemmed from Vella Templeton's religious convictions. She believed that self-reliance depended on making decisions for oneself, rather than letting others do the deciding. An active member of the Cumberland Presbyterian Church, she also had a deep commitment to another religious group, the fledgling Unity School of Christianity. From this source John learned some key lessons for his future. One of these was that happiness and success result from "thought control," concentrating one's mind on positive and productive things. Material success and wealth, said Unity founder Charles Fillmore, flow naturally from spiritual growth and progress.

That happiness stems from spiritual growth also follows from these ideas, and this is another of Sir John's suggested laws of the spirit, a law he seems to aptly substantiate and one that he feels should be researched and documented. It is a lesson he has learned well. William Proctor, in his book *The*

Templeton Prizes, makes the point that John Templeton has used his wealth to fulfill deeply held values, and this is the real secret of his happiness.

> But there is also another important side to the highest levels of happiness and success in investing — a side that encompasses far broader considerations than just the "nuts and bolts" techniques of accumulating wealth. As we'll see, it's essential to understand and affirm this broader dimension of making big money if you want to be *truly* successful and live happily with your wealth once you acquire it. Too often a person may forge ahead and do quite well in building up his personal assets. But then the unexpected pressures and temptations of his newfound wealth present so many problems that his "success" turns out to be not a success at all, but rather a curse in disguise.
>
> But Templeton has learned how to be comfortable with his riches. He's a self-made man who didn't have the benefit of a family tradition of "old money" and philanthropy, but he has avoided the danger of being "blown away" by his wealth because he has learned the secret of "successful living with success." Indeed, John Templeton provides one of the best living examples of how a person's wealth can become a satisfying extension of his inner drives and values.[3]

In addition to these two laws, Sir John would add two laws about giving. In the first he talks about love:

> The more love we give away, the more we have left. The laws of love differ from the laws of arithmetic. Love hoarded dwindles, but love given grows. If we give all our love, we will have more left than he who saves some. Giving love, not receiving, is important; but when we give with no thought of receiving, we automatically and inescapably receive abundantly. Heaven is a by-product of love. When we say, "I love you," we mean that "a little of God's love flows from us to you." But, thereby, we do not love less, but

more. For in flowing the quantity is magnified. God's love is infinite, and is directed equally to each person, but it seems to gain
intensity when directed to sinners. This is the wonder and mystery
of it, that when we love God we get an enormous increase in the
quantity of love flowing through us to others.[4]

To further validate this law, Sir John quotes from the first epistle of John,
the appeal to members of the early church to love one another as the proof
of their new relationship to God, and then concludes with a superlative quotation from St. Paul's first epistle to the Corinthians:

> And now I will show you the best way of all. I may speak in tongues
> of men and of angels, but if I am without love, I am a sounding
> gong or a clanging cymbal. I may have the gift of prophecy, and
> know every hidden truth; I may have faith strong enough to move
> mountains; but if I have no love, I am nothing. I may dole out all I
> possess, or even give my body to be burnt, but if I have no love, I
> am none the better.
>
> Love is patient; love is kind and envies no one. Love is never
> boastful, nor conceited, nor rude; never selfish, not quick to take
> offence. Love keeps no score of wrongs; does not gloat over other
> men's sins, but delights in the truth. There is nothing love cannot
> face; there is no limit to its faith, its hope, and its endurance.
>
> Love will never come to an end. Are there prophets? Their work
> will be over. Are there tongues of ecstasy? They will cease. Is there
> knowledge? It will vanish away; for our knowledge and our
> prophecy alike are partial, and the partial vanishes when whole-
> ness comes. When I was a child, my speech, my outlook, and my
> thoughts were all childish. When I grew up, I had finished with
> childish things. Now we see only puzzling reflections in a mirror,
> but then we shall see face to face. My knowledge now is partial;
> then it will be whole, like God's knowledge of me. In a word, there
> are three things that last forever: faith, hope, and love; but the
> greatest of them all is love (1 Corinthians 12:31–13:13).[5]

The second law about giving is a very familiar one. Sir John says:

> It is better to give than to receive. Giving is a sign of psychologi-
> cal and spiritual maturity. There are few diseases so childish and
> deadly as the "gimmies," a disease that separates us from friends
> and from God, and shrinks the soul. The secret of success is giving,
> not getting. To get joy we must give it and to keep joy we must
> scatter it. The greatest charity is to help a person change from
> being a receiver to being a giver.[6]

Being only a receiver does indeed separate us from our friends and from
God, and the resultant loneliness of body and spirit is the basis for another
suggestion for a law of the spirit: "Loneliness is the punishment for those
who want to get, not give. Helping others is the cure for loneliness. If we feel
lonely, we are probably self-centered. If we feel unloved, we are probably
unloving. If we love only ourselves, we may be the only persons to love us.
Whatever we give out, we get back."[7]

Along with the truth that self-centeredness leads to loneliness, Sir John
adds a law about the nature of forgiveness. "To be forgiven, we must first
forgive. Forgiving brings forgiveness. Failure to forgive creates a hell for the
unforgiver, not the unforgiven."[8]

Psychologists tell us that healing from a hurt someone has done to you
must begin with your forgiveness of that person. I recall once mentioning
to Sir John that a magazine article about him by a former employee was
unfair and untrue and that he should write a letter setting the record
straight. His response was, "I did write him a letter, but it was to wish him
well in his new job and to tell him I was praying for him!"

Then, of course, in this list of candidates for laws of the spirit, Sir John
included a law about thanksgiving.

> Thanksgiving opens the door to spiritual growth. If there is any
> day in our life that is not thanksgiving day, then we are not fully
> alive. Counting our blessings attracts blessings. Counting our
> blessings each morning starts a day full of blessings. Thanksgiv-
> ing brings God's bounty. From gratitude come riches — from

complaints, poverty. Thanksgiving opens the door to happiness. Thanksgiving causes giving. Thanksgiving puts our mind in tune with the Infinite. Continual gratitude dissolves our worries.[9]

Sir John has said that the attitude of thanksgiving has the potential for revolutionizing your life. It is a powerful tool for good, one that he uses continually, and one that his good friend Norman Vincent Peale stressed repeatedly from the pulpit of Marble Collegiate Church in New York City and through *Guideposts* magazine. In 1992, Sir John was awarded the Norman Vincent Peale Award for Positive Thinking.

We should not miss the connection between thanksgiving and giving, because, as John says, "Thanksgiving *causes* giving." When you are overwhelmed by the thought that God is making his infinite knowledge and love available to you, you want to share it with others. In a letter to Father Robert Sirico of the Acton Institute, Sir John explains his view of thanksgiving and its relationship to giving.

> Humility is especially rewarding when it is humility toward God. When you humbly admit that no human has ever known more than a tiny bit of the infinity and eternity of God, then you desire and seek to learn more. When you humbly admit that God is making available to you his infinite knowledge and love, then you want to become a clear and open channel to radiate this knowledge and love to others. Love shrinks when hoarded but multiplies when given away.
>
> People who are overwhelmingly grateful every day for their multitudes of blessings feel a desire to help others. When you are diligently trying to help others not only by producing goods and services but also by radiating love and knowledge, then, without any intention on your part, others will be attracted to you and you too will grow in prosperity and happiness.[10]

Becoming a channel of blessing to others brings prosperity and happiness to ourselves, he says. Then he adds another related law of the spirit, perhaps the most paradoxical of all: "Surrender to God brings freedom. It is in dying to our selfish selves (self-denial) that we are born to eternal life."[11] This law makes sense only if a person has put his or her trust totally in God. In *The Humble Approach*, Sir John quotes Jesus with these words:

> When Jesus was asked what is the greatest law, He said: "Thou shalt love the Lord thy God with all thy heart, and with all thy soul, and with all thy mind. This is the first and great commandment. And second is like unto it, Thou shalt love thy neighbor as thyself. On these two commandments hang all the law and the prophets" (Matthew 22:37-40).
>
> The law can be researched as a basic law of the spirit. A person who applies this law finds his life revolutionized. Opening our heart to God allows His love to flow through us like a mighty river. If we love God totally as He loves us, we will love each of His children without exception as Jesus Himself described (Luke 6:27-36). The happiest people on earth are those who love God totally.[12]

Here, then, are ten laws of the spirit, which are prime candidates for a program of research on spiritual information. To these, many more possible laws will be added. In fact, Sir John expanded the list to two hundred and published them in 1994 in the form of a book titled *Discovering the Laws of Life*; later he published a revised edition called *Worldwide Laws of Life*.

DISCOVERING THE "LAWS OF LIFE"

The initial impetus for the assembling of the expanded list of the laws of life came from Sir John's desire to build a component of moral and spiritual development into the curriculum of the world's schools. As a boy, he had the experience of seeing the laws of life in action in a Tennessee school. In April 1989 he wrote about this special school in *Plus*, a publication of the Foundation for Christian Living, the organization founded by Dr. and Mrs. Norman Vincent Peale.

I recall the Webb School, near where I grew up in Winchester, Tennessee. That school tried to teach more than reading, writing, and arithmetic. The school was started by an elderly man named Shaunee Webb. The motto of the school was "We Teach Character." Webb regarded as his principal purpose to teach students the "Laws of Life" along with Latin, history, and mathematics. Many graduates of the Webb School became nationally known, their success based on what they learned from the founder.[13]

Not surprisingly, Sir John's effort to bring a moral development emphasis into the schools was also begun in his home county, Franklin County, Tennessee. In the introduction to *Discovering the Laws of Life*, he talks of his hopes for the book and gives a little history of the essay program he began in Franklin County.

Following in the footsteps of Benjamin Franklin and others who have tried to pass on their learning to others, this book has been written from a lifetime of experience and diligent observation in the hope that it may help people in all parts of the world to make their lives not only happier but also more useful. It is intended for everyone, for the young who each day are being introduced to the laws that can make their lives more productive, as well as for the older and more experienced who seek confirmation and affirmation of the "Laws of Life."

... In this book, you will find two hundred major ones, culled from a list of many hundreds. They come from a vast array of sources — from the scriptures, from storytellers such as Aesop, from scientists such as Isaac Newton, from artists and historians. The poet Henry Wadsworth Longfellow wrote: "Lives of great men oft remind us that we can make our lives sublime and departing leave behind us footprints in the sands of time." The truth of this statement can be demonstrated if we look to the lives of the famous as well as to the unsung heroes of the past and present, for there we will find many models for useful, happy living. And, when we examine their words and deeds, we will discover the principles that inspired and sustained their benefits to future generations. . . .

Drawn from the scriptures of different traditions, as well as from schools of philosophical thought both ancient and modern, each quotation points to a particular law that holds true for most people under most circumstances. The essays are designed to inspire and encourage you — to help you consider more deeply the laws you live by and to reap the rewards of their practical application. The laws described here are like tools. When you apply them consistently, they have the power to transform your life into a more deeply useful and joyful experience. Even if your life is already working well, it's possible that it will work even better as you incorporate the wisdom contained in these pages. If I had found a book of two hundred basic laws of life during my college years, I could have been far more productive then and in the years that followed.

A few years ago, I began offering support for a "Laws of Life" essay contest in my boyhood home, Franklin County, Tennessee. Mr. and Mrs. Handy Templeton help in running the program. Prizes for the essays — they run from one hundred to two thousand words in length — are awarded semi-annually, with a first prize of $2,000, a second prize of $800, and a number of runner-up prizes. The response has been gratifying. The number of entrants for each six-month period has risen to its present size of six hundred students. It would give me a great pleasure to learn that your hometown wants to embark on its own version of the Franklin County program.

In my teenage years, I was inspired by the courage and vision of Rudyard Kipling's poem "If." This poem taught me to dream — but also to be master of my dreams. I learned from the great English poet that the earth belongs to us all and that, with courage

and enthusiasm, progress is likely to follow. The final stanza of
"If" still rings in my ears:

> If you can fill the unforgiving minutes
> With sixty seconds' worth of distance run,
> Yours is the Earth and everything that's in it,
> And — which is more — you'll be a Man, my son!

Behind this book is my belief that the basic principles for leading a "sublime life," to paraphrase Longfellow, can be examined
and tested just as science examines and tests natural laws of the
universe. I have a vision that by learning the laws of life and applying them to everyday situations, more and more people will find
themselves leading joyous and useful lives.[14]

A later chapter in this book will describe in more detail John Templeton's
plan for extending the "Laws of Life" program to high schools and colleges
in the United States, the United Kingdom, and most recently in Russia.[15] In
connection with the John Templeton Foundation's program of research on
spiritual laws, the "Laws of Life" projects are being included with the goal
of establishing the most useful and universally acceptable laws for promul-
gation through the schools. Sir John emphasizes that the laws of life are
only the beginning of the search for experimentally verifiable laws of a spiritual nature that are universally accepted and free of sectarian bias. Some of
these laws doubtless will not prove to be generally valid, and they will be set
aside. But research may show that a significant number of the laws have scientific validity, and these will be added to later editions of *Worldwide Laws
of Life*.

Sir John hopes that *Worldwide Laws of Life* can find its way into accredited
courses in some colleges and universities worldwide as a proven-effective
textbook. Sir John even envisions the development of a "World Council on
the Laws of Life" leading to a worldview agreed upon by educators and all
the world's religions.

CHAPTER 3

Research in the Sciences

❧

S IR JOHN HOPES that rapid progress in obtaining spiritual information ushers in a new renaissance for humanity and that joining
humility theology with science may be a key to success. Intrinsic to Sir
John's spiritual investment plan is a multifaceted research program, emphasizing rigorous scientific methodology and interdisciplinary thinking and
characterized by a willingness to take calculated risks in uncertain territory.
This strategy is not unusual for John Templeton. In the business world it has
made him one of the most successful investment counselors of all time. But
now, in place of exhaustive evaluation of a company's future business
prospects, Sir John thoughtfully examines the accelerating discoveries in
the sciences, which point so clearly to deeper reality. And, like the unbiased,
worldwide diversity of his Templeton Growth Fund, he now emphasizes
the essential nature of theology-science interaction where each side is lis-
tening to and learning from the other. And finally, the calculated risk, which
is always a part of profitable investing, but one that can be greatly mini-
mized by diversity and by careful research, must in this new context be
undertaken with daring and courage if the old entrenched ideas of traditional religion and sometimes dogmatic science are to be improved.

RESEARCH AT THE LIMITS OF SCIENCE

Of course, we have already discussed earlier some of the scientific discoveries that suggest that the visible and tangible may be only a tiny part of

underlying spiritual reality. Sir John seeks to encourage scientific research of this type, to obtain further evidence of the work and purpose of the fundamental, creative, spiritual reality through astronomy, physics, biology, and other hard sciences. He has already edited one book, *Evidence of Purpose*, with chapters by some of the outstanding scientists of the twentieth century, including Owen Gingerich, professor of astronomy and of the history of science at Harvard University and a senior astronomer at the Smithsonian Astrophysical Observatory; Sir John Polkinghorne, fellow of the Royal Society and former chair of mathematical physics at Cambridge University, who is also an Anglican priest and retired president of Queens' College, Cambridge; and Sir John Eccles, also a fellow of the Royal Society and the recipient of the 1963 Nobel Prize for physiology and medicine. Topics covered by these and the other seven contributors include new intimations from science that such ideas as design and purpose are very relevant to our understanding of the cosmos. Professor Paul Davies, a physicist at the University of Adelaide, contributes a chapter on the "Unreasonable Effectiveness of Science," pointing out the remarkable way in which the universe provides understandable answers to our queries. In other words, why should an incredibly complicated universe be governed by laws that can be described in terms of our mathematics? Then too, these laws prove to be special in a number of ways: by their coherence and harmony, their economy, and their universality and dependability. Yet, surprisingly, these same laws allow for a wide range of diversity and complexity instead of leading to total chaos.

In his introduction to *Evidence of Purpose*, Sir John writes:

> This book was written to bring a new scientific perspective to the age-old question of purpose. It had been assumed since perhaps the middle of last century that science had to put to rest any idea that there was a Creator whose design had brought the universe its form and process. Yet there have been powerful dissenting voices even among the great scientists. Physicists like Albert Einstein openly and movingly spoke of the religious attitude as essential to

good science and Sir James Jeans said that the universe was beginning to look not like a great machine but rather like a great thought. Astronomer Allan Sandage spoke of God in terms of the marvelous laws of nature, and Sir Arthur Eddington once wrote of a spiritual world that lies behind the universe we study.

But in the last twenty or thirty years, the number of scientists raising philosophical and religious questions as a result of recent scientific discoveries has multiplied. This volume contains some of those questions — searching, exploratory, tentative but often profound — about ultimate reality and purpose and meaning. The scientists who have contributed to this book cover a broad spectrum of theological and philosophical persuasion. Yet they all express something of the wonder of the universe we begin to know through science, and all see evidence for a deep meaning written into the laws and processes of nature.

It is to be hoped that the reader will come to this collection of essays with the same spirit of humility that characterizes all good science. As we begin to understand our own limitations as finite creatures in a vast universe of infinite complexity and intricacy, perhaps we can be released from our prejudices — whether scientific, philosophical, or religious — and open our minds to the great plan of which we are a part.

Science in the past few decades has revolutionized our view of the universe and our place in it. Just a century ago science appeared to be tidying up our world, dispelling the illusions of gods and inexplicable miracles and finally providing us with an "objective" view. Yet today the credo of objectivity, together with its tight little mechanisms and clockwork images, is gone. Matter has lost its tangibility, space and time are no longer separable entities, and quantum physics has shown our world to be more like a symphony of waveforms in dynamic flux than some sort of mechanical contrivance.

Anthropologist Loren Eisley talks about the illusions of science in his book, *The Firmament of Time*:

> A scientist writing around the turn of the century remarked that all of the past generations of men have lived and died in a world of illusions. The unconscious irony in his observation consists in the fact that this man assumed the progress of science to have been so great that a clear vision of the world without illusion was, by his own time, possible. It is needless to add that he wrote before Einstein, . . . at a time when Mendel was just about to be rediscovered, and before the advances in the study of radioactivity had made their impact — of both illumination and confusion — upon this century.
>
> Certainly science has moved forward. But when science progresses, it often opens vaster mysteries to our gaze. Moreover, science frequently discovers that it must abandon or modify what it once believed. Sometimes it ends by accepting what it has previously scorned. The simplistic idea that science marches undeviantly down an ever-broadening highway can scarcely be sustained by the historian of ideas.

Scientific progress is always attended by the corrections of error, by sharp shifts in direction and emphasis. And the nature of the correction is again only tentative, only partially truth. And the illusions could hardly be said to have been dispelled. In fact, in a very real sense, what we have started with as the tangible — matter, energy, space, and time — now seems to bear some of the mystery of an illusion. Things are not what they seemed. In the words of science writer K. C. Cole:

> So much of science consists of things we can never see: light "waves" and charged "particles"; magnetic "fields" and gravitational "forces"; quantum "jumps" and electron "orbits." In fact, none of these phenomena is literally what we say it is. Light waves do not undulate through empty space in the same way that water waves ripple over a still pond; a field is only a mathematical

description of the strength and direction of a force; an atom does not literally jump from one quantum state to another; and electrons do not really travel around the atomic nucleus in orbits. The words we use are merely metaphors. "When it comes to atoms," wrote Neils Bohr, "language can be used only as in poetry. The poet, too, is not merely so concerned with describing facts as with creating images."[1]

The most astounding thing about our recent discoveries in the sciences is that each answer seems not only to raise many more questions, but that the questions now seem to extend far beyond the capacities of ordinary previous experimentation to provide answers. If the answers sought before were only partial, the questions raised now are difficult to frame as scientific questions; perhaps we are peering into a whole new dimension, a new reality. Paul Davies deals with this phenomenon in the final chapter of his book *The Mind of God*, describing the frustration of some of his colleagues and the effort to avoid the whole issue on the part of many others. He concludes with some important thoughts about mysticism:

> Most scientists have a deep mistrust of mysticism. This is not surprising, as mystical thought lies at the opposite extreme to rational thought, which is the basis of the scientific method. Also, mysticism tends to be confused with the occult, the paranormal, and other fringe beliefs. In fact, many of the world's finest thinkers, including some notable scientists such as Einstein, Pauli, Schrödinger, Heisenberg, Eddington, and Jeans, have also espoused mysticism. My own feeling is that the scientific method should be pursued as far as it possibly can. Mysticism is no substitute for scientific inquiry and logical reasoning so long as this approach can be consistently applied. It is only in dealing with ultimate questions that science and logic may fail us. I am not saying that science and logic are likely to provide the wrong answers, but they may be incapable of addressing the sort of "why" (as opposed to "how") questions we want to ask.

The expression "mystical experience" is often used by religious people, or those who practice meditation. These experiences, which are undoubtedly real enough for the person who experiences them, are said to be hard to convey in words. Mystics frequently speak of an overwhelming sense of being at one with the universe or with God, of glimpsing a holistic vision of reality, or of being in the presence of a powerful and loving influence. Most important, mystics claim that they can grasp *ultimate reality* in a single experience, in contrast to the long and tortuous deductive sequence (petering out in turtle trouble) of the logical-scientific method of inquiry. Sometimes the mystical path seems to involve little more than an inner sense of peace — "a compassionate, joyful stillness that lies beyond the activity of busy minds" was the way a physicist colleague once described it to me. Einstein spoke of a "cosmic religious feeling" that inspired his reflections on the order and harmony of nature. Some scientists, most notably the physicists Brian Josephson and David Bohm, believe that regular mystical insights achieved by quiet meditative practices can be a useful guide in the formulation of scientific theories.[2]

Sir John believes these mystical experiences are just what one would expect from the Creator God who is bringing His plan for accelerating growth in spiritual knowledge to fruition. Research into these meditative insights, as well as a deeper probing of purpose and meaning in the universe, represents a major effort of the Templeton Foundation and hopefully of many others who will join the search in the years ahead. The benefits in terms of our deeper understanding of our selves and our purpose in the cosmos could be immense.

RESEARCH ON PURPOSE IN THE UNIVERSE

Another closely related human attribute with great benefit for study is purpose, the experience all of us share in our immediate planning for short-term goals and in our long-term dreaming of what could be. What is the source of this characteristic, if it is not a mark in miniature of the Creator in his creature? We should know much more about purpose, and especially reexamine our studies of other living organisms that seem to display purpose.

In his chapter in *Evidence of Purpose*, David Wilcox writes about the stubborn refusal of biologists to allow any teleological (purposeful) explanations into their science — "teleophobia," he calls it. Such bias, he says, has hampered important studies of probable built-in restraints in the evolutionary process and narrowed developments in this area of our understanding, especially as they might provide evidence for design.[3] This is probably just one of a number of areas of science in which empirical studies may be hampered by a selection against research that might provide data for purpose in the universe, just as scientists resisted the big bang theory for the origin of the universe because of its probable theological significance. An emphasis on freely conceived research, open to whatever direction the data takes, would be of great benefit to our understanding of our evolutionary past and in planning for a viable future for the human race. Further evidence for design in the evolutionary process would provide a temporizing and humbling influence on those scientists who are resistant to theistic arguments. It would also greatly challenge some members of the theological community who still shun scientific data as irrelevant or dangerous.

RESEARCH ON HUMAN CREATIVITY

John Templeton is also keenly interested in human creativity, in part because of its implication that we are the products of an incredibly creative process, which had us in mind, and in part because we may have been hampered in our creative development because of an unwillingness to fully explore human creative potential through empirical and statistical research methods. Neural science research is now showing that we use only perhaps 10 percent of our available brain cells at any one time. This strongly suggests that human brain function could be greatly enhanced if proper conditions could be found for mobilizing the remaining neural networks. This suggestion is also supported by limited data on so-called idiot savants, who show remarkable abilities in mathematics or in music, although their general abilities are quite limited. What is implied here is that the human brain can perform incredible functions under certain conditions. Finding these conditions for individuals with general mental abilities could be a tremendous potential benefit to the mental development of human beings. Beyond this lies the distinct possibility that research may demonstrate that spiritual attributes might also be greatly enhanced under certain conditions, thus leading to a greatly accelerated spiritual development of humankind.

In this connection, Paul Davies relates in *The Mind of God* what he calls mystical experiences, experiences that have happened to scientists in the course of their scientific theorizing. Davies mentions physicist Roger Penrose's description of his experience of mathematical inspirations as a sudden "breaking through" into a Platonic realm, and he also shares a report that mathematician Kurt Gödel spoke of "other relation to reality" by which he could directly perceive mathematical objects, like infinity, by meditative means. Perhaps his most interesting story is that of the famous cosmologist Fred Hoyle, who experienced what Davies calls "a truly religious (as opposed to merely Platonic) event" while driving through the north of England on his way to a vacation in the Scottish Highlands in the late 1960s. According to Davies, Hoyle had been working at Cambridge with his collaborator Jayant Narlikar on a cosmological theory of electromagnetism that involved some very challenging mathematics, and decided to take a break to go hiking with some colleagues. The story of his experience was later written in a report published by the University of Cardiff. Hoyle writes:

> As the miles slipped by I turned the quantum mechanical problem ... over in my mind, in the hazy way I normally have in thinking mathematics in my head. Normally, I have to write things down on paper, and then fiddle with the equations and integrals as best I can. But somewhere on Bowes Moor my awareness of the mathematics clarified, not a little, not even a lot, but as if a huge brilliant light had suddenly been switched on. How long did it take to become totally convinced that the problem was solved? Less than

five seconds. It only remained to make sure that before the clarity faded I had enough of the essential steps stored safely in my recallable memory. It is indicative of the measure of certainty I felt that in the ensuing days I didn't trouble to commit anything to paper. When ten days or so later I returned to Cambridge I found it possible to write out the thing without difficulty.[4]

Paul Davies analyzes Hoyle's experience as follows:

Hoyle believes that the organization of the cosmos is controlled by a "superintelligence" who guides its evolution through quantum processes. . . . Furthermore, Hoyle's is a teleological God (somewhat like that of Aristotle or Teilhard de Chardin) directing the world toward a final state in the infinite future. Hoyle believes that by acting at the quantum level this superintelligence can implant thoughts or ideas from the future, ready-made, into the human brain. This, he suggests, is the origin of both mathematical and musical inspiration.[5]

Others, too, have experienced these moments of clarity and insight. Davies says that Hoyle was told by the Nobel Prize-winning physicist Richard Feynman that several times he had experienced moments of inspiration, which were followed in each case by an intense feeling of euphoria lasting two or three days.

These are important data for the Templeton research program, because they strongly suggest that great resources of mind may be accessible if the conditions are examined carefully and systematically. Paul Davies is very impressed with the existence of mind in the universe. He concludes his book with these searching words:

The central theme that I have explored in this book is that, through science, we human beings are able to grasp at least some of nature's secrets. We have cracked part of the cosmic code. Why this should be, just why *Homo sapiens* should carry the spark of rationality that provides the key to the universe, is a deep enigma.

We who are children of the universe — animated stardust — can nevertheless reflect on the nature of that same universe, even to the extent of glimpsing the rules on which it runs. How we have become linked into this cosmic dimension is a mystery. Yet the linkage cannot be denied.

What does it mean? What is Man that we might be party to such privilege? I cannot believe that our existence in this universe is a mere quirk of fate, an accident of history, an incidental blip in the great cosmic drama. Our involvement is too intimate. The physical species *Homo* may count for nothing, but the existence of mind in some organism on some planet in the universe is surely a fact of fundamental significance. Through conscious beings the universe has generated self-awareness. This can be no trivial detail, no minor byproduct of mindless, purposeless forces. We are truly meant to be here.[6]

Of course, what Davies refers to as mind would have much of the character that John Templeton would define as spirit. The experiences of penetrating insight, of sudden appearance of solutions to seemingly intractable scientific problems, the euphoria that follows, the incredible creativity that musical and mathematical inspiration often entails, the sense of the presence of an awesome force (mentioned as the experience of physicist Russell Stannard, for one, in his book *Grounds for Reasonable Belief*[7]), the "cosmic religious feeling" of Albert Einstein, all are essentially spiritual experiences and seem most often to be so viewed by those who experience them. How can these spiritual experiences, which are so valuable to the individuals involved, be extended to a much wider segment of society?

CHAPTER 4

Research on the Role
of Spirituality in Medicine

S IR JOHN TEMPLETON'S desire to encourage progress in spiritual information through science also includes the expectation that medicine's great advances in treating physical illness can find complementary expression in the spiritual realm. Indeed, a strong move is currently under way in America to diversify medical treatment approaches to include a variety of previously excluded therapies, including spiritual ones. Beginning in 1991 the John Templeton Foundation gave strong support to studies conducted by the late Dr. David Larson, a psychiatrist with the National Institute of Mental Health who became director of a nongovernmental organization, the National Institute for Healthcare Research (NIHR), which was renamed The International Center for the Integration of Health and Spirituality (ICIHS) in 2001. These studies demonstrated that religious variables are neglected in clinical research and in the practice of medicine. In most cases they demonstrated a strong positive relationship between spirituality and health.

Progress has been slow but steady. In the November 10, 2003 issue of *Newsweek*, the cover story "God and Health: Is Religion Good Medicine? Why Science Is Starting to Believe" featured Dr. Harold Koenig, a Foundation advisory board member and editor of its *Science and Theology News*. Dr. Koenig says "religion has a place in medical school — and in practice." The article also praised Sir John's funding of exploration of the links "between science and God."

Has Religion Been the Forgotten Factor in Medicine?

In a lecture sponsored by the John Templeton Foundation for presentation at medical schools, Dr. Dale Matthews, then of Georgetown University School of Medicine, explained that a wall of separation has gradually come between medicine and religion. Yet it was not always this way. Medicine and religion had worked hand in hand for thousands of years. Illness was perceived in ancient societies as primarily a spiritual problem and religious and medical authority was vested in the same person (e.g., an Aaronic priest) who might himself become an object of worship (e.g., Imhotep, Ascalupius, Jesus Christ). This close relationship between medicine and religion remained until the seventeenth century, when empirical science challenged church authority with the eventual result that the religions generally relinquished concern for the physical body (and later still, the mind), leaving the soul as the church's domain. As Ian Barbour points out in his *Religion in an Age of Science*, by the twentieth century, religion and medical science were perceived as mutually exclusive and inharmonious; while science was portrayed as factual, empirically verifiable, and objective, religion was seen an ephemeral, subjective, and ambiguous. Indeed, the National Academy of Sciences, in its 1984 resolution concerning the teaching about origins, declared, "religion and science are mutually exclusive realms of human thought whose presentation in the same context leads to misunderstanding of both scientific theory and religious belief."

Contrasting Religious Attitudes of Patients and Healthcare Providers

But at the beginning of the twentieth-first century, change is again underway and a new rapprochement between medicine and religion is a distinct possibility. The reasons for this development lie for the most part at the doorstep of the medical scientific establishment, which is experiencing a loss of confidence and sensing a growing disillusionment among the larger society. According to the ICIHS, surveys indicate that the American people are highly religious; 95 percent believe in God, 80 percent believe the Bible is the actual or inspired Word of God, 72 percent agree that "my whole approach to life is based on my religion," 57 percent pray at least once a day, 46 percent describe themselves as having been "born again," and 42 percent attend worship services once a week. Furthermore, a significant number of Americans participate in religious healing activities. A 1986 survey of 586 adults in Richmond, Virginia, indicated that 14 percent reported physical healings such as recovery from viral infections, cancers, back problems, emotional problems, and fractures by means of prayer or divine intervention. And in another survey of 325 adults, 30 percent reported praying regularly for healing and for health maintenance.

In contrast to these observations, the surveys indicated that health professionals are significantly less religious than the general public. One study reported that 33 percent of psychologists, 39 percent of psychiatrists, 46 percent of social workers, and 62 percent of marriage and family therapists agree that "my whole approach to life is based on my religion," compared to 72 percent of the American public. Similar results have been found for 146 family physicians in Vermont in a 1991 study. The irony in these situations is, of course, that while most patients expect religious values to be addressed by their doctor, the average physician is not prepared to address the real contribution spirituality may bring to the healing process. David Larson and his colleagues published similar data in articles in *Mind/Body Medicine* (vol. 2, 1997) and in *Archives in Family Medicine* (1997) and in *Annals of Internal Medicine* (vol. 132, April 2000) and in *American Journal of Medicine* (vol. 110, 2001).

ATTITUDES OF MEDICAL SCIENTISTS

If we shift from medical practice to medical research, the same kind of neglect of religious variables was found by Dr. David Larson in an in-depth study of the clinical literature by a process called systematic review. One example of this work, titled "Systematic Analysis of Research on Religious Variables in Four Major Psychiatric Journals, 1978–1982," was published in the *American Journal of Psychiatry* in 1986. In the article, 2,348 psychiatric studies published over a five-year period were examined for religious variables. It was found that only 2.5 percent of the studies used a religious measure (e.g., denomination) while only 0.1 percent used religion as a central variable, and only one study used a validated, multidimensional measure of religious commitment. Seventy-two percent of these studies showed a positive effect for religious commitment.

The great value of Larson's approach to review lies in its more rigorous methodology, in which strict quantitative research methods are used to arrive at more objective results. This has been especially important in the case of social policy literature reviews, which previously had been done in a much less systematic manner with frequently biased results. Larson's approach, analyzing the clinical research work already published, has been of great interest to Sir John Templeton, and he provided significant support for Dr. David Larson and the NIHR. The John Templeton Foundation provided funding for a compilation of the current research conducted on spirituality and health. More than four hundred abstracts of published research articles were published over a three-year period (1993–95) in three volumes with the title *The Faith Factor: An Annotated Bibliography of Clinical Research on Spiritual Subjects*. Dr. Dale Matthews was co-author with Dr. Larson of the series. The chosen articles focused primarily on three areas of particular interest to Sir John: love or altruism, prayer, and well-being. The research gave strong support to the thesis that religious variables are neglected in clinical research and that there can be major benefits from religious commitment in terms of health care. In terms of overall benefits, consider the following:

> Of 212 studies examining the effects of religious commitment on health care outcomes, 160 (75%) demonstrated a positive benefit of religious commitment while 37 (17%) revealed a mixed effect or no effect, and 15 (7%) demonstrated a negative effect.

The positive benefits of religious commitment for psychiatric illness were even more striking. Dr. Matthews cites the results of the review as follows:

Positive effects of religious commitment were found in 15 of 15 (100%) studies of drug abuse, 18 of 19 (95%) studies of adjustment and coping, 20 of 24 (83%) studies of alcohol abuse, 15 of 18 (83%) psychopathology studies, and 13 of 19 (68%) studies of depression.

The forgoing suggested strongly to Sir John that a major research effort should be mounted to study the effect of prayer and other spiritual interventions under the most rigorous empirical scientific conditions with diverse populations and religions. Certainly, this area of study holds great promise in reestablishing the place of religion in the healing process.

Also of great importance is the changing of attitudes among medical scientists and clinicians. Already there are signs of change in the federal bureaucracy, with the establishment of the Office of Alternative Medicine within the National Institutes of Health, and the advent of a new journal, *Alternative Therapies in Health and Medicine*, edited by Dr. Larry Dossey, another close associate of Sir John. In his editorial in the first issue, titled "A Journal and a Journey," Dossey recalled some of the salient examples of scientists' intransigence in the face of new data and new ideas.

> History is also replete with examples of how scientists themselves can be part of the problem, just like anyone else. Marcello Truzzi, professor of sociology at Eastern Michigan University in Ypsilanti, Michigan, and director of the Center for Scientific Anomalies Research in Ann Arbor, Michigan, has said, "Many studies in the psychology of science . . . indicate that scientists are at least as dogmatic and authoritarian, at least as foolish and illogical as everyone else, including when they do science." Truzzi enumerates many examples from the history of science in which narrowness eclipsed open-mindedness. Lord Kelvin pronounced that X-rays would be a hoax. Thomas Watson, once chairman of the board of IBM, declared in 1943, "I think there is a world market for about five computers." In 1889 Charles Duell, commissioner of the U.S. Office of Patents, penned a letter to President McKinley

asking him to abolish the patents office since "everything that can be invented has been invented." Ernst Mach, the physicist whose ideas influenced the young Einstein, said he could not accept the theory of relativity any more than he could accept the existence of atoms. Thomas Edison, reports Truzzi, said that he saw no commercial use for the light bulb. When the French Academy of Science invited a demonstration of the phonograph, one scientist leaped from his chair, seized the exhibitor, began shaking him, and shouted, "I won't be taken in by your ventriloquist!" Lord Rutherford declared atomic power "moonshine." And so on.

The history of medicine includes numerous instances in which physicians have rejected new ideas, even in the face of compelling data. A dramatic example took place in the nineteenth century on the obstetric wards of Allgemeines Krankenhaus, a famous hospital in Vienna. The struggle involved a technique that was heretical for the time: handwashing. So high was the mortality rate from childbirth fever or puerperal sepsis at this hospital that women giving birth begged in tears not to be taken there.

One of the physicians, Ignaz Phillip Semmelweis (1818–65), noticed that the first obstetric ward was different from the second, which had a lower mortality rate in that students came into the first ward directly from the cadaver dissecting room with unclean hands, and made vaginal examinations of the pregnant women without washing. The second ward, in contrast, was devoted to the instruction of midwives, who devoted much greater attention to hygiene and personal cleanliness. Noting these differences, Semmelweis theorized that the students were spreading the disease. He immediately instituted hygienic precautions: simply washing the hands in a solution of calcium chloride while dealing with pregnant women in labor. As a result, the fatality rate in labor cases fell the first year from 9.92 percent to 3.8 percent and in the following year, to 1.27 percent.

In spite of the data, Semmelweis met with fierce opposition.

He was persecuted by many of the leading medical figures of the day. Essentially hounded out of Vienna, he went to the University of Budapest where in 1861 he published his immortal treatise on "The Cause, Concept, and Prophylaxis of Puerperal Fever," as well as his scathing "Open Letters to Sundry Professors of Obstetrics." The result proved devastating for Semmelweis: the strain of controversy brought on insanity and suicide. In spite of this sordid chapter in the history of unconventional medical practices, his contribution today speaks for itself. "He is one of medicine's martyrs," medical historian F. H. Garrison stated, "and in the future, will be one of its far-shining names, for every childbearing woman owes something to him."

Pharisaical, dogmatic objections often echo in the most hallowed halls of academic medicine, as when the handwashing debate erupted in a firestorm of controversy in Boston at the Harvard Medical School and in nearby Philadelphia. Here the central figure was Oliver Wendell Holmes, who was Parkman professor of anatomy. In February 1843 Holmes read a paper, "On the Contagiousness of Puerperal Fever," in which he affirmed that (1) women "in childbed" should never be attended by physicians who have been conducting autopsies or dealing with cases of puerperal fever; (2) the disease may be conveyed in this fashion from patient to patient; and (3) washing one's hands in calcium chloride and changing one's garments after attending a case of puerperal fever might prevent the disease from spreading. He was attacked by some of the greatest obstetricians of his time. Like Semmelweis, Holmes persisted. In 1855 he delivered his monograph, "Puerperal Fever as a Private Pestilence," reiterating his stance and citing Semmelweis's scientific findings which, as in Vienna, were slow in turning the heads of doubters.

These examples are a reminder that, when it comes to failures of judgment toward unconventional, alternative developments in science, everyone — lay persons and scientists alike — has dirty hands. For scientists, these lapses in clear thinking often take the shape of rejection-without-investigation, as one scientist, speaking about anomalies in parapsychology research, said, "This is the kind of thing that I would not believe in even if it existed." For lay persons, the error frequently lies in the other direction: uncritical acceptance without investigation. For both errors, science can be an antidote. Truzzi again:

> Despite serious questions about how well the system works, I believe in the process of science and scientific progress. Science is a self-correcting system. Encouragement of fair play and due process in the scientific arena will allow that self-correction to work best. A diversity of opinions and dialogue is extremely important. We cannot close the door to maverick claims.

> It would be naïve to suppose that medicine has ever been, or is likely ever to be, free of contentiousness. Indeed, it would be disastrous if medical science were an exercise in polite agreement. As Arnold Relman, former editor of the *New England Journal of Medicine*, has said: "Nothing would be further from the truth than to imagine that contemporary medicine is all cut and dried, an accumulated store of tried and tested facts and techniques. The truth is that medicine is, and always has been, in a continual state of ferment and remodeling. It is plagued by ignorance and therefore perpetually agitated by controversy. Controversy has in fact, always been an integral part of medicine, one of its most important and characteristic features. . . . Science and controversy are inseparable companions."

We agree with this point of view. Modern medicine is not fully formed, and we believe researchers in unconventional areas have much to contribute. Indeed, they always have. As Oliver Wendell Holmes observed in 1883 in his *Medical Essays* (albeit in language that today is considered insensitive):

> It (medicine) learned from a monk how to use antimony, from
> a Jesuit how to cure agues, from a friar how to cut for stone,
> from a soldier how to treat gout, from a sailor how to keep off
> scurvy, from a postmaster how to sound the Eustachian tube,
> from a dairy-maid how to prevent smallpox, from an old mar-
> ket-woman how to catch the itch-insect. It borrowed acupunc-
> ture and the moxa from the Japanese heathen, and was taught
> the use of lebelia by the American savage.

Alternative Therapies will enter the ferment that is medical progress, with the hope of contributing to the remodeling that is
incessantly occurring in the medical sciences. In so doing, we will
not advocate any particular alternative therapies; neither will we
be "selling" an exclusive point of view. Our challenge to both the
alternative and orthodox medical communities is the same: to
honor the tenets of science, to set aside preconceived biases, to
follow empirical evidence wherever it may lead.

In so doing, we hope to be guided by Plato's observation in his
Dialogues: "We are not simply contending in order that my view or
that of yours may prevail, but I presume we ought both of us to be
fighting for truth."

Please join us in this fight for the truth — upon which journey
this journal now begins.

Sir John Templeton would be quick to point out that humility in theology and in science has as much to offer the medical scientist in terms of a
challenge to prideful attitudes as it offers to theologians. We are all learners
in God's school!

CHANGING THE ATTITUDES OF MEDICAL EDUCATORS

Sir John also fostered another avenue of investment in changing attitudes,
again through the NIHR. This time the focus was on the American medical
educational establishment, whose attitudes toward religion are not unlike

physicians in practice and medical scientists in clinical research. To create a positive impact on these negative attitudes, Sir John has supported the development of an independent study guide targeted at professionals and graduate students in medicine, social work, psychology, and pastoral counseling.

The study guide is composed of seven study modules, which lead participants through published empirical findings on the relationship between spiritual factors and various aspects of physical and mental health. Introductory sections detail the historical neglect of spiritual factors by the healthcare profession and also discuss the complexities of measuring variables such as spirituality and religious commitment

In addition to this module series, there was also a NIHR-directed Faith and Medicine Program, including the lecture program mentioned previously, in which Dr. Dale Matthews lectured nationwide at medical schools concerning the beneficial impact that religious commitment can have on physical and mental health and discussed the relevance of religious factors in health care. In order to publicize the program, a mailing containing promotional materials on Dr. Matthew's lectures was sent to all 126 medical schools in the United States. A survey was also included in the mass mailing to ascertain the state of each medical school's curriculum concerning spirituality, religion, and health. Dr. Matthews received a surprisingly large number of calls in response to the mailing from medical schools nationwide, including John Hopkins University, Walter Reed Army Medical Center, the University of Maryland, Ohio State University, Vanderbilt Medical School, and the State University of New York Medical Center at Syracuse.

The second component of the Faith and Medicine Program included a competitive grant program funded by the John Templeton Foundation for the development of a curriculum that integrates religious components with medical care. This competition was advertised and promoted in Dr. Matthew's mass mailing as well as in several medical journals, including the *Journal of the American Medical Association* and the *Journal of General Internal Medicine*. As a result of these promotional activities, NIHR received more than forty inquiries regarding the competition for curriculum development.

A panel of judges evaluated each grant application, with five grants of $10,000 each awarded to the winning schools. In the second year, the Foundation awarded grants to twenty-five more medical schools in America. By June 2001, 80 medical schools out of 126 were addressing religion, a situation reported with amazement in the November 10, 2003 issue of *Newsweek*, which reported that only 3 had offered such programs a decade ago.

In 1998, the program became the responsibility of Dr. Christina Puchalski, assistant professor of medicine at George Washington University School of Medicine. She is also founder and director of the Institute for Spirituality & Health at George Washington University (GWish), a university-based organization working toward a more compassionate system of health care. GWish is changing the face of health care through innovative programs for physicians and other members of the multidisciplinary healthcare team, including clergy and chaplains.

A third component of the Faith and Medicine Program was a video exploring the relationship between religion and health. Produced by a public relations company, the video, *Body, Mind and Spirit*, contains interviews with Dr. Matthews as well as with many of the speakers who presented at a Templeton Foundation-sponsored conference on "Spiritual Dimensions in Clinical Research."

NIHR and its staff also began developing a model curriculum for psychiatric residents focused on promoting the importance of patient spirituality in psychiatric assessment, treatment, and care. Working in conjunction with a group of nationally recognized psychiatrists interested in encouraging clinical sensitivity to religious issues, NIHR completed the pioneering model curriculum and an accompanying study guide. The curriculum was sorely needed because all accredited psychiatric residency programs were mandated to include courses on sensitivity to patient religious issues as of January 1995. This opening to religious issues is encouraging given psychiatry's longstanding antagonism toward the religious sector, and it is hopeful that this model curriculum will help to better educate future psychiatrists as well as encourage a more accepting and open attitude toward religious issues in the clinical setting. The educational components of this program have also been moved to George Washington University School of Medicine under the direction of Dr. Puchalski.

NEW RESEARCH OPPORTUNITIES

The systematic review approach has proven very fruitful, and Sir John is eager to see it extended to other areas of health care. Given the importance to clinicians, researchers, and policy makers of the dynamics of living longer, NIHR undertook a systematic review of the longevity research in order to determine whether the religiously committed actually live longer than the non-religious. This work was done in collaboration with three of its research fellows, Dr. John Lyons, Dr. Jeffrey Levin, and Dr. Harold Koenig.[1]

In August 2001, NIHR was reorganized as the International Center for the Integration of Health and Spirituality (ICIHS). Sadly, less than a year later, on March 5, 2002, the president and founder, Dr. David Larson, died suddenly while exercising in the gym. He leaves behind a long line of dedicated healthcare professionals, including his wife Susan with whom he published extensively. Unfortunately, the new center closed its doors in August 2003.

One of Dr. Larson's colleagues, the previously mentioned Dr. Harold Koenig, has been a vigorous participant in the John Templeton Foundation's ongoing Spirituality and Health Initiatives Program. One component of the program is based at Duke University, where Dr. Koenig directs the Center for the Study of Religion and Spirituality. Under his direction, a landmark conference was organized in March 2001 entitled "Faith in the Future: Religion, Aging and Healthcare in the 21st Century." The aims of the conference were to explore how people envision their lives in "old age," specifically how the quality of their vision can effect their health and happiness and how these same attitudes could impact future healthcare resources. Could the old adage "Give to live; live to give" be a vital consideration in all strategic discussions regarding the future of health care in America? The conference provided examples of people who "live to give" and find joy and meaning in their lives by building networks of engagement and support. Discussions highlighted situations where people are happier and healthier overall and are providers of care rather than users of care. Speakers presented findings to support the building of spiritually inspired communities across the socioeconomic and health spectrum to provide resources of support and care. Conference participants had the opportunity to hear from a distinguished faculty of experts who examined the current and future health of the population over 65 years of age and the demands of health care as the population continues to age; solutions for providing care for the elderly by making full use of community resources, that is, religious organizations and municipal programs; the theological position on health care of the aging population and others in need; and the importance of the relationship between health and religion in later life.

Dr. Koenig has also written extensively in the health and spirituality field. Recent books include *Parish Nursing: Stories of Service and Care* (with Verna Carson), *Spirituality in Patient Care: Why, How, When & What, Faith in the Future: Healthcare, Aging, and the Role of Religion, Spiritual Caregiving: Healthcare as a Ministry* (with Verna Carson), *The Healing Connection: The Story of a Physician's Search for the Link between Faith and Healing*, and *Purpose and Power in Retirement: New Opportunities for Meaning and Significance*.

Meanwhile, Dr. Koenig has taken on a major responsibility for the Templeton Foundation as the editor-in-chief of an international newspaper entitled *Science and Theology News* (formerly *Research News and Opportunities in Theology and Science* until December 2003). Begun in the summer of 2000, with the able assistance of editor Karl Giberson, professor of physics at Eastern Nazarene College, the subscriber base for the thirty-six-page publication had reached 33,000 by March 2002 and had gained national media attention.

Another key player in this program of growth and recognition is Dr. Herbert Benson, author of the best-selling book *The Relaxation Response*, director of the Mind-Body Medical Institute, and associate professor of medicine at Harvard Medical School. Under Dr. Benson's direction, a major course titled "Spirituality and Healing" was convened in Boston in December 1995. It brought together several hundred healthcare professionals to learn about the current data on spiritual variables and health and then to hear a variety of perspectives from representatives of different cultural and religious groups. This three-day course offered continuing medical education credit and has been repeated several times with large attendance. Another in the series, "The Importance of Forgiveness," was held in November 2003 with the co-sponsorship of Dr. Christina Puchalski and the George Washington Institute for Spirituality and Health.

Finally, in the longer term, Sir John is looking for empirical studies of the impact of prayer, meditation, love, thankfulness, and many other characteristics of the spiritual life, all conducted under the most rigorous experimental protocols in a variety of cultural and religious settings. Encouraging the few trained investigators in this field and providing peer-reviewed journals in which they may publish their findings are among the highest priority goals of the John Templeton Foundation.

In any case, it is unlikely that Sir John's enthusiasm for medical research into the relationship between the spirit and healing will lessen, nor that the Foundation will be any less enthusiastic in years to come. Sir John's son, Dr. John M. Templeton Jr. (Jack), former professor of pediatric surgery at the University of Pennsylvania Medical School and president of the John Templeton Foundation, is likewise deeply concerned for the spiritual dimensions in medicine.

CHAPTER 5

A Call to Humility

Theology Is Often Resistant to New Ideas

So often scholarship is associated with pride. For many intelligent people, knowing more than others seems to be almost more important than the acquisition of knowledge itself. John Marks Templeton has observed that this tendency of the human ego has been especially destructive of progress in our knowledge of God. Disciples of the founding prophets of the great religions often took an exclusive view of their knowledge of God, and assumed that there was little new to be learned. Research has often been backward looking, focusing on the ancient foundation instead of on the future. In an interview with the publication *Second Opinion* in July 1993, Sir John was asked about his view that none of the great religions seem willing to experiment with openness.

> The main restraining influence has been and is personal ego — the concept that we are the center. For countless ages various people thought that the earth was flat, because it *looks* flat. For countless ages various people have thought that the sun revolved around the earth, because it *looks* that way. For countless ages people have thought that their god was the only true God. The Jews were not the only ones to think they were the chosen people. And the human ego has in effect said that God is understandable. Human ego has led most religions — I'm talking about forgotten religions — to say that they had the whole truth, they knew their mysteries.

Now astronomy has defeated human ego — we no longer think we are very important in a hundred billion galaxies. I would like to see that happen in our knowledge of God. I don't think we know much more about God now than we knew about the hundred billion galaxies 2,000 years ago.

Based on his experience as a trustee of Princeton Theological Seminary, Sir John applied the same approach to a possible solution.

I've been a trustee of Princeton Seminary for forty years. They don't appropriate anything for research in the same sense that a hospital or a medical school would. The research in the Princeton budget is for archaeology and ancient scriptures, which is nice. But it doesn't really lead us to know a lot more about God in the end. Since I couldn't find any organization concentrating on progress in religion, I've undertaken that. I may not succeed. It may not be feasible for anybody, but that's what I'm focusing on. The first step, twenty-one years ago, was to offer prizes for progress in religion. The progress has come in different fields, and out of the twenty-three winners so far, five have been in *science* and religion.

I hope that we can do research on many subjects in science and religion. We can't hope to foresee where God will reveal himself. Bob Herrmann and I published a book called *The God Who Would Be Known* with the idea that God is ready to reveal himself if we search with humility and in the right way. It never occurred to me to wonder *where* we should search — whether in astronomy or genetics or prayer or love. Almost no research has been done on love from a scientific standpoint, on its origin, nature, varieties, encouragement, or results. We are trying one thing after another to encourage people to do something that increases our knowledge of God, God's purposes, or God's love. Maybe 10 percent of the ideas we try will work. With that humble approach, it really never occurred to me to search, say, in astronomy and not in genetics.

SCIENCE IS PROVIDING EMPIRICAL AND SCHOLARLY
APPROACHES TO NEW IDEAS

John Templeton has become convinced that true progress in our seeking knowledge of God must take into account the incredible growth of our knowledge in the sciences. In the past few decades, science has revealed a universe of awesome size and complexity, and now some scientists are speaking out about the theological implications of these revelations. Professor Paul Davies of the University of Adelaide, a winner of the Templeton Prize for Progress in Religion, is one of the first of many scientists impressed with the unmistakable appearance of meaning and purpose in this new picture of our universe. And coupling this new theological impulse with the power of the empirical approach so essential to science would seem to provide a new and fruitful avenue of discovery for the theological enterprise as well. What Sir John envisages is nothing less than a supplemental theology, born out of this progressive exploratory approach — a new experimental theology to add to the wonderful testimony of holy scriptures. And such a program would surely be worthy of support at something near the magnitude of our researches in the natural sciences. Again in *The Second Opinion* article, he says:

> We are terribly ignorant. We should be anxious to learn, to experiment, to discover a little more about God. We should listen to anybody who thinks he knows something about God. More than a billion dollars a day are spent on scientific research. If one-tenth of that were spent on research in spiritual subjects, that would be a hundred million dollars a day. That would be visionary.

PRIZES FOR PAPERS IN HUMILITY THEOLOGY[1]

To promote this exciting vision, John Templeton began a program of prizes to encourage theologians and scientists to think and write and influence others in this new direction for progress in religion. An early step was to compile a directory of scholars writing and publishing in the interface between science and religion. This compilation, carried out at the Center of Theological Inquiry in Princeton, revealed more than eight hundred scholars who were working in the general field. For the support of this endeavor, John Templeton went to his longtime friend and colleague Dr. James I. McCord, former president of Princeton Seminary and at that time chairman of the Center. He also recruited Professor Harold Nebelsick of Louisville Presbyterian Theological Seminary, a pioneer in the dialogue between theologians and scientists, to assist him in editing the volume. Sadly, Harold Nebelsick died suddenly on March 26, 1989, and the volume was eventually completed by John Webster, a Princeton Seminary student, and published in 1992. John Templeton provided funding to support this work.

A second publication in support of the program has been the newsletter of the Foundation, *Progress in Theology*, for which I have been editorial coordinator. Our major involvement has been the publication of abstracts of winning papers, some two dozen in the course of the last three years. During this period we have received numerous letters and some manuscripts from our readers, many accompanied by pleas to help in the publication of new ideas in the area of theology and science. In reviewing the nature of these requests and the character of the manuscripts, we have come to realize that scholarship and the normal structure of publication, with its attendant research into the ideas of others and required peer review, is an essential ingredient of publication in humility theology. In the editorial for the March 1994 issue of *Progress in Theology*, we outlined our philosophy about and commitment to the highest scholarship in encouraging the development of new ideas. The editorial, albeit somewhat lengthy, is reprinted in full below because it carefully explains our position.

> One of the difficulties in any publishing endeavor is deciding which of many ideas should be presented in a specific forum. Ideas about progress in theology are no exception, and our editorial office has been favored with a rather bewildering array of papers presenting new concepts or old concepts in new forms. Our difficulty is even more acute than usual because, on the one hand, we

wish to encourage novelty and creativity, but on the other hand, we feel that such ideas should be somehow anchored to the world of scholarship.

The approach we have taken thus far in our program of publication is to invite material from recognized scholars, and particularly from those whose ideas and concepts have undergone editorial and peer scrutiny. Those of us who have a scientific background are very aware of the importance of interaction with colleagues and of a thorough literature search in the course of formulating new hypotheses. The subsequent submission of our best effort to a refereed journal is the most important step of all.

Some have argued that there are no avenues of publication for papers with progressive ideas about religion, but our experience suggests that that is rarely the case for well-thought-out and thoroughly documented papers. Publications that accept this type of material can be found by reviewing the journals listed in the publications of authors included in *Who's Who in Theology and Science*, published in 1992 by Winthrop Publishing Company (Framingham, MA, ISBN: 1-879302-00-4). The importance of publication has also been emphasized in another program of the Center, the Call for Papers on Humility Theology. The Center's advisory board has strongly recommended that only papers published in scholarly, refereed science and religion journals be considered for awards in this program.

A second avenue that potential authors should consider is the critical interaction with a group of interested scholarly individuals. Membership in one of the science/religion organizations listed in Directory C of *Who's Who in Theology and Science* is an excellent way to develop a group for such interaction. For academicians, another approach is to interact with students by developing a rather open-ended course in science and religion. The Humility Theology Information Center [now the John Templeton Foundation Advisory Board] is conducting a program for the development of academic courses in which science and religion are taught together. Here the emphasis is placed on a balanced treatment of the two disciplines, again with an effort to promote good scholarship.

The tension between the ideas of an individual and the collective views of a scholarly community will surely always be with us. Perhaps, as an example of humility theology, we need willingly to subject our most cherished ideas and convictions to the evidence of the past and the criticism of the current community of scholars. It is our hope that by this mechanism not all novel and original thinking will be suppressed, but rather that new ideas in theology will by their sheer power and grandeur find acceptance and become one means toward a new, spiritual renaissance.

The Call for Papers in Humility Theology program was announced in 1991, with the stipulation that entries had to have been published in the prior three years in a reputable scientific or theological journal and would be judged on the basis of their contribution to our greater understanding and appreciation of the new climate of humility engendered by the sciences, and the theological openness which that awareness demands.

The announcement was mailed with a cover letter to the people listed in *Who's Who in Theology and Science,* and advertisements were placed in several science-theology journals, including *Zygon, Perspectives on Science and Christian Faith,* and *Science and Christian Belief.* Sixty-four authors submitted 130 papers in the first year of the program. Twelve papers were awarded prizes.

In the second year of the competition, we saw a definite improvement in the number and quality of submissions. More than 100 authors submitted 131 papers; 47 of them qualified for an award. In the third year, 65 papers were submitted and 35 prizes were awarded. The lower number involved in the third year is generally attributed to the fact that a new program inviting academics to submit courses in science and religion was running concurrently, and this new emphasis clearly diverted the attention of some potential "Call for Papers" participants.

Professor Howard Van Till of Calvin College, one of the judges of the first three programs, undertook direction of the program in its fourth year. The emphasis broadened to include a second area of humility theology, the constructive interaction of religion and the health sciences. The criteria for this enlarged program had the following domains of concern:

- Epistemological concerns — assessing the possibility, character, or extent of progress toward knowledge in theology, religion, science, and their mutual interactions;
- Empirical concerns — assessing the probative force of empirical investigation in the evaluation of theories regarding the mutual relevance of theology/religion and the sciences;
- Methodological concerns — assessing the methodologies appropriate to research on the relationships among theology, religion, and the sciences; and
- Constructive exploration — constructing, in a manner both creative and intellectually responsible, a novel perspective or way for growing in our understanding of God, ourselves, and the vast universe in which we live. This constructive exploration might well constitute one's response to the question, "Is it not possible that the unseen (the full array of spiritual realities that are not directly perceivable by our senses) is far more vast than the seen (the physical realities that can be sensibly perceived)?"

As we look at the results, it is instructive to realize that we have accessed a very large number of theological and scientific journals and involved a large number of scholars in this program. In 1993 the winning papers were published in thirty-four different scholarly journals, and in 1994, twenty-six different journals were represented. Furthermore, the majority of papers came from theological faculty, indicating some attention by theology and religion departments to the possibilities of humility theology. Admittedly, there is still much to be done, but it would seem that influencing theological scholarship may be part of the 10 percent of ideas that Sir John thinks may work.

CHAPTER 6

Discovering the "Laws of Life"

O NE OF SIR JOHN TEMPLETON'S major goals in his quest for
progress in religion has been to deepen the spiritual research of
high school and college students worldwide. His view of spirituality, however, goes well beyond Sunday school teaching or college classes in religion.
Rather, he sees a need for a broad-based emphasis on research for spiritual
realities and also on the "laws of life," spiritual laws that have served as
guidelines for countless generations of people in all cultures and political
settings. These laws, he believes, have been deeply embedded in human history, with a similar kind of permanence and given-ness as the physical laws
that appear to govern our universe. For example, he visualizes the Golden
Rule, as taught by Jesus in the Sermon on the Mount — "do unto others as
you would have them do unto you" — as a universally accepted law to live
by. Agreed on in the three major monotheistic religions, Judaism, Christianity, and Islam, it is also proposed by all of the Eastern religions and
philosophies. Many other spiritual laws have this same kind of acceptance,
and they have been the mainstay of countless successful political, business,
and professional leaders all over the world. The problem, as Sir John sees it,
is that these spiritual laws have gradually lost prominence in our educational
systems as societies have become more secular and programs to build character and moral strength have been seriously crowded out.

A HIGH SCHOOL ESSAY PROGRAM

One of John Templeton's approaches to a solution began with a teenage essay contest in Franklin County, Tennessee, which was developed with the help of his niece and nephew, Becky and Handly Templeton. At a 1986 meeting of the Foundation advisory board, John talked about the background of this emphasis:

> We started the essay contest on the spiritual "Laws of Life" some years ago in the county in Tennessee where I grew up and it had an amazing effect on that county. Because America may be the only nation in the world that forbids teaching religion in the schools, we did not work through the schools. We just made it publicly known that teenage boys and girls could win cash by writing essays on how they planned to lead their future lives — the spiritual principles they were going to use in their lives.
>
> Two things made it work: one was the prizes — not large, $2,000 for the first prize with nine prizes scaled down to $100. We offered these twice a year. Students of that age get terribly excited about winning $100 or $1,000. This idea just swept the county with three-quarters of the students of that age writing essays twice a year on the spiritual principles they expected to use in their lives. But, in addition, the other working principle is this: We don't tell them the spiritual principles. We ask them to tell us! Now there's magic in that because people of that age love to tell you, but they sometimes resent *your* telling them. It also causes them to think.
>
> If they have to think it up for themselves, they understand it better than if they just read about it in a book. Also, they go to their parents and say, "Tell me what are the spiritual laws of life." Some of the parents have to think more than they would otherwise. It's the same with the teacher and the teachers have to think. Following the writing period, the prize-winning essays are announced on the local radio and in the local newspapers. Then

we put on a banquet at the country club and give out honors and plaques to the prizewinners.

This program is having just a transforming effect on this county. It's been so remarkable that we've prepared a handbook about how to organize an essay program. Similar programs were started in Bradley County, Tennessee, and in Jackson, Mississippi, which have also been very successful.

Dr. Jack Templeton, Sir John's son, added his own enthusiasm:

Students who, in many cases, were not doing well in their classes found for the first time that the assignment was not directed at them but that the idea was to come out of them. One set of parents said, "Our daughter hasn't talked to us in two years and now she's interested in things that are important to our family." So families are really growing in the experience. Some students not particularly distinguished in their academics and some who were even disruptive in their classes became focused on the idea that someone cared about what they had to say. These students were often not those who were the most polished writers. Their grammar and punctuation may not have been perfect, but sometimes the content was so deep that often someone who was at best a C student could be a prize winner. This did a tremendous amount for their self-esteem, and with the public recognition both at the dinners and in being identified in the school newspapers, the students' own academic achievement began to go up because they found a measure of appreciation for their own productivity. . . .

Our real hope is that this will be like dropping pebbles in a pond; that there will be a big ripple effect so that with the help of a new managing director of the program we can take this idea to centers around the country. We will talk to individuals and organizations like the Rotary Club to undertake this with their county or their school district. Part of what has worked well in Franklin

County is that it has brought together public schools and private schools to interrelate in this project. There's a lot to be gained in the local areas when people realize that there's more hope and concern in the younger generation.

The Laws of Life Essay Contest program has continued to expand. Dr. Arthur Schwartz has been joined in this program by Ms. Peggy Veljkovic. By December 2003, over 122 individual contests took place in 27 states and 54 countries around the world, including the United Kingdom, Canada, Argentina, Uganda, New Zealand, and Russia. The program has been endorsed by the National Association of Secondary School Principals, a forty-thousand-member organization of principals and vice-principals in sixty countries around the world and with affiliates in every state in the United States.

Mrs. Amy Butler, a Templeton Foundation member, pioneered the establishment of contests in Georgia. In September 2003, 21 high schools with an enrollment of 33,000 students were participating. Of these, 15,400 students submitted essays. The program has formed a coalition with the Georgia Center for Character Education, and also recently benefited from a newly passed state law requiring character education at elementary and secondary school levels. The events in Georgia suggest that the character education movement may represent a great opportunity for this program.

Elsewhere, Sir John Templeton's daughter Dr. Anne Zimmerman and her husband have been strong proponents of the laws of life program in Wyoming, where thirty-one of the state's forty-nine high schools participate.

JOHN TEMPLETON'S OWN DISCOVERY

As for John's own part, being brought up in the hill country of Tennessee was probably not a bad way to gain strength and direction for life. For example, in the farming community where John Templeton grew up, truthfulness was a law of life. Your word was your bond. People of character would never promise something and then go back on their word. A contract between two parties did not have to be put in writing; there was no need for a court or a judge to enforce it. Civilization, as many then perceived it, was a place where the handshake was sacred.

Sir John says that doors and windows in his hometown of Winchester were never locked. For that matter, any hardware store would sell skeleton keys that worked in almost 90 percent of the door locks. Every home had a Bible — sometimes as the only book. Motion picture theaters showed only films that taught ethics — the hero always won and, in the end, the villain always lost. Prohibition precluded any home having alcoholic drinks under penalty of jail. And in his seventeen years of growing up in Winchester, he remembers only one person who was a drug addict.

John's father was a paragon of thrift yet was ever willing to sponsor the worthwhile projects John thought up. As already mentioned, his mother was quite unusual, being very well educated for the time and for rural Tennessee. After college, she then tutored for two years for a wealthy Texas family before returning to Winchester to eventually marry Harvey Templeton. Vella was the first family member to become interested in the Unity Movement, with its emphasis on the positive, on possibilities, and on the virtues of material prosperity. Unity emphasized "thought control," the ability to discipline yourself, to focus your mind on those things that are positive and most productive. Physical healing, wealth, inner peace — Unity teaches that almost anything is possible if your mental processes are in tune with the great divine principles of the universe. The capacity for greatness is within, where God is ever present.

Acting on these principles, Harvey and Vella Templeton gave young John almost total freedom to do what he thought best. He was never given advice about ethics, religion, or conduct, though he was active in the Cumberland Presbyterian Church and had ready access to the literature of the Unity Movement and to a set of the *Book of Knowledge Encyclopedia*.

Only once in John Templeton's school career was he asked if he'd done his homework assignment. His mother once asked him if he'd finished his work. He hesitated, but finally told her, "Mother, all my life I've gotten nothing but As. Even in Latin. Not a single grade lower than an A. So please leave it up to me. I love you for your solicitude, but you needn't worry." She never asked him again.

John Templeton understood the virtues of promptness and perseverance at a tender age. When he was in the first grade, he took his report card home and showed his father, with understandable pride, that all of the subjects were marked A. His father was very pleased and said that he would like to set up a contest. On each of John's half-year reports that showed nothing lower than A, he would give his son a bale of cotton. Each time there was a grade lower than A, however, John would have to give his father a bale of cotton.

The theory was that the son would wind up owing his father many, many bales of cotton, which would be a lesson to John. But the older Templeton did not reckon with his son's will power, desire to succeed, and his early ability to get the most out of the minutes in an hour.

He worked hard at his lessons, he was always prompt with them, and he went through grammar school and high school without a single grade below an A. Eleven years later his father owed him twenty-two bales of cotton. But then, in the Great Depression, when John's father could give no more tuition money beyond supporting his first year at Yale, John refused to accept those twenty-two bales.

John's mother was in many ways a superb teacher of self-reliance. One summer, for example, when John was 12, his mother loaded him, his 15-year-old brother, and a couple of cousins in the car and took them on an extensive two-month trip throughout the Northeast. They traveled about one hundred miles a day, camped out, and did their own cooking. But this was not a parent-controlled vacation. The kids were in charge just as much as Vella Templeton, with each person participating in selecting the routes and activities and setting up the day's campsite.

Even though they had a lot of fun, the trip was by no means merely a relaxed, carefree sort of affair. Every moment was scheduled, and myriads of stimulating sights and experiences were packed into each day. For example, every time they arrived in a big metropolitan area like Washington, New York, or Philadelphia, they would hit all the museums — and that meant every room on every floor of every major museum.

It was a hectic two months, but such high-powered activity, combined with intensive learning experiences, was what young John learned to expect and love as a boy. And that trip served to set the stage for still another summer adventure a few years later.

When John was 16, his mother loaded up the car again — this time with John, Harvey Jr., and one classmate — and they headed west. Their goal: to see *everything* west of the Mississippi — all the historic sites, national parks, national monuments, and the Pacific Ocean. Again, they were gone about two months, and they camped out every night.

This kind of intensive study of one part of the country or one area of knowledge was part of a regular pattern in John's childhood. It not only instilled self-confidence in him, but also inspired a love for travel and an outward look, which in later years gave him an advantage in international investing.

John's youth was a time of great activity — crammed with projects and experiments and meaningful learning experiences. It is not surprising that he covets this self-discovery for the young people of today. Noteworthy, too, is his avoidance of television or radio entertainment.

THE HONOR ROLL FOR CHARACTER-BUILDING COLLEGES

In 1989, Sir John Templeton initiated a second program for character building and moral development — this time in the nation's colleges and universities. His idea was to select approximately one hundred schools whose educational programs and campus activities showed the greatest commitment to the personal growth and moral development of their students. For example, the *U.S. News and World Report* national survey that periodically rates America's best colleges uses the opinion leader approach, and its results are widely accepted in the academic community. Regardless of the approach taken, one of the clear benefits of the review process is that each institution learns a great deal about what others are doing in terms of character building and personal moral development. Specific courses dedicated to personal ethics, applied ethics, the psychology of human development, moral reasoning, or human values are often listed. Programs are often outlined for community involvement, overseas missions, and campus ministries for the handicapped and those with pressing personal problems.

In 1995, applicant institutions were evaluated according to the following five criteria:

- Encourages students to explore an individual moral reasoning process;
- Fosters positive attitudes and overall well-being;
- Encourages spiritual growth and moral values;
- Promotes community-building values; and
- Advocates drug-free lifestyle.

The Foundation received applications from 325 institutions. About half listed specific courses in character building and personal ethics. Most institutions were religiously affiliated; only about 20 percent of the 325 were state-supported or private secular institutions. However, these nonreligious schools had a higher proportion of courses or programs in personal and applied ethics. In 1995, 124 schools made the Honor Roll.

CHARACTER BUILDING AND SPIRITUAL DEVELOPMENT

A full-scale program to encourage courses in character formation and spiritual development is underway. This program, under the direction of Dr. Arthur Schwartz, is termed the College and Character Initiative Program. Under the auspices of the Florida State University's Institute on College Student Values, a guidebook has been published by Templeton Foundation Press entitled *Colleges That Encourage Character Development: A Resource for Parents, Students, and Educators* that profiles 405 exemplary college programs in ten categories that inspire students to lead ethical and civic-minded lives, as well as 50 college presidents selected for their leadership in this area and 100 colleges named to the Templeton Honor Roll. Schwartz reports that the rigorous selection process for inclusion in the book has evolved into a highly competitive process, garnering high interest among college administrators.

The College and Character Initiative has also established a relationship with the National Association for Counselors and Admissions Officers, with the goal of emphasizing character development as a criterion parents and students should consider when choosing a college. A relationship is also being developed with the American College of Education in order to focus on the college president's role in prompting character development on the campus.

In fall 2001, Dr. Schwartz published an article on the resurgence of interest in spirituality and religious values on college campuses. The article, entitled "Growing Spiritually during the College Years," appeared in *Liberal Education*, a publication of the Association of American Colleges and Universities. The article recognizes that although college students' attitudes toward organized religion often may be negative, interest in spirituality is increasing on campus. Indeed, for some students, he says, "spirituality is a compelling and generative term that captures our most heartfelt aspirations." Lived out in our lives as a "search" for the truth in our time and place, spirituality can dynamically shape our thoughts and actions. This change suggests that there are new opportunities on the campus for an emphasis on character education.

In March 2002, a landmark workshop, Exploring Prayer and Spiritual Formation during Adolescence, was convened at Princeton Theological Seminary. The workshop had three goals.

1. To explore the relationship between the adolescent spirit and the Creator Spirit.
2. To explore whether prayer serves as an effective motivational resource during adolescence.
3. To focus theological and scientific attention on adolescents who have clearly developed a convictional faithfulness in the midst of a secularized and relativized society.

The Foundation recently awarded a major grant to Professor William Damon, director of the Center on Adolescence at Stanford University, to research the development of purpose in the lives of young people. The Foundation also awarded a grant to Dr. Peter Benson, president of Search Institute, to explore the science and theology of spiritual development during childhood and adolescence. Another major grant was awarded in 2002 to the Higher Education Research Institute at UCLA to design and implement a national survey on the religiosity and spirituality of college students. Titled "Spirituality in Higher Education: A National Study of College Students' Search for Meaning and Purpose," the initiative is designed to involve and engage colleges and universities interested in expanding and enhancing opportunities for college students to grow spiritually and religiously. The hope is that other foundations interested in education will follow the lead of the Templeton Foundation in emphasizing spiritual values on the campus.

CHAPTER 7

Bringing Science and Religion
Together on Campus

THE GAP BETWEEN SCIENCE AND RELIGION

JOHN TEMPLETON'S enthusiasm for progress in spiritual information and research finds a challenging arena in the world's institutions of higher learning. Over the past century most of our universities and colleges have gradually shifted their allegiance from a religious worldview to a scientific one. The scientific view most generally presented the world as a clock-like structure ruled by natural laws. Everything that happened seemed resolvable into cause and effect. There seemed no need for God. Objective science became the supreme arbiter of truth, the source of progress, the frontier subject. Religion came to be viewed as looking backward, almost irrelevant to the modern age.

To Sir John, this was a sad and largely unrealistic state of affairs. The nine judges for the Templeton Prize for Progress in Religion awarded that prize on several occasions to university theology professors. This highlights the fact that there still were forward-looking pioneers in academic religion departments. Among them were Sir Sarvepalli Radhakrishnan, Oxford professor of Eastern religion and ethics, who received the prize in 1975; Thomas Torrance, professor of Christian dogmatics at the University of Edinburgh, who received the prize in 1978; and Ralph Wendell Burhoe, professor of theology at the Meadville/Lombard Theological School's Center for Advanced Study in Chicago, who was awarded the prize in 1980. But for

John Templeton these three prizes represented only a small token of his enthusiasm for progress in spiritual information and research.

In his book *The Humble Approach*, Sir John talked about the enormous creative opportunities that lie before us and placed the blame for the present narrow outlook of most religious people squarely on human egotism. By contrast, he said, many or most natural scientists have displayed an open-minded, exploratory, tolerant, and searching attitude, and he strongly recommended that theologians could benefit from their example. In the introduction he writes:

> We are perched on the frontier of future knowledge. Even though we stand upon the enormous mountain of information collected over the last five centuries of scientific progress, we have only fleeting glimpses of the future. To a large extent, the future lies before us like a vast wilderness of unexplored reality. The God who created and sustained His evolving universe through eons of progress and development has not placed our generation at the tag end of the creative process. He has placed us at a new beginning. We are here for the future.
>
> Our role is crucial. As human beings we are endowed with mind and spirit. We can think, imagine, and dream. We can search for future trends through the rich diversity of human thought. God permits us in some ways to be co-creators with Him in His continuing act of creation.
>
> There is, however, a stumbling block: egotism. The closed-minded attitude of those who think they know it all inhibits future progress. Natural scientists, by and large, have overcome this hurdle. They are more open-minded. They research the natural wonders of the universe, devising new hypotheses, testing them, challenging old assumptions, competing with each other in professional rivalry. The physical future of human civilization is in their professional hands, guided by relatively tolerant and open minds.
>
> This is not equally true concerning our spiritual future. Some

theologians, religious leaders, and lay people are frequently blind to the obstacles they themselves erect. Many are not even aware that the spiritual future could, or should, be different from anything that has ever been before. Many do not realize that spiritual reality can be researched in ways similar to those used by natural scientists. Some do not want even to consider the possibilities of a future of progressively unfolding spiritual discoveries.

Why not? Many devoutly religious people are not devoutly humble. They do not admit their worldview is limited. They are not open to suggestions that their personal theology might be incomplete. They do not entertain the notion that other religions have valuable insights to contribute to an understanding of God and His creation. When people take a more humble attitude, they welcome new ideas about the spirit just as they welcome new scientific ideas about how to cure headaches, how to heat and cool their homes, or how to develop natural resources.[1]

Sir John feels that the future of our spiritual understanding is far too important to be left in the hands of people of restricted vision or people who are preoccupied with protecting their turf. This period in our history is the blossoming time, when the human enterprise is bursting into flower and the growth of human knowledge is accelerating at an incredible pace.

Yet this explosion in our scientific knowledge has not brought about a conviction among most scientists that we have learned all there is to learn. There may be a few zealots like Stephen Hawking who suggest that we are approaching a theory of everything, which will bring the "end of physics" and "then we shall know the mind of God."

But the vast majority of working scientists realize that we are only beginning to be aware of the extent of our ignorance. The past few decades have brought most scientists to a sense of awe and to a new humility. And some are once again looking at their science for philosophical and theological meaning, almost in the way many of the early scientists spoke of their scientific endeavors as opening the book of God's works.

Given this remarkable recent change in attitude among many scientists, John Templeton sees the stage set for a new dialogue between scientists, philosophers, and theologians, especially on university and college campuses. More than this, he sees the opportunity for the revitalization of religion, theology, and science departments. Given the new world that science has brought to us, these disciplines should, he says, be the most exciting focus for new ideas and concepts in the university. All of this would be possible if we adopted a new spirit of humility, open to the God of a universe infinitely greater and more complex than we could ever have dreamed. Sir John gives us another side of this new challenge to theology in another chapter of *The Humble Approach* titled "The New World of Time." In it he mentions Teilhard de Chardin's view of God's activity as a progression from the geosphere to the biosphere to the noosphere—the sphere of the mind—and then to a consummation in Omega Point. But, Sir John asks, what if there is no Omega Point, but other spheres and other worlds instead.

> The twentieth century after Christ may very well represent a new renaissance in human culture, a new embarkation into future cultures. Persons born in this century can hardly imagine the small amount of knowledge and the limited concept of the cosmos man had when the scriptures of all the five major religions were written. Do old scriptures need reinterpreting to accommodate an expanded notion of the universe?
>
> More important for theology is the expanded concept of history. When all the scriptures of all major religions were written, the history of the universe was conceived as only a few thousand years. Now geologists and paleontologists who think in hundreds of millions of years read history in visible form sometimes more reliable than history books or scriptures. And cosmologists think in billions of years. Because light travels a hundred and eighty-six thousand miles a second, we can see the sun not as it is now, but as it was some eight minutes ago. We see some stars as they were when Christ was born. We see some galaxies as they were six mil-

lion years ago. Such a revolution in our conceptions of time and history is beginning to shape our theology.

What existed before this universe began? What will exist after the sun has grown cold? After minerals there emerged plants, and after plants, animals, and after animals there emerged minds; and minds began to participate in the creative process. What comes next? Is there evidence that minds are developing into even more miraculous spirits and souls? These are not only questions of science but also of theology — a new type of theology not yet taught in seminaries.

Consider the cold, inert world of minerals, the throbbing world of life, the curious, searching realm of the intellect. What next? This may be the most important question facing us at the end of the twentieth century. To answer it, scientists are daily engaged in new scientific experiments that will help us know more about the vast unseen. Theologians, too, answering Chardin's call for a new religion, must begin to explore the vast unseen dimensions of our evolving universe; they must plumb the very "depths of God's own nature."[2]

In some ways, the university may be ready for a new dialogue between the sciences and the humanities — with special reference to religion. Robert Sollod, at Cleveland State University, published an article in *The Chronicle of Higher Education* calling for a reconsideration of religion and spirituality as integral parts of college curricula in this era of curriculum reform.[3] Additionally, Stephen Cain, staff reporter for the *Ann Arbor News*, reported on a conference at the University of Michigan that called for the reincorporation of values, ethics, morality, and organized religion into the life of the university. University regent Laurence Deitch said at that conference, "There has been a breakdown of values in our society with little counter force from any point of view other than the religious right. Values can and should be taught at the university."[4]

John Templeton has proposed that we get more religion departments to take a scientific view of their subject, opening their minds to the new scientific discoveries with their challenging voices for theology. He has proposed a number of ways that this might be encouraged by the Templeton Foundation. One of the most fruitful so far is a program to encourage the development of new and improved courses joining science and religion.

THE SCIENCE AND RELIGION COURSE PROGRAM

Begun in 1994, the first phase of the program involved the identification of academic courses in science and religion that could serve as models or guides for faculty interested in the development of new and improved courses in institutions worldwide. Sir John chose the broad-sweep approach, surveying all catalog offerings in colleges, universities, and seminaries in the United States and Canada. The search team found 943 science and religion courses. Questionnaires were sent to the course managers, department heads, or deans, requesting syllabi and additional information about the courses. Prizes of $5,000 each were offered for the best five courses identified.

Descriptions of the model course winners and their courses were published in the science-religion journal *Zygon*. The article was written by freelance science writer Margaret Wertheim and appeared in the September 1995 issue.[5]

The second phase of the program was announced in June 1994 in the various science and religion journals and newsletters: *Zygon, Perspectives on Science and Christian Faith, Science and Christian Belief,* the *Journal for the Scientific Study of Religion, Science and Religion News,* and *Progress in Theology.* In addition, personal letters were sent to some five hundred faculty listed in *Who's Who in Theology and Science.*

Sir John was eager to get participation by a broad segment of the academic science and religion communities, so he made the generous offer of up to one hundred prizes of $10,000 each — $5,000 for the course manager and $5,000 for the institution — for new and improved courses that followed the criteria that had been set for the model courses. Winners were required to attend an all-expense-paid workshop on course design the following summer, with the intent that a network of faculty in the field could be established and liaison with the Foundation maintained.

Then, in September, Sir John decided that we should add an additional workshop, this time for applicants who might be new to this interdisciplinary area but interested enough to travel at their own expense. Sir John was quite sure they would, given the incentive of the $10,000 prize, half of which was designated for the institution. Surely institutions would support the travel expense if it represented an investment toward the award. And of course he was right! More than 150 faculty members inquired and nearly 80 attended the workshop.

By every criterion, the workshop was a success. There was excellent leadership by Robert Russell and John Albright, superb facilities, and an atmosphere of excitement as like-minded faculty (who thought they were alone in their interest in religion and science) found each other. The attendees' evaluations were very positive. Furthermore, they gave every indication of being teachable — even the few who had been involved with a science-religion course for many years. They certainly were very appreciative of the Templeton Foundation's vision. And perhaps of most importance, more than half the attendees were from secular schools, and more than half had never taught a formal science-religion course.

The response to the second phase of the award program was equally enthusiastic. A total of 184 applications were received and 173 were reviewed for an award. The largest number of courses, 72, came from faculty in religion and theology departments, amounting to 42 percent of the total. Science departments accounted for 18 percent and philosophy departments 16 percent of the total. Of the remainder, the largest percentage originated in various interdisciplinary programs. More revealing, perhaps, the percentage of applications from secular institutions was greatest for interdisciplinary programs, suggesting that faculty in secular institutions intending to initiate courses in science and religion may find good possibilities in the great variety of interdisciplinary programs that were then being developed at secular institutions. Overall, 43 percent of the applications came from secular institutions. Applicants for new courses predominated, with philosophy departments and interdisciplinary programs applying primarily with new courses, while science, religion, and history departments brought almost equal numbers of new and improved courses to the competition.

In 1998, the Foundation decided to give the program a more global emphasis and turned over its administration to the Center for Theology and the Natural Sciences (CTNS) in Berkeley, California. The director of CTNS, Dr. Robert J. Russell, had been a strong supporter of the Foundation's programs and especially the Science and Religion Course Program from its beginnings in 1994. In the Center's column "Bridge Building," in the November 2000 issue of *Research News*, CTNS recounts some of the early innovations it brought to the course program. In part they say:

> In the spring of 1998, the Templeton Foundation made a four-year, $12.6 million grant to the Center for Theology and the Natural Sciences (CTNS) in Berkeley, California, "to develop and expand course programs in science and religion at universities worldwide." At that time, CTNS earmarked over 70 percent of its grant for directly supporting regional and international programs in science and religion education. Robert John Russell was designated principle investigator and Ted Peters, professor of systematic theology at Pacific Lutheran Theological Seminary, became program director. Peter Hess was named associate program director as well as competition director for the Science and Religion Course Program (SRCP).
>
> On receiving the grant at CTNS, Russell identified three main goals for the program's future:
>
> 1. Expanding the program to Europe, Asia, Australia-New Zealand, and Latin America;
> 2. Broadening the impact of the course program by bringing it to faculty in 25 of the leading research universities and 15 of the leading divinity schools and seminaries in the United States, Canada and England.
> 3. Strengthening the program where it has been most successful so far.

CTNS has moved forward aggressively to meet these goals.

The course program has dramatically changed the appearance of the field since the days when only a few scholars were engaged in interdisciplinary work. More than 600 course award winners have been enabled to participate more fully in the dialogue, teaching an estimated 12,000 students in courses on science and religion. With a vast range of courses now being offered in colleges, universities, and seminaries on every continent except Antarctica, this has truly become a global conversation.

The fundamental objective of the course program remains what it was at its inception: to enable course award winners to exercise an enduring influence on the curricula of their colleges, universities, and seminaries. A 1999 CTNS survey showed that, since 1994, semesterly offerings of science and religion courses increased by 125%, annual offerings by 285%, and bi-annual offerings by 54%.

Even more remarkable than numerical growth has been the evolution of the field in terms of its diversity. What began largely as a Judeo-Christian discussion — or at least a discussion conducted within a monotheistic context — has now been broadened to include scholars from many theological traditions. New scientific disciplines have also emerged. While cosmology and evolutionary biology retain their places in the discussion, fascinating questions are now being raised by genetics, neuroscience and cognitive science, and other disciplines.

As reported in the June 2002 issue of *Research News* (now *Science and Religion News*), considerable progress has been made in extending SRCP to most parts of the world. Many projects are in development. Workshops and conferences have been held in Pune, India; in Pueblo, Mexico; in Adelaide, Australia; in Islamabad, Pakistan; in Seoul, Korea; and in Kuala Lumpur, Malaysia.

By June 2002, the course program had awarded over 700 grants for establishment of academic courses. In 2002, 53 grants were made, with 64 percent of the winning proposals coming from outside the United States. In April 2002, 10 grants of $10,000 each were also awarded to consortia of European scholars for both teaching and research.

Foundation support for these programs ended in August 2002 after a total of eight years of "community building." There were forty course program leaders at the final staff meeting in June, and program director Ted Peters summed up their contribution with a commendation for having made "a deliberate attempt to plant seeds for the future."

PART II

The Making of a World-Class Investor

CHAPTER 8

The Winchester Years

S IR JOHN TEMPLETON drove a small red rental car out of the long sweeping drive of the big brick house at 600 South High Street in Winchester, Tennessee, and proceeded down High Street. It was the beginning of two days of travel down memory lane — to recount for me some of his experiences growing up in a small town in middle Tennessee. The big brick house had been built by John's father for his parents, Dr. John Wiley Templeton of Beech Grove, Tennessee, and Susan Jones Templeton, formerly of Canton, Mississippi. Dr. Templeton had received one year of medical training in Nashville, and had been a regimental surgeon in the Confederate Army during the Civil War. After the war he practiced general medicine for some forty years in Wartrace, Tennessee, and then retired to live in Winchester.

The first stop in our trip was almost immediate: the house next door, where John grew up. It was a large stone house built by John's father for Vella Handly two years after they were married. Harvey Templeton and Vella Handly had begun their married life living with the older Templetons, and when she moved to the new house, she made the most of it. The house was set closer to the road, and had a long, low, double limestone wall designed as a planter with an earth-filled center. Vella's love of flowers took the form of a cascade of hanging petunias, which draped the full length of the wall.

The newlyweds' property was six acres in all, including an entire acre of flowers, as well as pecan trees and plantings of a variety of vegetables and fruit. Just beyond the Templeton property in the old days was a field of sedge and wildflowers that attracted many butterflies, the collection of which became one of John's many hobbies that continue to this day. Turning right at the end of the block, we soon encountered a series of small houses built by John's father; John, at age 11, and his brother Harvey, at 14, had wired the houses as part of the construction work. Both boys were remarkably knowledgeable about electricity, which along with such things as auto repair, gardening, astronomy, butterfly collecting, hunting, fishing, and travel, made the Templetons a very interesting family.

At the next corner we turned right again and soon reached the town cemetery. At a site near the road was a well-kept plot with the graves of John's father, mother, and maternal grandfather. The plot was originally purchased by Vella's family. Her father, Robert Clinton Handly, had been a businessman in Winchester, with a busy grain mill on Boiling Fork Creek. The Handlys were also prominent politically. John's maternal grandmother, Elizabeth Marks, was the sister of Colonel Albert Marks, governor of Tennessee. John can even boast of a Revolutionary War-hero ancestor, Virginia-born Samuel Handly, whose parents emigrated from northern Ireland in 1740. Samuel fought the Cherokee Indians, who were believed to have been incited by the British at the beginning of the Revolution, and later he was involved in a decisive victory over British forces at King's Mountain, North Carolina. He is buried in Belvedere, Tennessee, and his tombstone records that he was also "a member of the first convention that formed the Constitution of the State of Tennessee."

Just after we passed the cemetery, Sir John pointed out a row of low-income houses on the other side of the street. Several of these were built by his father with the lumber he purchased when the old courthouse was torn down. According to John, this was a bit of fulfilled prophecy. Like John's father, John's Uncle Jess was also a lawyer in Winchester, with offices in the Farmer's National Bank building where John's father had his offices.

> Uncle Jess was several times judge of the county court. I helped in
> the hard-fought political campaigns when he was elected judge
> and was always surprised that the judge's salary was only $900 a

year. One of his opponents, Judge Frank Lynch, (the father of John's main high school sweetheart, Katrine Lynch) told people "Do not elect Jess because if you do, his brother Harvey will wind up owning the courthouse." Sure enough, a few years later during the Great Depression the federal government made a grant to Franklin County for the purpose of building a new courthouse. Accordingly, the old courthouse was put up for demolition and auction and was bought by my father, who used the materials to build rental houses on the edge of Winchester.

A little farther along, the road dips down and to the left, to the old railroad station and a junkyard, which was the site of another of John's father's enterprises, a cotton gin. The location was referred to locally as Gin Bottom, and it was here that some one hundred local farmers brought their cotton to be ginned for two dollars per bale. As many as two thousand bales were ginned there in a single season in the 1920s. Mr. Harvey, as John's father was often called, also stored cotton for the government and over the years bought a number of farms at auction. These enterprises, along with his practice as a self-educated lawyer, allowed Harvey Templeton to provide a quite adequate standard of living for his family. Although not rich, his was certainly one of the more prosperous families in Franklin County in John's childhood years. When Buicks were first sold in Franklin County in 1916, his uncle bought the first one and his father the second.

Continuing our journey, we turned right and climbed the hill from Gin Bottom into the center of Winchester. The typical square, with courthouse in the center, seemed like many others I've seen in recent years. There was still the old theater on one corner and a few restaurants, jewelers, and banks interspersed with a number of vacant storefronts. Back in John's childhood days, this was the center of activities. Vella Templeton's brother owned a dry goods store here and Vella worked in the store as the maker of ladies hats.

Just a block from the center of town we passed the Knies hardware store. It was across the street from an abandoned building that had been, during John's childhood, the Knies Blacksmith Shop, complete with forge, where

John watched horseshoes being "hammered out in the old-fashioned way." Once more around the square, we turned onto Dinah Shore Boulevard, named after the singer-actress, the other famous person of that generation who hails from Tennessee. Dinah's family ran the only clothing store in Winchester when John was growing up. John tells the story of meeting Dinah many years later, in 1988, at a special county homecoming celebration. As they were sitting together at the head table at dinner, Dinah remarked about John's fame as a world-class investor, perhaps implying, as so often happens, that he might give her a hot tip about the stock market. He responded, "If you promise not to ask me about investments, I'll promise not to sing."

It was on that same occasion that John announced the idea of a laws of life essay contest for Franklin County.

Just after turning onto the boulevard, John pointed out the old jailhouse, now a museum, and just below it the pond that was part of Boiling Fork Creek, where he went frog hunting as a kid. A mile upstream on that creek, Vella Templeton's father had his corn-grinding mill. All of that is changed, John said, because of the damming of the Elk River and its tributaries as part of the huge Tennessee Valley Authority project.

After some brief shopping on the boulevard, we returned to the big brick house on South High Street, now the home of John's brother, Harvey Templeton Jr., to spend the afternoon and have dinner with the family.

REMINISCING AT THE OLD HOMESTEAD WITH HARVEY AND JEWEL TEMPLETON

Harvey Templeton is John's older brother, a former nurseryman turned racecar driver, now retired. Almost his first words to me were "sit down and reveal the meaning of life." It was clear from the conversation that followed that he is not the man of faith that John is. He sees religion as many do, as judgmental and austere, and sees himself as something of a free spirit. One would certainly have to credit him for showing a lot of courage and daring, leaving a prosperous nursery business in his late fifties to begin a career as a racecar builder and driver. Nor was his wife Jewel at all a hindrance in this new career, as she was a climber and skier and something of a daredevil behind the wheel. They later took me out to the "smokehouse," which has long since exchanged its role of curing ham and bacon to become a machine shop and garage for Harvey's last Ford Formula 4 racecar and for Jewel's Lotus sports car. Back in the house are racing pictures — in one Harvey is arm in arm with Paul Newman with their cars behind them — and quite a few cups commemorating successful races at Daytona Beach and elsewhere. It is easy to see that Harvey and John both inherited some rather creative genes, though John's early love for engineering in the form of refurbishing old cars, wiring houses, and putting on "electric shows" was gradually shifted in the direction of entrepreneurship — raising cash crops, selling fireworks, building a savings fund for various projects, sponsoring home dances during high school, and organizing camping, hunting, and fishing adventures.

The two Templeton families have kept close ties over the years. John's three children — Jack, Anne, and Chris — spent several childhood summers in Winchester, staying with Harvey and Jewel, and enjoying all kinds of activities with their five children — Jill, Harvey, Handly, Avery, and Ann. During my visit, Jewel had great fun recounting some of the antics of the kids, especially when they traveled with her to Florida in Jewel's big black hearse, which she christened Queen Mary.

John and Harvey joined in, describing their travels with their parents, including two winter vacations in Florida when John was 6 and 7 and two camping-out motor trips, which John's mother devised when John was 14 and 15 to visit the Northeast and California. Travel from Tennessee to Florida was something of an expedition in those days; plans had to be laid carefully and preparations for the unexpected had to be thorough. For their first Florida trip, in 1919, Vella wrote well ahead of time to Chicago for the *Blue Book*. In it were detailed directions for travel throughout the country. Because there were virtually no road signs on the seven hundred-mile route from Chattanooga to St. Petersburg (part of the Dixie Highway from Chicago to Miami), a guide book was of equal importance to the very essential spare tubes, patches, and tire irons needed to keep the wheels turning.

There were no paved roads outside the few big cities. And the part of the trip from Winchester to Chattanooga was so hazardous that John's father and another man drove the car to Chattanooga, a four-day trip of only seventy miles by road and river barges, while Vella and the two boys reached Chattanooga by railroad. As the motor trip began, John's father and the two boys would sit in front, while John's mother would sit in the back, reciting the directions from the *Blue Book*. ("She was the original back-seat driver!" quipped John.) The directions were fascinating in their detail, and made it quite evident that the *Blue Book* had to be frequently updated. John read the section for leaving Winchester: "Once you leave Winchester you are on 7 and College Street at the far side of the Courthouse. Turn rt. On College St., go 0.1 mi., come to 4 corners, turn left, passing a school on the right, go another 0.1 mi., at end of road turn rt., cross the RR, then 0.7 mi. to a fork and bear rt. . . ."

Sometimes the directions were less detailed, as in the following description of travel from Monteagle — farther along the road — to Jasper, a town close to Chattanooga: "Monteagle, 4 corners, station on the left, keep close along the RR, end of rd. turn rt., shortly descending Cumberland Mountains on a long easy grade. End of rd., turn left on macadam. Jasper courthouse on the left."

Besides getting lost, one had also to worry about getting stuck in the mud — which John said occurred about every hundred miles — and about finding places to sleep. But farmers along the well-traveled routes were quick to help with mules for towing for a fee, and often allowed camping on their property overnight. Food was less of a problem, especially if you were as resourceful as the Templeton boys. John and Harvey often took turns perching on the running board of the moving car and shooting rabbits that had strayed onto the road!

All of this might seem a rather adventurous and risky undertaking for the parents of two small children, but it turns out to be perfectly consistent with the style of upbringing employed by Harvey and Vella Templeton. They gave the boys maximum freedom and every encouragement to try out new ideas and to design a variety of potentially useful projects, even if there were risks involved. Beginning with his butterfly collection, John was allowed to purchase cyanide for his killing jars from the local druggist, and soon after, he was buying ammunition for his rifles and shotguns as well as gunpowder for fireworks displays. He and his brother were also extended unlimited credit in all the local stores, although John is quick to point out that they were very careful to buy very little. John says of his early training: "I can remember no time when my parents or teachers ever volunteered to me even one sentence of advice on ethics, religion, conduct, behavior, business, thrift, dress, hours, or homework. Of course my multitudes of questions as a child were answered thoughtfully; but after age 12 rarely did I ask."

John's performance in school continued to be exceptional. Valedictorian of his class at Central High School, he also received four out of the five gold medals awarded — for debate, public speaking, citizenship, and scholarship.

What John's parents and teachers gave him was a remarkable self-confidence, an assurance that he could realize high goals and leave a mark on the world. One of his favorite poets, one he first read in high school, is Henry Wadsworth Longfellow, and he particularly likes several stanzas of "A Psalm of Life."

> . . . Tell me not, in mournful numbers,
> Life is but an empty dream!
> For the soul is dead that slumbers,
> And things are not what they seem.
> Life is real! Life is earnest!
> And the grave is not its goal;
> Dust thou art, to dust returnest,
> Was not spoken to the soul.
> . . . .
>
> Lives of great men all remind us
> We can make our lives sublime,
> And, departing, leave behind us
> Footprints on the sands of time.
> . . . .

> Let us, then, be up and doing,
> With a heart for any fate;
> Still achieving, still pursuing,
> Learn to labor and to wait. . . .
> (stanzas 1, 2, 7, 9)

John's vision for his life began to take focus early in his high school years.

> As a high school freshman, I decided to try to go to Yale, but this required taking examinations by the College Entrance Examination Board, which no one from my high school had ever taken. From the Board I bought copies of the old examinations for the four years past. Then each year when high school finished about May 20th, I began to study the subjects eight hours a day. Each year for three years I took the three-day College Entrance Board Examinations in Nashville the third week in June. Entrance to Yale required a minimum of four years of Latin, four years of English, and four years of mathematics. Central High School offered only three years of math, so the principal agreed to offer solid geometry and trigonometry as a fourth-year class, provided I would teach the class and recruit at least eight friends so that the class would meet state requirements. The principal set the examinations for us, and graded them, and all of my students passed.

But the old saying about all work and no play making Jack a dull boy could not be said about the blossoming John Templeton. Upon entering high school, he also discovered girls, and with the help of one pretty high school junior, he learned to dance. Subsequently he began to invite a small group of students to his home for dances. John and Mary Mark Mowry, daughter of the president of the Farmer's National Bank, alternated locations — one weekend at Mowry's, the next at Templeton's. John also attended dances at the University of the South in Sewanee, and joined the Sigma Phi Omega fraternity at Sewanee Military Academy, preparatory to starting a chapter in Winchester.

Despite his mere 130 pounds, John also played on the Central High football team for three years. In a small school of fewer than two hundred it was not easy to find twenty-two boys who would commit the time to a rather demanding sport.

ON THE ROAD AGAIN WITH JOHN TEMPLETON

The next morning, promptly at nine, Sir John and I embarked on another motor tour of Winchester. This time we traveled farther along on South High to the new cemetery, which John's brother had developed during his nursery days. There we saw the Templeton mausoleum. John's second wife, Irene Butler Templeton, who died in 1993, is buried there, along with her son Malcolm, who died suddenly in 1995. The inscription, "God is Love, and he who dwells in love, dwells in God and God in him," is taken from one of John and Irene's favorite passages from the New Testament (1 John 4:16).

John and Irene and their families came together through the matchmaking efforts of John's son Christopher. John and his three children were living in Englewood, New Jersey, on the same street as Irene Butler and her two children. Four years earlier, John lost his wife, Judith Dudley Folk, through a tragic accident. Irene was divorced at the time.

> When my Christopher was 6, I had been a widower four years. His favorite playmate was Malcolm, who lived with his sister and devoted mother Mrs. Irene Butler, also on Chestnut Street in Englewood. One day, to Irene's great surprise, he phoned to ask if he could come to tea with her alone. After they drank tea together, Christopher said, "If you ever think of getting married again will you please consider my father?" Three years later Irene and I had a big church wedding in her St. Paul's Episcopal Church with all five of our children, ages 8 to 18, as attendants. After our honeymoon at Jupiter Island Club, we all lived in my home and the Fisher's Island summer home with my Tennessee ladies, Rosezella Romney as governess and Mattie Whitworth as housekeeper.

Irene and I wanted our five to feel more like a family, so we planned eight weeks driving all over Europe for the seven of us. We could not find in Europe an auto adequate for seven people plus luggage, so I bought a ten-passenger Volkswagen bus. Thus, we were able to invite my brother's three older children, Jill, Harvey III, and Handly. With no room for much luggage inside our bus, we bought a roof rack plus tarpaulin to keep the bags dry. All ten of us were limited to a single suitcase for eight weeks, including Irene, who often traveled before and after this trip with five or more pieces of luggage.

We knew our children were peculiar in the fact that each child wanted his own way. So we made each child the total boss of some activity. John Jr., aged 18, was the only one of the eight to have traveled in Europe, so he was in charge of choosing cities and hotels. Although that July and August were the busiest Europe ever had, he wanted to make no reservations. Each day about five we would stop at a teashop so he could have thirty minutes to get hotel rooms for the ten of us. To our great surprise, only thrice did he fail. In Frankfurt, the best we could find was a former bomb shelter. Irene felt panic at the thought of not having windows but we all were good sports. When Jack could find no hotel in Ljubljana, in Communist Slovenia, we all slept on cots in corridors of a high school. Jack found only a hayloft on Bank Holiday in Hemel Hempstead, England, but Irene charmed a male long-distance phone operator who did find four rooms in a public house twenty miles away after ninety minutes of trying.

Jill, age 18, was boss of all finances and paid all bills and pocket money. Harvey, age 17, was boss of the timetable, maps, and guidebooks. Anne, age 15, was boss of mail and travel history, and wrote five hundred words every other day about our adventure so my secretary in Englewood could make photocopies and mail them to all our friends. Wendy, age 15, was boss of everything relating to food. Handly, age 14, was boss of the bus and drivers.

Malcolm, age 9, was cameraman, and took many pictures daily to mail to my secretary for distribution. Christopher, age 10, was famous for complaints, so he was in charge of "no grumbling." If any of the ten of us said anything negative, his job was to call us down. Before the complainer could continue, he or she had to say two pleasant things. After that only rarely did anyone want to continue his or her complaint.

Irene and I kept for ourselves only the hardest job, which was to keep our mouths shut while witnessing hundreds of childish mistakes. Each morning we would pack our single bag and sit on the back seat of the bus while the youngsters made all the usual mistakes about bills, maps, tips, etc. However, I made the only serious mistake. When I gave Jill $500 for expenses the first week, all the youngsters were excited by more money than they had ever seen in cash, so they asked what to do with a surplus any week they did not spend it all. I said I would be so pleased by such careful management that they could reward themselves by dividing the week's surplus among the eight. From that moment, they would not let us rent a room with bath and we bought food at grocery stores. Handly decided his saving would be enough to buy his first used auto when he returned home. When I paid extra for Irene to have a room with bath during our two days climbing Gross Glockner mountain in Austria, all eight children lined up to use her bathtub.

At the end of the trip, we sold the bus for a hundred dollars more than we paid for it in Germany. Anne took the photos and her thirty adventure stories to make for each of us an illustrated history of the eight weeks, which welded our family together. My classmate at both Yale and Oxford, Arthur Gordon, was then editor at *Cosmopolitan*. He wrote a great story of our adventure and sold it to *Good Housekeeping* for $1,500 and gave me half of that fee.

After John and I left the cemetery in Winchester, we drove across town to North High Street, to the site of the Handly house where John's mother was born. When Vella was a girl, her father sold the mill in Boiling Fork Creek and built a one-story home here on a half-block of land. Turning back into town, we passed the Cumberland Presbyterian Church, where the Handlys were longtime members. John's mother was a staunch supporter of this church, often cooking and serving dinners to various groups. Sometimes the church could not afford a minister, so services depended on students from the School of Theology at the University of the South in nearby Sewanee. But Vella also earned enough money to pay half the cost of supporting a missionary in China named Gam Sen Qua. Vella and her sister Leila also provided much of the leadership of the church, as the following letter from the daughter of one of the ministers attests:

Dear Mr. Templeton:

The article about you in the December 30, 1973 issue of the *Nashville Tennessean* brought back some wonderful memories.

Miss Vella and Miss Leila, as "women elders," were a new experience for my father, the Rev. W. B. Spraker, when he became their pastor at the Winchester Presbyterian Church in 1937. However, it did not take long for him to realize and appreciate their worth and faithfulness. Their prayers, coupled with their hard work, held that little church together for many years.

The garden Miss Vella grew to help you get to Yale also fed her pastor's family — as well as half the poor in Winchester. I wish I could tell you of the many happy memories I have of her. Her religion, pure and undefiled, has had a tremendous influence on my life.

This I am sure of . . . Miss Vella would be enormously proud of your success but not at all surprised at it nor at the fine person the article portrays you as having become.

My very best wishes for your continued usefulness and happiness.

Sincerely,

Alma Spraker

John's mother also got him involved at Cumberland. At the age of 15, he was elected Sunday school superintendent, though he felt a bit uneasy about the post. As he expressed it: "This caused me to begin to develop some conscience, because I felt badly standing in front of all these good people knowing that I was not a very good Christian myself . . . My thoughts were too often about girls, sports, and possessions."

Vella also introduced her family to the writings of Lowell Fillmore through the Unity School of Christianity, then a new movement centered in Kansas City. Unity teaching stressed the power of faith and the potential of the individual, both of which have been powerful influences in John Templeton's life. To understand John's parents' hands-off attitude, one must first understand that Vella's faith included the belief that God can do what we can't if we give freedom and encouragement to our families and communities. Ideals of thrift and discipline and self-sufficiency therefore came to John early in childhood, yet were always tempered by a sense that all we had came from God, so it should be accepted with humility and thankfulness.

One aspect of humility was reflected in the way Vella dressed her two young boys. Only on Sunday did John wear good clothes. The rest of the week the two youngsters wandered around town in overalls. When it was warm, they went barefoot. On at least one occasion this lead to some embarrassment. When a government social worker came to town to evaluate the needs of the poor in the community, she and Vella happened to meet in the town drugstore, and discussed how to clean up the poor children. To illustrate the need, she pointed out the window at two small boys in overalls and bare feet. To Vella's embarrassment, they were John and his brother Harvey. One sometimes pays a price for humility!

Riding back to Harvey and Jewel's for a second afternoon and dinner, I thought again about some of the other advantages John had had growing up in Winchester, Tennessee, in the teens and twenties of this century. This was "small-town America." Families didn't lock their doors. Motion pictures were wholesome. Television did not yet exist. There was essentially no drug problem and, until 1933, when prohibition was repealed, there was little drinking of alcoholic beverages. On a personal level, John's mother was a leader in the local chapter of the Women's Christian Temperance Union, and John's father offered a reward of twenty dollars for the arrest of anyone with a whiskey still.

But perhaps the most significant thing — and maybe it's still true in some parts of "small-town America" — is that phenomenon so rare in the business world . . . trust. John Templeton learned the importance of trust from his parents and from an utterly powerful and trustworthy God, and used it as a powerful testimony in the investment world of our day.

CHAPTER 9

Reaching Out: Yale, Oxford, and across the World

W HEN JOHN GRADUATED as top scholar from Central High School in Winchester, Tennessee, in 1930, the world of economics and business was just beginning a long-strangling depression, which followed the stock market crash of 1929. But part of the tuition for his first year at Yale had already been set aside through a systematic savings plan devised by John's parents during the First World War. As John explains, "In the First World War citizens were asked to invest five dollars daily in war bonds, so my parents offered to give my brother and me (aged 8 and 5) each a dollar to put in ten-year bonds every day during the war when we did not fight with each other. Ten years later we used this to help with college tuition."

Because these savings were modest, John embarked on an ambitious plan to sell magazine subscriptions door to door. After responding to an advertisement in a magazine, he became one of a group of seven teenage boys who were driven from town to town by an employee-trainer of the Hearst Publishing Company. Their magazines were popular ones, *Good Housekeeping* and *Cosmopolitan,* and each subscription cost two dollars for the year. But most housewives were careful with their money in those hard times, and so a bargain was struck between Hearst Publishing and the boys. If each boy sold two hundred subscriptions in eight weeks, the publisher would pay room, board, and transport for the eight weeks and send two hundred dollars toward college tuition. Not only was this an almost impossible goal from an economic standpoint, it was also a forceful sales approach that John found distasteful. As he put it, it was "against my nature." For example, their trainer actually required them to run from house to house so that they would be breathless and so seem excited and forceful in their sales pitch. John guesses that perhaps a quarter of the housewives didn't even know what they had bought, only that some poor college student needed their help. John was one of only four boys who finished out the eight weeks and sold at least two hundred subscriptions. The income was only about 5 percent of what he needed for college, but the experience taught him special lessons about hard work and self-confidence. His brother Harvey jokes that the eight weeks had warped John's "Southern gentleman" personality. Actually, John Templeton seems not to have lost any of his Southern charm; he has been soft-spoken and gracious throughout his life. What those eight weeks really contributed, he says, was an important lesson in the perseverance needed for the trials of life.

John's first year at Yale was a new challenge, making new friends and settling down to work for a degree in economics. He had never been to New England and he encountered a new kind of elitism; two-thirds of Yale's 825 freshmen had attended private schools in the East in preparation for Ivy League colleges. This meant that many of them had friends in their class and in the upper classes as well. Because of this, John says, no public high school graduates were invited to join a fraternity. He is quick to disclaim that discrimination was involved, and actually, the next year he and various public high school graduates were invited.

Sophomore year at Yale was a very challenging one, with the economic crisis deepening all over the country. Back in Winchester, John's father was beginning to feel the pinch as a landlord and landowner, and that summer he announced that he would not be able to provide any tuition for Yale for the coming year. But as before, John responded with his unique form of resourcefulness and self-confidence. As he tells the story:

> At the beginning of sophomore year (which was two years after the great stock market crash of 1929) my father told me with regret that he could not contribute even one dollar more to my

education. At first, this seemed to be a tragedy; but now, looking back, it was the best thing that could have happened. It caused me to begin studying really hard to get top grades and thereby maintain two scholarships to help with the expenses. Mother had saved a little cash from selling vegetables and eggs, and I borrowed two hundred dollars from my Uncle Watson, which Mother paid back years later. This enabled me to travel to New Haven and to apply to the very well-organized Yale Bureau of Student Employment, which was run by a capable man named Ogden Miller, who later became headmaster of the Gunnery School. He helped me to get scholarships and also to earn money at various jobs, such as being senior aide of Pierson College and chairman of the *Yale Banner and Pot Pourri* yearbook.

During these Great Depression years, one bank in which I had an account, the Broadway Bank, failed. Friends in New Haven said the safest bank in which to open a new account was the Mechanics Bank. About six months later, when walking by that bank, I saw a long line of people extending half a block from the front door. In those days, this meant that there was a "run on the bank" and, of course, no one could get near enough to the cashiers' windows to withdraw money. Economics textbooks at that time said that savings depositors in Connecticut were paid off in bankruptcies at two dollars for each dollar paid to checking account depositors. Accordingly, I went to the savings deposit window where there was no one and opened an account by transferring to savings my entire checking account.

Although Yale was known as a rich boy's college, there was no discrimination of any kind against those of us working our way through. In fact, in those depression years, 42 percent of the students were earning at least part of their expenses. By hard study, I became the top scholar in the class by the end of junior year, which was helpful in being elected president of Phi Beta Kappa. This, in turn, was a great help toward selection for a Rhodes scholarship.

I was tapped for the Yale Senior Society called Elihu and served as assistant business manager of the comic magazine called the *Yale Record*. When majoring in economics in 1932, I chose investment counsel as a profession because of deep interest in the difficulty in judging the true value of any shares of corporations. As a senior at Yale, I earned one thousand dollars as the first senior aide of Pierson College. This was a tremendous help because it covered one-half of all that year's expenses. When the 1934 accounting for the Yale yearbook was finished, about eight hundred dollars in profit was distributed to me as chairman, which I used to open an account with my roommate, Jack Greene. He was then senior partner of a stock brokerage firm in Dayton, Ohio, called Greene and Ladd because his father had died during Jack's junior year at Yale. This account is now forty-two years old, but the name of the firm has changed to Cowen and Company. My first purchase of any stock was the seven-dollar preferred stock of Standard Gas and Electric Company, which was selling at 12 percent of par because of the Great Depression. From that original eight hundred dollars and later savings have grown all of the investments I now own.

John's years at Yale would have to be characterized as tremendously energetic and full of enterprise. He readily admits that he was relieved when his excellent grades qualified him for scholarship money. After all the pressure and uncertainty at Yale, Oxford, with expenses paid by Rhodes, would seem like a bed of roses.

OXFORD AS A RHODES SCHOLAR

As senior aide at Pierson College at Yale, John guided students who were earning their tuition. In this capacity, and because he was top scholar at Yale as a junior, he was encouraged by Alan Valentine, master of Pierson College and a member of the Rhodes Connecticut Selection Committee, to compete for a Rhodes scholarship. Only two students from each of the six New

England states were allowed to compete for the four New England scholarships. John was one of those selected. After the interviews, the group had six hours to wait for the results, so John and Bob Michellet, an applicant from Dartmouth, decided to go to nearby Wellesley College. Surprisingly, they discovered that they both wanted to visit the same girl, Judith Dudley Folk of Nashville. Bob wanted to visit the girl recently voted the "most dated" girl in the Wellesley class of 1934, and John wanted to visit the girl who had been his sweetheart for two summers while she was staying at her family's summer home at Monteagle Sunday School assembly grounds in the mountains not far from Winchester, Tennessee. John and Judith were secretly engaged the next summer, and married three years later.

The sad part of the story is that Bob Michellet, whom John would have invited to be a groomsman at the wedding, died heroically while trying to rescue boys from a burning Dartmouth fraternity house, and the Rhodes scholars that year were one scholar short.

On arriving in Oxford, the Americans found a very different kind of academic setting; compared to the hectic pace of Yale, Oxford seemed like a rest period. The Rhodes scholarship was sufficiently generous that it was not necessary to work, which was fortunate, because it was not considered proper for Oxford students to work for money. In fact, John says that at that time it was beneath the dignity of a student even to carry a parcel home from the store! At Oxford there were no grades and no examinations, and no classes to attend for two years until the formal examinations. Instead, instruction was by tutorial, and in John's case, this involved meeting one hour each week with a Mr. Tyler, a brilliant legal scholar at Balliol College. The choice was made for a program leading to a Bachelor of Arts degree because there was no program available in the study of business and certainly nothing on investments.

Many years later, John Templeton returned to Oxford to found Templeton College as the first college of the university devoted to postgraduate management studies. The beginnings of this institution date back to 1965, when the Oxford Centre for Management Studies was established in Kennington, Oxford, about a mile from the town center. In 1982, John was approached by Dr. Uwe Kitzinger, later to become president of Templeton College, and asked to become founder of what was to be the first Rhodes scholar college at Oxford. John agreed, but with several important stipulations that display his keen foresight and investment prowess. Dr. Kitzinger wrote in *The American Oxonian* in its winter 1987 issue:

> John Templeton was interested in making a partnership contribution — keeping us on our toes and encouraging us still to find other benefactors — rather than supplying the totality of our needs. We were talking about a gift of $5 million and suggesting re-naming ourselves in memory of his mother and father, Harvey and Vella Templeton. But the Fellows of the Centre and John Templeton thought it wise to follow through the thought expressed in the *American Oxonian* article and call it, in the future, a College. The governing Council of Management (on which the business community is strongly represented) after serious consideration, agreed: and in 1984 the University gave us the right to matriculate up to twelve postgraduate students in management each year.
>
> It quickly became clear that John Templeton was actively interested in what that College could actually do to advance management studies at the University, revitalize the British economy, and help people the world over manage their affairs better and escape from poverty, famine, and disease. And these concerns were urgent. He therefore made it explicit in the deed of gift that the money was not only to be spent rather than hoarded (the parable of the talents is one dear to his heart), but also that it was to be spent "effectively and expeditiously."
>
> Instead of handing over this gift to a Board of Trustees for long-term investment in farms or in stock market securities, and then only using the income derived from them, we were to invest it as working capital in ourselves — thus not just gaining for management education the net profit from others' corporate operations, but increasing the volume of management education by the whole

extent of our own additional turnover. The deed of gift shows how widely John Templeton interprets the concept of working capital: It includes quite explicitly not only such physical investments as buildings and equipment, but also such academic investment as funds to enable Fellows to use their sabbaticals to best advantage, such commercial investment as public relations, and such institutional investment as fund-raising.

The Templeton deed also has another, closely related innovative feature: the "roll-over principle." There is always the temptation to devote unrestricted funds not to the most urgent purposes, but to those for which it would be most difficult to find specific donations. To free us from that concern, the trust deed therefore expressly allows us to use the gift in whatever is the most effective way for the realization of its ultimate purposes: if later we find another donor to fund any particular investment already being financed by the Templeton benefaction, we are always still able to accept another gift, and name that particular item of investment — be it a student hall of residence or an executive center or a new institute or fellowship — according to the next donor's wishes. The original funds are then rolled back into the Templeton benefaction to be used for the next most urgent purpose.

Templeton College was dedicated as a college of Oxford University in October 1984, in a ceremony attended by Keith Joseph, Britain's minister of education, and Lord Jenkins, the chancellor of the university. My wife and I were fortunate to be in attendance, and I remember that amid the various speeches, John Templeton's stood out, both for its remembrance of his parents, for whom the new college was dedicated, and for Sir John's characteristically public thanks to God for the manifold blessings we have all received. It raised some eyebrows, but I thought it was the high point of the ceremonies.

Because Oxford gave six weeks holiday at Christmas, six weeks at Easter, and fourteen weeks in the summer, John and his fellow Rhodes scholars had the time and good fortune to meet some fine English people and to explore the historic and artistic sights of Europe in a way few tourists would. The contacts with English society were arranged by Lady Francis Rider, who had initiated a program during World War I to introduce young American officers stationed in England to the best of English society. When the war was over, she arranged with the Cecil Rhodes Trust to invite Rhodes scholars to participate, and each year, at a tea party at Rhodes House in Oxford, the new scholars were invited to select families and dates and places the young men would like to visit. Among the possibilities were families with country homes and horses and others with castles by the sea, and the stay could be for a day or a weekend or for as long as two weeks. Formal invitations were mailed shortly thereafter, and included clothing suggestions — dinner jackets or formal white tie and tails, morning suits for some city homes. According to John, these visits were exciting and sometimes embarrassing, but always tremendous learning experiences.

The second kind of learning involved a series of well-planned trips, taking advantage of used copies of *Baedeker's* guidebooks for each of the European countries. John and his colleagues would study the guides thoroughly, then buy student railway tickets for unlimited mileage. They also took advantage of information supplied by the guidebooks about places to stay — inexpensive hotels, youth hostels, and YMCAs. These intensive learning experiences were achieved at very little expense and so were doubly satisfying to John, who carried his ideal of thrift well beyond the confines of Winchester and Yale.

In fact, John's thriftiness enabled him to save four hundred dollars while at Oxford, and to persuade a former Yale classmate, James Inksetter, who was studying at Cambridge, to join him in a seven-month trip through thirty-five countries after graduation from Oxford. As for thrift, John's expenses for that trip were an incredibly low ninety pounds. Hotels averaged only twenty-five cents per night, and by living at the poverty level, John and James learned much about the life of the masses in the rest of the world. The decision to make this never-to-be-forgotten trip was not made lightly.

The years at Oxford had only served to reinforce John's decision to become an investment counselor, and he was already preparing for the job he wanted when he returned to America. Before leaving on the trip, he wrote a letter of introduction, setting forth his qualifications and goals, and mailed it to one hundred American brokers and investment advisers, asking for appointments when he returned from the trip. Furthermore, the trip itself was made with an eye to future investment opportunities, and given the international success of John's later investments, those seven months may have been the most educational period of his entire career.

Preparation for the trip also included decisions about how much they would carry, and how it could be protected. James Inksetter took a knapsack and John hired a seamstress to sew an over-the-shoulder roll like the one his grandfather, Dr. Robert Clinton Handly, carried in 1860 as a Confederate army surgeon. One side of the roll was a sleeping bag and the other side held one shirt, underwear, socks, raincoat, four *Baedeker's* guidebooks, and a Bible. To reduce the risk of robbery, they used 80 percent of their money to buy traveler's checks, which they mailed ahead to American Express offices in Athens, Jerusalem, Hong Kong, and Tokyo.

The trip began with travel through northern Europe, and included a six-day stop at the 1936 Olympic Games in Berlin. There each morning the stadium resounded with "Seig Heil!" for fifteen minutes as the Nazi party demonstrated its allegiance to Adolph Hitler. From Germany, the two traveled through Hungary and Austria, then via boat on the Danube through Yugoslavia and Romania, then by third-class rail through Bulgaria, and then by coastal boat to Greece. At each of the cities where John and James planned to stay overnight, they discovered their porters, wearing caps advertising inexpensive hotels, could be bargained with at the train stations. In this way, despite the language barrier, they were able to find fairly reasonable places to stay at very low cost. The least they paid for a bed was ten cents in Changsha, China, but the bed was made of wooden boards and the pillow was a wooden block. "At least they were very clean!" John said.

Such was not the case in Bucharest, Romania, where an unfortunate mishap landed them in jail. Their problems began when they misread the train schedule, thinking the daily train to Varna, Bulgaria, left at 10 p.m. rather than 10 a.m. They had carefully spent all their Romanian money before walking to the station, so they crossed the street to sleep in the park for the night. Unfortunately, their choice of outdoor "hotel" made them look more like vagrants than anything else. In a few hours the local police appeared and asked them what they were doing in a language the two men couldn't understand. Eventually, they were hauled away to the police station, where they spent the rest of the night in a flea-infested cell. When they awoke the next morning, thousands of fleas were crawling over them, and they seemed to have at least as many flea bites. Some people might have given up at that point and gone home, but not these two adventurers. After picking the fleas off each other as thoroughly as they could, they left for Varna a little worse for the wear.

The most exciting and perilous part of their investment tour occurred in the Middle East, where John had a close brush with death and almost precipitated an international crisis. John recalls the experience:

> After diligent study of the antiquities, history, museums, economy, and people along the Nile, we bought third-class bus tickets for the trip across the desert to Jerusalem. The British were then protecting the [area], so the bus was protected by an armored car. From the Bible we read carefully every mention of the disciples James and John and then tried to visit each location where they are mentioned and do what they did. In each letter to my mother, I tabulated the chapter and verse so she could read what James and I were now doing daily. James and John were called by Jesus when they were fishermen on the Sea of Galilee, so we found a Jewish boy who spoke English and Arabic, who, in turn, found for us two Arab fishermen from the Golan Heights who agreed to help us catch a fish. The innkeeper told James this was dangerous, but I went boldly back to their rowboat.
>
> I took an oar to help the two fishermen row, but by sign language they insisted I sit on a pillow in the prow. I thought we

Sir John Templeton reading the *Wall Street Journal* at the exact North Pole, July 27, 1996. Russian icebreaker *Yamal* is in background.

Relatives attending Sir John's eightieth birthday celebration, 1992. *Front row (l to r)*: Hillary Brooks, Admiral Winston Folk, USN Ret., Sir John Templeton, Irene Templeton, Gregory Carrol, Jewel Templeton, Cameron Brooks. *From second to back (l to r)*: Colin Brooks, Sander Brooks, Irene Reynolds Butler, Anne Dudley Zimmerman, Wendy Brooks, Virginia Templeton, Amy Butler, Heather Templeton, Christopher Templeton, Mrs. Gäbriel Flynn, Gäbriel Flynn, Josephine Templeton, Jennifer Templeton, Ann Cameron, Jennifer Cameron, Gail Zimmerman, Renee Zimmerman, Richard Sidman, Jill Sidman, Lauren Templeton, Rhonda Zimmerman, Eva Zimmerman, Harvey Templeton III, Becky Templeton, Jason Flynn, Derek Dietz. *Top row (l to r)*: Michael Zimmerman, Malcolm Butler, John M. Templeton Jr., Handly Templeton

Managers of Templeton Foundation, Bahamas, 1997: Mrs. Mena Griffiths, Sir John Templeton, and Mrs. Mary Walker

Templeton Foundations staff, Radnor, Pennsylvania 1997 (*l to r*): Anne Heilman, Karyl Wittlinger, Bryant Kirkland, Aideen Quigley, Judith Marchand, Fran Schapperle, Charles Harper, Joanna Hill, John Templeton, Jr., Arthur Schwartz, Laura Molina, Linda Kelly, Andrea Beckerman, Joann DiIullo, Pat Laird. Not pictured: Pam Lairdieson and Patricia Hotz.

Harvey Maxwell Templeton, 1930

Vella Handly Templeton, 1908

Harvey Templeton, Jr. *(left)* and
John Marks Templeton, 1914.

John Marks Templeton ca. 1916

John Marks Templeton,
1930

Judith Dudley Folk Templeton
wedding, Nashville, Tennessee
1937

Portrait of John
Marks Templeton,
1950

For my dear friend
John Templeton —
ever as kind as
he is wise —
which is saying
a lot, indeed!
All the best,
always,
Lou Rukeyser

John Templeton and Louis Rukeyser, 1992

Board of Directors of Templeton Investment Funds. *Front row (l to r)*: Baron von Diergardt, Harold Siebens, John Galbraith, Sir John Templeton, William James, Lloyd Blachford, John Goldstone. *Back row (l to r)*: Bruce Clark, Bruce McGowan, Mark Holowesko, Jay Bradshaw, Harry Kuch, Gary Motyl, Leroy Paslay, Tom Hansberger, Dr. John M. Templeton, Jr., Richard Tottenham.

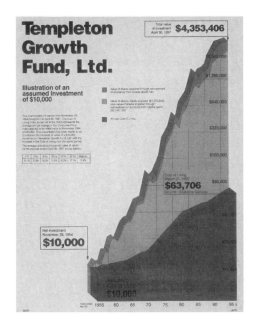

The growth of the Templeton Growth Fund, Ltd., as compared to the Cost of Living Index.

Portrait of John Marks Templeton
at home, 1980

Portrait of Irene Reynolds Butler
Templeton, 1961

One branch of the
Templeton family.
Seated (l to r): Pina,
Heather, and Irene.
Standing (l to r): John
M. Templeton, Jr. and
John Marks Temple-
ton, 1978

could catch a fish in half an hour and be home before dark. But they rowed for three hours from Tiberius to the Golan Heights and then took me to their family's home, a tent of burlap for shade from the hot sun and a row of carpets inside covering the dessert floor. Their mother ground a few coffee beans in a shallow cup with a spoonful of water and handed it to me. I drank it, although I do not normally drink coffee. That was a mistake, because the mother had to start over with another saucer handed around the family circle and then to me for each of us to take a taste. This was a lifesaver because it apparently meant that the family was giving me its protection. Soon great shouting started on the shore from a group of fishermen who had been mending nets. Brandishing long knives, they came toward us, apparently having decided I was either Jewish or English and therefore I should die.

With tremendous shouting and wrestling, the men from my tent held them back until another boy who spoke English could be found; meanwhile, I prayed. Fortunately, I carried my American passport and with that the boy persuaded them to return to mending their nets peacefully.

The rowboat was pushed about fifty yards offshore and by sign language the men told me to sleep on the pillow. Because of the excitable fishermen on shore, I did not sleep but prayed until they thought they were waking me two hours before dawn. After rowing a mile offshore, they put their net in the sea in a great horseshoe shape with us at the mouth. They then asked me to make maximum noise with the tin pan from which we had all eaten mush by hand the night before while they pounded on the boat sides to scare the fish who ran into the net; its holes were just large enough that the larger fish heads could go through but then the gills kept them trapped. By pulling in the net, we caught twenty-three good-sized St. Peter's fish of about two pounds each. Then by rowing two hours we returned to the spot we had started from. They insisted I keep the largest fish and I bought several packs of cigarettes to give each fisherman. With great smiling and bowing, they said goodbye, and I then returned to the little inn where James and the innkeeper were overjoyed to see me.

John says that his mother had a premonition of his brush with death, and her dream had been so vivid that she literally gave him up for dead. Perhaps she could read between the lines of his daily letters and realized how explosive the situation was in Palestine.

The rest of the trip took John and James through India, China, and Japan. Here again they were able to meet the people and gauge their attitudes and lifestyles in a way that traveling first class would not have allowed. John came away with a better grasp of the grassroots economies and practical political systems of a variety of nations. It would have a major impact on his pioneering decision to search the world for investment opportunities. Returning home, the two travelers told their story to a classmate, Arthur Gordon, who wrote an article about their adventure and sold it to *Good Housekeeping* magazine. Arthur shared the proceeds with John and James, which in turn paid half the cost of their seven-month trip.

MARRIAGE TO JUDITH DUDLEY FOLK

When John returned from his around-the-world trip in the spring of 1937, plans for his marriage to Judith Dudley Folk were well under way. The wedding was to be a major event in Nashville society, and the local society pages were full of pictures and stories of the garden parties and white-tie dinners and dances that occurred over a period of perhaps ten days as the wedding party assembled. John and Dudley, who preferred to be called by her middle name, were married by the Episcopal bishop of Tennessee on April 17, with a reception following at Belle Meade Country Club. There were twelve bridesmaids and sixteen groomsmen and ushers, including many of John's friends from Yale and Oxford. John borrowed his mother's Pontiac, and he and Dudley drove for their two-week honeymoon to the floating gardens of Xochimilco near Mexico City. In May the two went to New York to find jobs. Dudley found a job earning $150 a month at Young and Rubicam, an advertising agency in the Chrysler Building. John got a job, also at $150 a month, in the newly formed investment counsel division of Fenner and Beane in Wall Street.

At this point, the emphasis shifted sharply back to what for both John and Dudley were high priorities — saving for investment with the emphasis on thrift.

CHAPTER 10

The Growth Years

O N ARRIVING IN NEW YORK CITY, John had interviews with several investment counsel firms. Twelve had expressed interest based on the one hundred letters he had mailed out before the seven-month world tour. He received five job offers, and took one of the lower-paying jobs, at Fenner and Beane, where he thought there was more opportunity to learn. But after three months a very special opportunity came up. A fellow Rhodes scholar, George McGhee, was working in Dallas for a seismograph exploration company called the National Geophysical Company. George told his boss, William Salvatori, about John, and he was so impressed that he offered John a job as secretary-treasurer of the company at $350 a month. John talked over the offer with Dudley and with his associates at Fenner and Beane, and made the decision to move to Texas. While in Texas, Dudley opened an advertising agency of her own.

John and Dudley had committed themselves to saving 50 percent of their incomes for investment, and so, when they returned to New York two years later, they were already in sight of their goal of starting an independent investment-counseling firm. They continued to hold unflinchingly to the principle of thrift, and even made a game out of finding fantastic bargains in cars and houses and home furnishings.

ESMERALDA AND OTHER BARGAINS

John started bargain hunting early in life. When he was just 12 years old, he and some friends were playing in a hay barn about a mile from his house when he stumbled on an old broken-down Ford. Seeing a potential bargain in the making, John asked the farmer who owned the barn if he would like to sell the car. The farmer replied that he would sell it for ten dollars, so John went home, withdrew some of his savings, explained the situation to his always-agreeable mother, and bought the car. But now came the hard part — finding another Ford of the same model to use for spare parts to get the first one in working order. Finally, John located a matching Ford. If possible, it was in even worse condition than the first, but it had one virtue — it too only cost ten dollars.

With his equipment and parts assembled and tools borrowed from brother Harvey, John and his eighth-grade friends moved to stage two of their plan — transferring the parts from one of the cars into the other. They were confident that they were smart enough to put a car together. If they got stuck in their effort to assemble a workable jalopy, they ran down to the local Ford dealer and pored over his repair manuals until they were clear on the principles to follow. They got to know the mechanics around Winchester and picked up valuable tips to help them complete their project.

After nearly half a year of working afternoons and weekends, John and his friends finally got one of the cars to run. They painted it orange and green and named it Esmeralda. And, surprisingly, with the help of constant and careful maintenance, the car they had rebuilt performed for four straight years, long enough to take the boys to and from classes and to play in out-of-town high school football games until they graduated from high school.

John, always aware of the importance of thrift, had recognized a bargain in those two cars and, with the help of his friends, had turned his dream into a reality, for only a twenty-dollar investment. As a matter of fact, the first five cars he owned were secondhand and none cost more than two hundred dollars. He never paid more for a car until his net worth exceeded a quarter of a million dollars.

Thrift and bargain hunting went hand-in-hand in every aspect of John's life.

> Of course we paid all cash. We had been always scrupulous never to borrow. We paid all cash for autos and houses and everything

else, so we would always be receivers and not payers of interest. In 1941, after the first of our three children was born, we found a fifteen-year-old house in a good part of Englewood, New Jersey, with three bedrooms, two baths, and two-thirds of an acre of garden for $5,000 all cash, on the bus line within five miles of the George Washington Bridge to Manhattan. Five years later we were able to find a fifty-year-old twelve-room home in the best residential area with one-and-a-half acres of garden for only $17,000 total all cash. Then we sold the $5,000 house for $17,000. Number 124 Chestnut Street was home until my partners and I sold our investment counsel companies to the Richardson family of North Carolina in 1959. Then we built our permanent home at the Lyford Cay Club in the Bahamas and began to build the Templeton Group of investment mutual funds.

The twenty years during which he saved 50 percent of his income were not drudgery for John. In fact, he describes the early years in New York, when he and Dudley were setting up house, with great enthusiasm.

To make thrift a joy rather than a burden, we made a game of it by telling our plan to all friends and relatives, who then gave us ideas. We found a furnished Manhattan apartment with a view of the East River for fifty dollars monthly. Our friends helped us find "blue plate" dinners in restaurants for fifty cents. In 1940, the only Manhattan apartment we could find for fifty dollars was on the sixth floor of a no-elevator building on East 88th Street. To furnish five rooms, we could budget only twenty-five dollars. Our friends watched newspapers for furniture auctions when people were moving away. At such auctions if anyone bid one dollar for a chair we said nothing, but if no one bid we said ten cents. Our costliest purchase was five dollars for a two hundred-dollar sofa bed, which was so good we used it for twenty-five years. With such joyous games we furnished five rooms with mismatched furniture and carpets for twenty-five dollars.

The Early Investment Years

In September 1939, when Germany and Russia invaded Poland, it was obvious to John Templeton that a second world war had begun. From his study of investment history, it also became clear that war was a time when even the least efficient businesses revive, because everything is in great demand regardless of price.

Accordingly, John decided to buy one hundred dollars worth of every stock on the stock exchanges that was selling for no more than a dollar per share. To finance this venture, he borrowed ten thousand dollars from his former boss, Dick Platt of Fenner and Beane, a somewhat unusual move for someone who ordinarily paid cash for everything. But this was borrowing of a different sort — borrowing money for a business venture in which the funds would be used to make money. John had great confidence that the stock market would behave as he predicted, with stock prices rising in the face of wartime boom. Furthermore, John had the collateral to back up the loan; his and Dudley's personal investment portfolio was then worth more than thirty thousand dollars.

Dick Platt agreed to John's proposal, although he remarked that 37 of the 104 companies in which John proposed to invest were currently in bankruptcy. It seemed a high-risk move to Platt but, as it turned out, only 4 of the 104 companies became worthless. Within a year, John was able to pay back the money he had borrowed. After he had sold all the stocks, an average of four years after he bought them, the original ten thousand dollar investment had grown to more than forty thousand! John wished later that he had kept some of the stocks much longer, a lesson he put to good use with the Templeton Group of Investment Funds. John says of the 104 stocks:

> The best was the seven-dollar preferred stock of Missouri Pacific Railway. When first issued, investors paid one hundred dollars a share for seven dollars yearly preferred dividend. But in bankruptcy, my one hundred dollars bought eight hundred shares. Gradually railways began achieving good earnings again. When

the stock went up from one-eighth to five dollars a share, I felt grateful and sold out. Then, within five years, the price rose about $105 per share.

The idea of letting money work for you fascinated John Templeton. He would spend hours studying compound-interest tables and playing mental arithmetic games. He even figured out how much the Indians would have made if they had taken the twenty-four dollars in trinkets they had received in 1626 from the Dutch for Manhattan Island and invested it at 8 percent annual interest. According to his calculations, they would have had $255 billion by 1926, or about sixty times as much money as the U.S. federal budget in that year. This meant they would have been able to buy all 14,000 acres of Manhattan back for $15 million per acre — and still have billions left over!

John's opportunity to launch his own investment counseling company came a year after he and Dudley had returned from Texas. He heard that an elderly man, George Towne, owned an investment counsel firm with only eight clients, and so he offered him five thousand dollars for his operation. The name was changed to Towne, Templeton and Dobbrow, and for the first time, John "had his name on the door." Two years later his firm merged with Vance, Chapin and Company and the name changed to Templeton, Dobbrow and Vance. John remembers that those years were lean ones in his investment world. At times the young firm could not earn enough to pay him any salary, so he was forced to rely on savings. However, his focus was on building a sound investment organization, and to make money for his investors. One of his top priorities was to build a research library, but the cost could be prohibitive. He heard that his old firm, Fenner and Beane, was merging with Merrill Lynch, and would no longer need its library. John offered twenty dollars for the research material and twelve bookcases, and his offer was accepted. Any one of the bookcases would have cost one hundred dollars new. John had caught his old company in the midst of a move when bargaining for unneeded books and furniture had no priority. A research library for twenty dollars. What a bargain!

John's habit of thrift pervaded his new investment firm. When he opened his investment counsel office in the RCA building in New York's Rockefeller Center in 1940, he told his secretary never to buy a new typewriter. The value of typewriters declined 30 percent to 40 percent the day they leave the store. They bought reliable, secondhand machines, most of them no more than a few months old, for an average of 40 percent below retail price.

The typewriter principle, John reasoned, could be applied to office space. He didn't need to spend on show, on something glittery and new. He simply needed the right amount of room in which to function. When he found that he'd outgrown his space in the RCA building, he decided that it would be more economical to have the research department near his home in Englewood, New Jersey. He found space in an old building above a drugstore, and because it was in disrepair, he was able to rent it for one dollar per square foot per year. Templeton spent a few hundred dollars fixing up the entrance to lend it an air of dignity. And, most important, he had more than two thousand square feet of office space for two thousand dollars a year.

Because of his devotion to thrift — in small items like typewriters as well as in large ones like office space — John Templeton's corporation operated at a profit every year after the first two years.

John and Dudley's first child, John Jr., was born in New York City in 1939. Two years later, Anne Dudley was born, and five years after that, Christopher Winston, also in New York City, although the Templetons lived at that time in Englewood, New Jersey. They joined the First Presbyterian Church of Englewood, and John became involved in fundraising and serving, first as a deacon and later as an elder. At that time he also took on the chairmanship of the board of trustees of the YMCA of Bergen County. In 1940, he was elected to the Commission on Ecumenical Mission and Relations of the National Presbyterian Church and soon after was chairman of the managing committee for its $50 million endowment funds. Through meeting national church leaders, John was invited to many meetings of the General Assembly and the National Council of Churches; he was even a guest at a World Council of Churches meeting in Geneva, Switzerland.

These were hectic years for the Templetons, with the investment corporation demanding more and more of John's time just when he was involved with a growing family and with community activities. The only vacation John and Dudley had had since their honeymoon was a ten-day trip to Nassau in the Bahamas while they still lived in Texas. John's business was going well; they had accumulated $150,000 by the time he bought Vance, Chapin and Company. So it seemed appropriate to take another vacation — this time in Bermuda. But then, just when everything seemed to be going well, tragedy struck. In February 1951, Dudley was severely injured in a highway accident as she and John toured Bermuda on motorbikes. She had suffered severe internal head injuries and died in the hospital. Recently, their oldest son, John Jr., a pediatric surgeon and trauma expert, told me that his mother was the victim of what was then a poorly understood type of injury.

The three children were devastated by the sudden loss of their mother. John, of course, had not only the pain of her loss, but also the problem of going on. As he explained his predicament:

> I had three young children. I didn't know how to be a mother to them, but I had to try. I couldn't spend all day with them because I was in the midst of trying to build a business and earn a living. So I asked one of our two servants, Rosezella Romney, to become the governess for the children. After the first few weeks, I found that the best thing to do was to go back to work, to fill my mind with business. It was much better to keep my mind full of serving clients than to worry over what had happened.

The tragedy was doubly painful because it came just a few months after John's mother's death, in September 1950. In less than a year, he had lost the two most important women in his life. Some people in such circumstances are bewildered if not embittered. But others, like John, are fortunate enough to have deep spiritual resources. Not only did he go back to investment counseling with vigor and determination, but he also accepted a position on the board of trustees of Princeton Theological Seminary, as a ministry to the church. Here he met gifted ministers with spiritual strength and insight, like Dr. Bryant Kirkland, then minister of the Fifth Avenue Presbyterian Church, and brilliant scholars like Dr. James McCord, who was president of the seminary for thirty years. Soon John became chairman of the seminary's endowment investment committee and served in that capacity for thirty-eight years. He also served as chairman of the trustees for twelve years. Princeton was a very important experience for John. Through interaction with Kirkland and McCord and other trustees, half of whom were ministers, John formulated much of his own plans for charity programs and foundations to emphasize the acquisition of new spiritual information through research.

During this period, two other things occurred that helped ease the loss of Dudley for the family. One was the purchase of a summer home on Fishers Island, New York, in Long Island Sound. There the three children spent each of the next six summers together, along with their governess and cook and sometimes a theology student who provided instruction in golf, tennis, swimming, and boating. John was away for most of these summer weeks, but flew in on the weekends. Incidentally, the house on Fishers Island was another bargain hunter's dream. Purchased at the time of a busy and threatening hurricane season, it cost $18,000 and was sold by the children for $630,000. But John is quick to point out that real estate is not generally a good investment. It's "too individualistic," he says.

The other important event of that period was the initiation of a new business association, the Young Presidents Organization (YPO). John was invited to a luncheon at New York's Waldorf-Astoria by a stranger, Ray Hickock, president of Hickock Belt Company of Rochester, New York. After lunch, Hickock said to his fifty guests that his father had died and left him in charge of the belt and leather company and, at the age of 25, he felt the need to talk to other young executives about management issues and techniques. He asked if any of the young presidents in the room thought they could learn from each other at semi-annual conferences. Seventeen people raised their hands and put their names on a list for future meetings. John thought the story would end there, but Hickock had his public relations agent write a news story about the meeting for the *New York Times*. The response was

overwhelming, with more than one hundred more young presidents want-
ing to be involved. Thus was born the Young Presidents Organization, which
grew to more than seven thousand members worldwide, with five-day meetings held twice yearly and other special meetings on occasion.

At first, a prospective member had to have become president of a corporation before he reached the age of 40. At the same time, his company had
to have a sales volume of at least $3 million a year or more than one hundred
employees. While these last two criteria have changed over the years, the
age requirement has remained the same.

Another qualification for membership was that you had to drop out when
you reached age 49. When John and some of his colleagues reached that age,
they decided they wanted to continue their friendships, so they formed an
alumni organization called the Chief Executives Organization. All members
were graduates of the YPO and there was no upper age limit. Hoping to have
conventions where they all knew each other and their spouses, they limited
membership to one thousand. However, soon a duplicate group called the
World Presidents Organization was formed; it too was open to every person
who had been a member of YPO. This organization eventually grew to be
much larger than the Chief Executives Organization.

Making many new friends through YPO was a great tonic for John, not
only for his business dealings but also in his social and spiritual life. Conversations often drifted easily from stocks and production quotas to personal
subjects and even religious concepts. John said that these organizations were
"marvelous ways to learn from each other how to be better presidents and
share the joy of seeing old friends again." This would seem to be one of the
hallmarks of John Templeton's approach to social life. Good friends, good
conversation, but always with an eye to what is more worthwhile and life-
changing: What is a good investment?

These, then, were the growth years, full of potent and challenging experiences for a wise, disciplined, and extremely energetic man. It was not
illogical that they would lead to an extraordinary investment program
called the Templeton Growth Fund Ltd., which John started in November
1954. The achievements of this common stock mutual fund have been

phenomenal. To illustrate, Leroy Paslay invested $100,000 Canadian at the beginning and, with distributions reinvested, his family owned shares worth $37 million Canadian on April 30, 1996. This performance is believed to be the world's greatest mutual investment fund performance for that time period.

CHAPTER 11

Investing with John Templeton

THE TEMPLETON INVESTMENT PHILOSOPHY

JOHN TEMPLETON'S financial investment years began a second phase with the initiation of the Templeton Growth Fund in 1954. It was a global fund from its inception, and it was immediately successful because John saw foreign markets, especially Japan, as bargain-priced investment opportunities. Recalling his travel experiences, he reasoned that countries with thrifty, hard-working people like post-World War II Japan would have many growing companies. William Proctor, who wrote the 1983 book *The Templeton Prizes*, tells us a little of John's bargain-hunting approach.

> Templeton's basic formula is to divide the total value of a company by the number of shares the company has distributed. This calculation will give you the *true* value of a company's stock, and if the market price is lower, then it's a bargain. . . .
>
> At one point, for instance, Templeton decided that he liked the Yasuda Fire and Marine Insurance Company in Japan. He came to this conclusion after he took all the investments they owned, added up the listed market prices of those investments, and then divided this sum by the number of Yasuda shares outstanding. As a result, he discovered that the shares were priced 80 percent below their liquidating value. Now, that was a bargain, according to Templeton.
>
> But many companies and other investment opportunities can't

be evaluated in such a straightforward way. Like many savvy investors, if Templeton is evaluating retailing companies, for example, he looks to see the extent to which the geographical area is changing; the number and character of the people moving in and out of the vicinity; the nature of the company's competition; and the stability and competence of the management. And this is only the beginning. The more information Templeton collects about a specific company or industry, the better he is prepared, he feels, to make a final decision.

So he tends to fill all his "dead time" — the minutes and hours he spends on airplanes and buses, or waiting for appointments — with a sheaf of reports, graphs, and analyses on various companies and managers. He reads, studies, and weighs the pros and cons of each potential investment in light of these mountains of information. And then he decides. Only in this way can he have the confidence that he is using his personal gift of good judgment wisely, effectively, and accurately.

When Templeton is checking up on oil and gas companies, the wealth of information is still of prime importance. But the specifics are different from the specifics for a retail store chain. For oil and gas, he concentrates on the company's cash flow. Cash flow provides more reliable comparisons between oil producers because reported net profits are distorted by many arbitrary choices regarding accounting methods and exploration programs.

Each industry and company, then, has its own requirements when it comes to determining worth and bargains. When evaluating grocery chains, Templeton looks at net earnings. With mining companies he collects information on the ore bodies to estimate how long it will be before the minerals are depleted. The key point underlying his bargain-hunting methods is that his system of evaluating stocks is dependent on extensive research and sound judgment. There really is no easy formula that can be applied across the board to find a good investment value.[1]

John Templeton's keen analysis of investment opportunities gave him a significant edge over his competitors, but it also put a high priority on his time. As anyone who has handled many private accounts will tell you, the telephone never stops ringing. Each account represents a unique set of objectives and sensitivities to taxes, timing, and risk. Each client quite rightfully makes claims on a money manager's time. And for Templeton, time has always been a thing to be treated as a gift. Templeton's close associate John Galbraith says that:

> by nature, he doesn't want to waste time — so you don't ever find yourself sitting around exchanging small talk. You always have a sense that he has more things to do than time to do it. We noted that our meetings with him would always begin within a few minutes of the designated time, and always ended on schedule. Just as he respects his own time, Templeton extends that respect to the time of others. John Hunter, one of his Canadian stock brokers, says that when he tells him he will call at 9:15 Canadian time, the call will invariably come through at precisely that time — from wherever Templeton is traveling in the world. In fact, to ensure that he is prompt, he has always set his watch ten minutes fast.

Sir John's desire to use his time effectively and to help others through good money management found its logical expression in mutual funds — a means for "everyman" to stake a claim in the market. In a sense, he saw this field not only as a very good business, but as an opportunity to help families of many income levels save money and acquire wealth and security. A newspaper story covering a Templeton address to a Chicago financial group reported that among the stockbrokers and financial planners seeking his autograph was a young accountant who told Templeton, "my daughter is two weeks old, and we just put $500 in your fund for her college education." Templeton shook his hand, saying, "We'll do our very best for you." He seemed genuinely concerned, and the man walked away with the satisfaction that his daughter's funds were in caring and capable hands.

The Principle of Maximum Pessimism

John Templeton is one of the most optimistic, up-beat people I have every met. But he works in a world all but defeated by a dour pessimism, gripped by prophets of doom who have, like the newspapers and television news programs, almost always looked at the bad side. He does not deny that there is a bad side, but suggests that dwelling on good things leads to power, peace, and success, whereas a focus on the negative leads to weakness, pain, and failure. However, he has used the prevalent negative tendency of others — especially investors — to forge a successful philosophy of investment. He calls it "the principle of maximum pessimism."

In 1978, John Templeton was featured on the cover of *Forbes* because the superb performance of the Templeton Growth Fund was then becoming well known through the marketing activities of his colleague John Galbraith. John Templeton was again on the cover of *Forbes* in 1995, and the related article talked about his optimistic view of the world economy and how he used it in a counterintuitive way to find the best investment bargains.

> When we last featured Templeton on our cover, in 1978, the Dow industrials were around 800, the economy was stagnating and some business publications were proclaiming the death of equities. Templeton's advice was unequivocal: Buy U.S. Stocks. They were then among the cheapest in the world. If U.S. Stocks did no more than get back to their traditional levels of around 14 times earnings, we would have a Dow of around 2800 by 1986. That's what he said. It sounded ridiculous at the time. Smart people were buying gold and collectibles and real estate, not stocks. Would stocks ever get that high again? "They always do," was Templeton's calm answer. And indeed they did.
>
> But it's 1995 and U.S. Stocks are no longer cheap by historical standards. On the other hand, the economy looks pretty strong. So, of course, we asked John Templeton: Where are the good buys now?
>
> "People are always asking me where is the outlook good, but

that's the wrong question," he responds. "The right question is: Where is the outlook most miserable?" Templeton calls this approach to investing "the principle of maximum pessimism." Others might call it contrarianism. He explains it this way: "In almost every activity of normal life people try to go where the outlook is best. You look for a job in an industry with a good future, or build a factory where the prospects are best. But my contention is if you're selecting publicly traded investment, you have to do the opposite. You're trying to buy a share at the lowest possible price in relation to what that corporation is worth. And there's only one reason a share goes to a bargain price: Because other people are selling. There is no other reason. To get a bargain price, you've got to look for where the public is most frightened and pessimistic."[2]

John Templeton's optimistic expectations for the stock markets of the world have been thoroughly justified. Investment counselor Gary Moore, in his 1996 book *Ten Golden Rules for Financial Success*, quotes a *World Monitor* article of February 1993, in which John wrote:

There will, of course, be corrections, perhaps even crashes. But over time our studies indicate stocks do go up — and up — and up. With the fall of communism and the sharply reduced threat of nuclear war, it appears that the United States and some form of an economically united Europe may be about to enter the most glorious period in their history.... Business is likely to boom. Wealth will increase. ... By the time the twenty-first century begins — it's just around the corner, you know — I think there is at least an even chance that the Dow Jones Industrial Average may have reached 6,000, perhaps more. Despite all the current gloom about the economy and about the future, more people will have more money than ever before in history.[3]

By 1997, the Dow had reached 8,000.

THE MOVE TO THE BAHAMAS

Phase two of John Templeton's investment program ended in 1968 with his decision to move his permanent home to Lyford Cay on the Island of New Providence in the Bahamas. The 1960s were a time of spiritual renewal for John. He and Irene Butler had married in 1958, four years after he had started the Growth Fund, and in 1959 he sold his New York investment counsel firm to an insurance company. John sought the move as an opportunity to devote more time to spiritual progress; as he put it, "I had spent my early career helping people improve their personal finances, but helping them to grow spiritually began to seem so much more important."

John and Irene built a beautiful home on a hill in Lyford Cay, overlooking a fine golf course and the Lyford Cay Club, a private club of 1,100 members from twenty-four countries. The native Bahamians are a people of deep spirituality and, so that Sir John could participate fully in this new country, then a British colony, he became a British citizen. He also began a program of spiritual training for Bahamians interested in the Christian ministry, providing a number of fellowships for study in the Bahamas and at Princeton Theological Seminary. Later he founded Templeton Theological Seminary, the first theological college in the Bahamas.

But John Templeton didn't shift completely away from financial investment management, since he still owned one mutual fund, the Templeton Growth Fund. As it turned out, the Growth Fund performance in the Bahamas was even better than before. John smiles as he recalls that at the start his "office" was two rooms rented above a barbershop in the Lyford Cay shopping center. Mena Griffiths, who is with him still, was his half-time secretary. It also turned out that Lyford Cay had other advantages. As he says:

> With the advantage of hindsight now, I think there are two reasons for this success. One is that if you're going to produce a better record than other people, you must not buy the same things as the other people. If you're going to have a superior record, you have to do something different from what the other security ana-

lysts are doing. And when you're a thousand miles away from Wall Street in a different nation, it's easier to be independent and buy the things that other people are selling, and sell the things that other people are buying. So that independence has proved to be a valuable help in our long-range performance.

Then, the other factor is that so much of my time in New York was taken up with administration and in serving hundreds of clients that I didn't have the time for the study and research that are essential for a chartered financial analyst. And that was the area in which God had given me some talents. So now in the Bahamas I had more time to search for the best bargains.

Another very important aspect of John Templeton's continuing success in the investment world relates directly to his growing spiritual commitment. For instance, he never overlooks the importance of prayer.

We start all our meetings, including our shareholders' meetings and our directors' meeting, with prayer. If you start meetings with prayer, the meetings are more fruitful and more productive — you reach decisions that are more likely to help everybody concerned. There is less controversy if you begin a meeting with prayer. Or, as I like to say, "Prayer helps you to think more clearly."

It goes back to my concept of God and His creative process. God is infinite. Maybe everything that exists in the universe and much more *beyond* the universe *is* God. This means that the whole visible universe may be a small part of God and is itself a manifestation of God. By the word "manifest" I mean that which is able to be known by a human being. So one little piece of God has become known to us through light waves and other things that enable us to perceive a few features of the universe.

We ourselves seem to be a recent creation of God and a little part of God. If we realize this and try to bring ourselves into harmony with God, with the Infinite Spirit — if we try to be humble tools in God's hands and become clear channels for His purposes —then we can accomplish much more. And what we do accomplish may be more permanent and lasting.

Whatever you do in life—whether you get married, bring a case to a law court, operate on a child, or buy a stock—you should open with prayer. And that prayer should be that God will use you as a clear channel for His wisdom and His love. You should open with prayer that every thought in your mind and every word and action that is taken will be in tune with what is right in God's purposes, and for the benefit of all God's children and not just a selfish goal.

And if you pray this way, everything you do following such a prayer is likely to be more successful. Your mind is not twisted by conflicts. You're less likely to disagree with your associates or do something you'll regret next year. So your decision making may be improved if you try to bring yourself into contact with the Creator, into harmony with His purposes.

If you make this basic effort to be in harmony with God and all of His children through prayer, then it's far more likely that anything you do in life will turn out for the best, including your selection of stocks. When we have directors' or shareholders' meetings or business meetings to discuss investment selections—whatever we do—we begin with prayer. We don't pray that a particular stock we bought yesterday will go up in price today, because that just doesn't work, but we do pray that the decisions we make today will be wise decisions and that our talks about different stocks will be wise talks. Of course, those decisions and discussions are not always wise—no one should expect that when he opens with prayer, every decision he makes is going to be profitable. Evidence shows that more of them are good if you open with prayer than if you don't.

Evidence also shows that John has been fair in his dealings with others. In more than sixty years in the corporate world, neither he nor any of the dozens of corporations controlled by him has ever sued or been sued. This may reflect Sir John's policy of ethics, peace, harmony, and love for everyone without exception. John Templeton has derived great strength from a regular prayer life, not only evidenced at all his investment meetings, but in his private life as well. Here are parts of his daily prayers,

> Almighty God, our loving heavenly Father, through faith and the Holy Ghost I am totally one unity with Thee. I am completely whole in mind and body.
>
> Thou are all of me and I am a little part of Thee. Every little cell, every little vibration which is me is only an outward expression of Thy divine will in perfect health and harmony.
>
> Thou art always guiding me, inspiring me to make the right decisions in family matters, in business matters, in health matters, and especially in spiritual matters.
>
> And dear God, I am deeply, deeply grateful for Thy millions of blessings and millions of miracles with which you surround each of us.
>
> Today and every day, I am especially grateful for the miracle of prayers answered and for the joy of being a humble servant of Thine on earth.
>
> Help me to see more clearly how to use these marvelously increasing assets and talents to accomplish the very most for Thy purposes on earth.
>
> Dear God, help me to open my mind and heart more fully to receive Thy unlimited love and wisdom, and to radiate these to Thy other children on earth especially today and every day this year.
>
> And thank Thee dear God for blessing and protecting all my travels and public appearances so that all will be safe, on time, and useful.
>
> Dear God, thank Thee for blessing and inspiring each person

concerned with the Templeton programs to help religion and freedom.

Thank Thee for my redemption and salvation and for Thy gift of the Holy Ghost by grace, which fills me to overflowing and increasingly dominates my every thought, and word and deed.

To Thee we pray in the name of Thy beloved Son whom I adore and seek to imitate, my savior and my God, Christ Jesus. Amen.

The result of Sir John's merging of his spiritual and professional lives seems to have made both his efforts in the spiritual domain and his investment activities prosper. John set a schedule that divided his time equally between religious and philanthropic activities on the one hand, and overseeing family investments and the mutual funds on the other. He had begun a program of double tithing in the mid-1960s (in fact, John regularly gives to charity twenty times as much as he spends on himself), but now he was giving his time as well.

The Rise to International Prominence

John Galbraith joined John Templeton in 1974, at a time when the Growth Fund had reached $13 million in assets, but was, like all other mutual funds, in a market slump. It was Galbraith who brought the necessary marketing skills to bring the Templeton record of success to the wider public. The success of this combination was meteoric: In just four years the assets of the funds reached $100 million; when the funds' management corporation was finally sold in 1992, there were $22 billion in assets; and in 1997, the funds' assets had grown to the extent that more than four million people worldwide owned $80 billion.

In 1960, John Galbraith had been an accountant working in the earlier mutual funds managed by the investment counsel firm John Templeton had sold to the Richardson family. But in 1974, the Piedmont Company, as it was called, chose to move to the west, so Galbraith began looking for a new job. He approached John Templeton with a proposition to market the Tem-

pleton Growth Fund, setting up a U.S.-based network of brokers and deal-
ers. His business plan was presented to John Templeton at Lyford Cay in
that same year. Galbraith noted that the Growth Fund had only grown from
$7 million to $13 million in assets during its first twenty years, despite its
outstanding performance. The problem, he said, was marketing. He proposed to multiply the assets of the fund tenfold in ten years. If he succeeded,
Galbraith would buy the management of the fund, paying for it over the
next three years. If he was unsuccessful, John Templeton would keep it all.
According to Galbraith, John responded, "Did you bring your swim trunks?"
Whereupon they went off to the Lyford Cay Club for a swim. As they sat on
the beach, John said, "There are lots of people who want to buy my company, but I don't want to sell. Why don't you do everything you proposed,
but buy 20 percent of my company?" John Galbraith says he went home a bit
disappointed, and told his wife Rosemary, "I went for the whole loaf and I
got half." But then he quickly added, "What I thought was half a loaf turned
out to be *many loaves*."

In 1978, John Templeton started a second fund, the Templeton World
Fund, at John Galbraith's suggestion. In subsequent years additional mutual
funds were introduced to focus on small companies and development of foreign nations. Stockholders' meetings were held in a variety of locations,
including the World Trade Center in New York, with the help of Galbraith's
longtime associate Milton Steren, although the biggest meetings continued
to be in Toronto. In 1997, seven thousand stockholders in five cities
attended the Toronto annual meeting by closed-circuit television. The Templeton Growth Fund in Canada has been a longtime success story, with
strong leaders in accountant Bruce MacGowan, the first full-time employee
in the Toronto office, and manager Donald Reed. The Canadian fund has a
significant share of all mutual fund business in Canada. John Templeton has
been an active presence at all the stockholder meetings, and he has encouraged his son, Jack Templeton, to participate as well. Despite Jack's demanding medical career, he has taken an active part in the meetings of the
Templeton Funds and has opened the meetings with prayer since 1985.

By 1978, John Templeton's investment workload had increased to such an extent that he hired Tom Hansberger, a Ft. Lauderdale, Florida, investment counselor, to assist him. They worked together, dividing the work between the Lyford Cay office and the office in Ft. Lauderdale. In 1985, John Templeton hired Mark Holowesko, a young Bahamian-born investment counselor. At 25, Mark was one of the youngest chartered financial analysts. In 1992 he became director and chief investment officer of Templeton Worldwide, Inc. In 1986 the two operations, John Templeton's in Lyford Cay and John Galbraith's (by then located in St. Petersburg, Florida), merged to become Templeton, Galbraith and Hansberger, Ltd.

In 1992 all management and marketing activities of the Templeton family of mutual funds was sold to Franklin Resources, Inc., a larger mutual fund manager in San Mateo, California. At that time, the many Templeton Funds had assets of $22 billion, managed by some of the top talent in the field of investment. This helped Franklin Resources, Inc. to become one of the largest and most respected investment companies worldwide, with offices in fourteen nations and more than five thousand employees.

Throughout this monumental phase of John Templeton's investment career, several salient features are evident. One is his frequent reference to common sense as a part of decision making. Time and again, says Bruce Mac-Gowan of the Toronto office, John would respond in the question-and-answer period of stockholder meetings with the words, "it's just common sense," and then follow those words with a clear, concise, but sensitive answer. One of John's longtime business friends, Burton Morgan, a fellow member of the Young Presidents Organization, recalls such an encounter at a YPO shipboard seminar titled "Mergers and Acquisitions." In the question and answer period, Morgan shared a major problem he was facing. He says of the encounter:

> I was number four to raise my hand. I said, "I started this company, Fasson, and now own 15 percent of the stock. I originally bought 5 percent for cash and two options of 5 percent each, giving me the 15 percent. My total options would give me 25 percent, but my partner never meant to give me so much. I am an

employee and stand to make a million dollars. He has asked me to give up the last two options, and I have refused. The only way he could not pay is to fire me, because the options are good only if I am employed. He will not buy my shares for fear I will start up again, so he has my money, and I have no job. What can I do?

John replied, "Take your shares and go to an investment banker. With these shares as collateral, he will give you 25 percent of a new company and provide $500,000 in equity for his 75 percent. You can then borrow $500,000 from a bank and get a contractor to lease you a new plant."

"You mean I can really do this?"

"Certainly. Next!"

This gave me the courage to take what I had and to start Morgan Achesin from scratch. Before I met John, I had given up. I was out looking for an engineering job, and I felt that I would never again get a real entrepreneurial chance.

This was the single greatest boost of courage I have ever had and I have never forgotten John Templeton.[4]

John Galbraith, too, lauds John Templeton's performance at meetings with brokers and salesmen as well as stockholders. In fact, he arranged for Templeton to appear on the television program *Wall Street Week* with Louis Rukeyser in 1980. John has been on the program many times since, more times than any other guest, and Louis refers to him as "one of the authentic heroes of Wall Street."

John was back with Louis Rukeyser for an interview published in *Louis Rukeyser's Wall Street*, a monthly financial newsletter, in January 1998. Rukeyser's friendship and appreciation of Sir John is evidenced by his introduction:

The world is not just John Templeton's oyster, it is his mission. In the strictly financial sense, it is he who has prodded Americans for 57 years not to let their investing horizons stop at the border. In the spiritual sense, it is he who for 25 years has funded the non-sectarian Templeton Prize for Progress in Religion, the world's largest philanthropic monetary award. Central to his beliefs, and to his life, has been the often-unfashionable idea that free enterprise not only is in no way the enemy of humane values but is, in fact, its true best friend.

Sir John, as this 85-years-young dynamo is known to Queen Elizabeth and his neighbors in the Bahamas, has been technically retired for five years, since he sold (and severed all ties with) the Templeton mutual funds. But, as you'll see below, his brain is as crisp as when he moved from Winchester, Tenn., to Yale to a Rhodes Scholarship at Oxford more than six decades ago. He is an old friend of mine — a record 15 appearances on *Wall Street Week with Louis Rukeyser*, charter membership in its Hall of Fame — and of this publication, where his regular appearances over the years have offered exclusive opportunities to find out the latest thinking of one of the century's most incisive — and kindest — minds.

In the interview that followed, Sir John made it clear that he is still very much in the stock market, though now as a private investor rather than as a manager of mutual funds. He still believes mutual funds and diversification are the best tools for the average investor. He still thinks that global investing is the safest approach in the long term.

CHAPTER 12

The Templeton Prize

W HILE THE TEMPLETON MUTUAL FUNDS were making headlines in the financial world, John was also busy in the spiritual domain. In 1972, he created the Templeton Prize for Progress in Religion, an annual cash gift exceeding in value the Nobel prizes to honor individuals making a significant contribution to progress in religion. His first thoughts of a prize for religion stemmed from a recognition that many of his friends — especially the best educated and most successful — seemed to be neglecting religion. He recalls that "they thought of religion as uninteresting and old-fashioned, or even obsolete."

In contrast, some of the work he was doing with religious organizations like the United Presbyterian Church Commission on Ecumenical Mission and Relations and the Princeton Theological Seminary called his attention to, in his words,

> the marvelous new things going on in religion. There were new churches being formed; new schools of thought arising; new books being written on spiritual matters; new religious orders being established; and new denominations appearing. And I thought, how wonderful it would be if my friends could hear about these things and read about them. They couldn't help but be uplifted and inspired if they could just be informed about what was happening.

Then, too, the general tone of press coverage around the world seemed to

ignore or even run counter to the religious movements that John Templeton was noticing. He says, "I struggled with this issue for a long time.
Finally, I decided that, because I had limited resources and was just one person, the best I could do was to try to single out some of these wonderful
people and help them to become more well-known — not so much for their
own benefit, but for the benefit of people who might be inspired by them."

So, just as Alfred Nobel had done at the turn of the prior century, John
placed in his will a stipulation that, after his death, his trustees would award
a prize for progress in Christianity. "But then I began to realize that it was
a mistake for me to leave the assets for later use," he says, "because 'later'
might be a long, long time away; I might live twenty years, and in that case
the world and my living friends would miss out in hearing about these wonderful religious movements and people." So John sought advice from his
longtime associate Dr. James McCord, the president of Princeton Theological Seminary, and also from Lord Thurlow, the former governor of the
Bahamas. Both of them encouraged him to go ahead with the program of
prizes while he was still alive. At the same time, John decided to broaden
the religious base of the prize. He says, "It was during those formative years,
particularly when talking with friends in the World Council of Churches,
that we decided also that it would be a prize for progress in religion of all
types, so no child of God would feel excluded." To confirm this idea, John
convened a panel of nine prestigious judges, with at least one judge from
each of the five major religions. In addition, at least half the judges would
not be religion professionals. "In this way," he said, "they would be more
likely to be receptive to new ideas." John also set up an extensive system of
nominators representing all the denominations of the Christian Church and
several other religions. Lastly, John found a very distinguished person to
award the prize:

> In my early conversations with Lord Thurlow and Dr. James
> McCord, both of whom were selected to serve on our first board
> of judges, I said, 'If we had a really famous person to award the
> prize, it would be beneficial to a much larger number of people.'

With the help of Lord Thurlow's friend, Sir Robin Woods, then dean of Windsor, His Royal Highness Prince Philip, husband of the Queen, graciously consented to award the first prize in 1973, and has continued to do so each year.

Some of those who have served as judges for the Templeton Prize include Presidents Gerald Ford and George Bush; Baroness Margaret Thatcher, former prime minister of Great Britain; the Dalai Lama of Tibet; U.S. Senators Orrin Hatch, a Mormon, and Mark Hatfield, an evangelical; Her Majesty Fabiola, Queen of the Belgians; Sir Mohammed Khan of Pakistan, former president of the International Court of Justice at the Hague; Lord Yehundi Menuhin, violinist from England; the Reverend Dr. Norman Vincent Peale, minister of New York's Marble Collegiate Church; the Reverend Dr. Arthur Peacocke, former dean of Clare College, Cambridge, and subsequently director of the Ian Ramsey Center, Oxford; and Princess Poon Pismai Diskul of Thailand, the former president of the World Federation of Buddhists.

The early recipients of the Templeton Prize, including Mother Teresa of Calcutta, the first recipient, in 1973, are described by William Proctor in his book *The Templeton Prizes*. Since that book was published in 1983, there have been many more winners, one each year except for 1989 and 1990 when two individuals shared the prize.[1] Among this group of winners are several who have been leaders in the recognition of the impact of current science on theology. These include Sir Alister Hardy, who was knighted for his work in marine biology but who was also a leading researcher into the nature and extent of religious experience. Stanley Jaki, a Benedictine priest and a professor of astrophysics at Seton Hall University, has written several books about science, philosophy, and faith. Professor Carl Friedrich von Weizsäcker of Starnberg, Germany, received the award for his work on the relationship of physics and cosmology to theology. Professor Charles Birch, an Australian biochemist at the University of Sydney, has found process theology compatible with current science. The 1995 winner was mathematical physicist Professor Paul Davies of the University of Adelaide, who has written more than a dozen books revealing how physics, mathematics, and cosmology point to purpose and meaning in the universe. Recognizing the importance of scientific research, the prize was later renamed The Templeton Prize for Progress Toward Research or Discoveries about Spiritual Realities.

PAUL DAVIES

Each occasion of recognition of the prizewinner has been memorable, and I am fortunate to have been present for all the recent ceremonies. I especially remember the ceremony for Paul Davies, who for me exemplifies the Templeton Prize winners. I also had the privilege of reporting on the event in the newsletter *Progress and Theology*.[2]

On May 3, 1995, Paul Davies became the twenty-fifth recipient of the Templeton Prize. The ceremony was held at London's Westminster Abbey, and in his acceptance speech, Professor Davies remarked that it was a special thrill to be standing just a few meters from the remains of Isaac Newton, one of the "great heroes" of his own discipline, physics.

Many people working in the science-religion field look at Paul Davies as a new kind of hero in physics, one who has opened the way to a new arena of dialogue in which scientists, philosophers, and theologians look at each other's disciplines with new respect and at their own discipline with a fresh kind of humility. For Paul Davies, that humble probing spirit has been evident throughout his many excellent books, of which some of the best-known are *God and the New Physics, The Cosmic Blueprint, The Mind of God, Other Worlds, About Time,* and *Are We Alone?*

In his acceptance speech for the Templeton Prize, Paul Davies noted with great appreciation that one of the judges for the prize, Baroness Margaret Thatcher, had also been involved in an earlier award, when she, as a member of Parliament, had presented him, then a schoolboy, with a copy of *Norton's Star Atlas* for his proficiency in his O-level exams. He says it was a deciding point for him — the beginning of a long and exciting career in science.

Readers of his books also know that his career has gone well beyond that of most of his colleagues in probing the nature of the universe. What he has found is a universe that is unceasingly creative yet incredibly lawful. And he

The dedication of the Templeton Hall of the Princeton Theological Seminary, 1990. (*l to r*): Dr. Thomas Gillespie, president; John Marks Templeton, former chairman; Mrs. Irene Templeton; Dr. David Watermulder, chairman.

Templeton Hall of the Princeton Theological Seminary, 1990.

On the occasion of Sir John Templeton's election as an Honorary Fellow of Templeton College, Oxford. *Seated:* Sir John Templeton, Lady Irene Templeton, U. Kitzinger. *Middle row:* I. Kessler, B. Prodhan, E. Howard, S. Dopson, R. Undy, S. Jennings, R. Martin. *Back row:* R. Davies, J. McGee, C. Cowton, P. Anand, G. Fitzgerald, J. Purcell, J. Reynolds, R. Stewart, K. Blois.

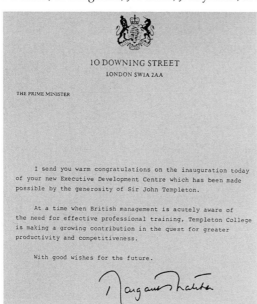

Letter from Margaret Thatcher recognizing the establishment of Templeton School of Management at Oxford University.

The Templeton Prize for Progress in Religion was awarded to Dr. Billy Graham in 1982. (*l to r*): John Marks Templeton, Mrs. Billy Graham, Dr. Billy Graham, HRH Prince Philip.

The plaque with three gold medallions bestowing knighthood on John Marks Templeton.

Sir John and Lady Templeton
leaving knighthood ceremony
at Buckingham Palace, 1989.

In 1992, Sir John was honored with
a festschrift, a collection of articles
by some of his most respected
friends and colleagues, which included this foreword written by
HRH Prince Philip.

The Templeton Window, donated by Sir John, at Lady Chapel, Westminster Abbey, 1996.

Westminster Abbey, London, where Sir John served on HRH Prince Philip's Restoration Commission, 1996.

John M. Templeton, Jr.,
Anne Templeton Zimmer-
man, and Christopher W.
Templeton in Casper,
Wyoming, 1990.

Dr. Anne Templeton Zim-
merman and Dr. Gail Zim-
merman on their wedding
day in Tucson, Arizona,
1979.

Drs. Jack and Pina Templeton and their daughters, Heather (*left*) and Jennifer, 1996.

Front row (*l to r*): Rhonda Zimmerman, Anne Zimmerman, Gail Zimmerman, Heather Templeton, Jennifer Templeton, Lady Templeton, Virginia and Susan Judith Templeton, Pina Templeton. *Back row* (*l to r*): Mike Zimmerman, Eva Zimmerman, Renee Zimmerman, Sir John Templeton, Jack Templeton, Christopher Templeton, Gäbriel Flynn, Jason Flynn.

Sir John Templeton with his son Christopher's daughter, Susan Judith.

Sir John and Lady Templeton, Mr. and Mrs. Harvey Templeton, Jr., and descendants in Winchester, Tennessee, 1992.

believes this discovery is of deep significance for both the scientist and the theologian. Of the scientific enterprise, he has said,

> A lot of people are hostile to science because it demystifies nature. They prefer the mystery. They would rather live in ignorance of the way the world works and our place within it. For me, the beauty of science is *precisely* the demystification because it reveals just how truly wonderful the physical universe really is. It is impossible to be a scientist working at the frontier without being awed by the elegance, ingenuity, and harmony of the law-like order in nature.
>
> In my attempts to popularize science, I'm driven by the desire to share my own sense of excitement and awe with the wider community; I want to tell people the good news. The fact that we are able to do science, that we can comprehend the hidden laws of nature, I regard as a gift of immense significance. Science, properly conducted, is a wonderfully enriching and humanizing enterprise. I cannot believe that using this gift called science — using it wisely, of course — is wrong. It is good that we should know.

For the theologian, Paul Davies sees profound significance in the creativity and intelligibility of nature. At Westminster Abbey, he also said,

> Now some of my colleagues embrace the same scientific facts as I, but deny any deeper significance. They shrug aside the breathtaking ingenuity of the laws of physics, the extraordinary felicity of nature, and the surprising intelligibility of the physical world, accepting these things as a package of marvels that just happen to be.
>
> But I cannot do this. To me, the contrived nature of physical existence is just too fantastic for me to take on board as simply "given." It points forcefully to a deeper underlying meaning to existence. The emergence of life and consciousness, I maintain, are written into the laws of the universe in a very basic way.

This occasion was a very special one for Sir John Templeton as well, for he has been a friend and encourager of Paul Davies who, in turn, is an advisor to the Templeton Foundation.

Indeed, these have been exciting times for the goals of the Templeton Prize, for as John Templeton realized so very early, science is opening up a whole world of opportunity for acquiring new spiritual information and hence for progress in religion.

In fact, the last four Templeton Prize winners have been individuals with a deep commitment to the science-religion dialogue. In 1999, the winner was physicist-theologian Ian Barbour, and the public ceremony was held for the first time in Russia, in the Krestovaya Hall in the patriarchal chambers of the Kremlin. Given the state of turmoil in Russia at that time, Sir John was offered a caravan with armed guards but characteristically decided instead to walk across Red Square from the Hotel Metropol with a company of perhaps a dozen of us who had been invited to the ceremony. We arrived without incident and were received by dignitaries of the Russian Academy of Science and The Russian Orthodox Church and were also treated to sacred music provided by the choir of Moscow University's St. Tatiana Chapel.

The introduction of Dr. Barbour was made by Dr. John Templeton, president of the John Templeton Foundation. He said, in part:

> Until his retirement, Ian Barbour was professor of religion and professor of science, technology and society at Carleton College in Minnesota, USA. Professor Barbour has been one of the world's pioneers in the integration of science and religion. His books and articles are helping to expand the field of theology, not only for Christians but also for other faiths.
>
> Born in China, Ian Barbour has had a distinguished academic career culminating in his Gifford Lectures in Scotland in 1989, and the American Academy of Religion Award for Excellence in the Study of Religion in 1993.
>
> Professor Barbour has shown that in the contemporary world, science offers an enormous resource for growth and deepening of religious knowledge. At the same time, no fact of

our understanding of God is immune to the potential challenge science raises against the very credibility of religious belief.

Nominated for the Templeton Prize by Emeritus Professor John B. Cobb Jr. of the School of Theology at Claremont, California, USA, Ian Barbour joins a select group of recipients who have, over the past fifty years, forged a new relationship between science and religion.

Ian Barbour sees a great need to continue the dialogue between religion and science that seeks integration of the two. As John B. Cobb Jr. has written:

> No contemporary has made a more original, deep and lasting contribution toward the needed integration of science and religious knowledge and values than Ian Barbour. With respect to the breadth of topics and fields brought into this integration, Barbour has no equal.
>
> As physicist, philosopher, theologian, ethicist, environmentalist, technologist and worshipper in the biblical tradition, Ian Barbour embodies the best of the many worlds he spans. No one has contributed more to overcoming the split between science and religion and to developing a new synthesis than he. If there is a paradigm for the new relationship between science and religion at last emerging, and so clearly contributing to progress in religion, it is that of Ian Barbour.

Also in attendance at the Moscow ceremony were two distinguished recipients of the Templeton Prize, Mr. Alexander Solzhenitsyn and Professor Paul Davies.

FREEMAN DYSON

The following year, the prize was conferred upon another physicist, Dr. Freeman Dyson, professor emeritus of the Institute for Advanced Studies, Princeton. As one of the outstanding physicists of our time, he has also written extensively on the meaning of science and its impact on religion and ethics.

In that year I was serving as a judge for the Templeton Prize, so had the privilege of attending the private ceremony at Buckingham Palace that ordinarily precedes the public event. His Royal Highness, Prince Philip, the Duke of Edinburgh, was there as usual to present the prize, and the occasion provided an illustration of Prince Philip's easy manner and Dr. Dyson's humble spirit.

The palace ceremony was an occasion for a rather jovial exchange between the Prince and the prize recipient in which Freeman Dyson said he felt like a returning prodigal son, having been born and raised in England (where his father was a leader in music education in London) and educated in Cambridge, but having spent most of his professional life in America. Prince Philip's response was to ask why he hadn't studied music, to which Dyson slyly replied that he and his father had agreed that he had "absolutely no talent."

The public prize ceremony and the reception preceding it saw Dr. Dyson in the same relaxed, jovial mood, clearly enjoying the occasion and the opportunity to meet with many well-wishers. The event was held in conjunction with the John Templeton Foundation annual meeting, so many of the members and trustees were also present for the festivities. Four former Templeton laureates were also present: philosopher Michael Novak, physicist Paul Davies, diplomat and businessman Sir Sigmund Sternberg, and physicist-theologian Ian Barbour.

At the public ceremony at Washington's National Cathedral, Dr. Dyson delivered his acceptance speech, thanking Sir John and the Templeton Foundation for the honor and the Institute for Advanced Study at Princeton for supporting him while he "strayed into other areas remote from physics." Like a number of other prizewinners, Dyson focuses his theological interest on those mysteries which lie beyond science. "The greatest unsolved mysteries are the mysteries of our existence as conscious beings in a small corner of a vast universe. Why are we here? Does the universe have a purpose? Whence comes our knowledge of good and evil?"

At the end of his speech, Dyson added a prayer: "This is my vision, and it is the same vision that inspired Francis Bacon four hundred years ago, when he prayed that through science God would endow the human family with new mercies."

Sir John Templeton followed up Dyson's address with the following thoughts:

> The Templeton Prize is awarded annually to a living person of any religious tradition or movement. The Templeton Prize does not encourage syncretism, but rather an understanding of the benefits of diversity. It seeks to focus attention on the wide variety of highlights in present-day religious thought and work. It does not seek a unity of denominations or a unity of world religions; but rather, it seeks to encourage understanding of the benefits of religious and spiritual progress.
>
> From its beginning, the Templeton Prize was made larger than the Nobel prizes. This was a way of saying that progress in religion is more important than progress in any other area. While the winner each year will benefit from the prize, the vastly greater benefit is for the millions of readers whose spiritual growth is enhanced by studying the life and work of each awardee. Millions of readers may learn that religion is progressive and dynamic. Nothing is more important than the need to learn more about our infinite, omnipotent, and all-loving Creator; and also, to learn more about how we can be helpers in divine creativity.
>
> The Templeton awards are open to every child of God. There is no limitation in regard to race, creed, sex, or geographical background. Each year the selection is made by a panel of distinguished judges from at least four major religions. The judges first ask, What has this person done that was entirely original? Secondly, Was it primarily spiritual rather than humanitarian? Lastly, Did this original contribution by the nominee result in a great increase of either humankind's love of God or understanding of God? To clarify this important difference: for example, if a church

should found a hospital, that is humanitarian, but if a hospital were to create a new kind of church, that would be originality in religion. Many other awards honor wonderful humanitarian works, but this award is reserved for originality of research in religion or spirituality.

Each of us should be deeply grateful that God allowed us to be born in this generation when the quantity of knowledge is increasing and accelerating. Nevertheless, great humility is needed because we have so much to learn about God and his nature and purpose. While he is infinite, we are very tiny and limited. No person may even know one percent of the Infinite Creative Spirit. To learn anything, we must first become humble and rid ourselves of the egotistical idea that we already know everything about God.

Do multiplying discoveries indicate that reality is more basic, complex, and vast than some things tangible or visible? Can all the wonderfully beneficial ancient scriptures be supplemented over one hundredfold partly by science research for spiritual information and verification? Can all religions learn to be so humble as to be enthusiastic (rather than resistant) to new spiritual information?

Likewise, can new information from science research on basic spiritual truths and realities reduce conflict between religions? Can religious conflict vanish if people come to recognize, from science research, spiritual information that is universal to all people? In this way, all religions can embrace the motto, "How little we yet know, how eager to search and learn?"

ARTHUR PEACOCKE

The 2001 Templeton Prize was awarded to another scientist, this time a biochemist, and, as was the case with Ian Barbour, to an individual formally educated in theology as well. The Reverend Canon Dr. Arthur Peacocke was

presented with the 2001 Prize by the Duke of Edinburgh at a private ceremony in Buckingham Palace on May 9, 2001.

Arthur Peacocke, in his acceptance remarks, dwelt at some length on the
appreciation due Prince Philip for his support of the positive interaction of
science and religion. At one point, Arthur was interrupted by the Prince,
who laughingly inquired as to who was getting the prize.

The public ceremony was held in Guildhall, London. Speakers from three
major faith traditions delivered the addresses in honor of Dr. Peacocke to
over eight hundred guests gathered in the Great Hall. The welcome on
behalf of the Templeton Foundation was given by Dr. John Templeton, followed by a stirring address by Arthur's longtime friend and associate, John
Hedley Brooke, the Andreas Idreos Professor of Science and Religion at the
University of Oxford.

In his remarks, Professor Brooks recalled Peacocke's fifty years of reflection on the relation of scientific worldview to Christian belief. Combining
careers in biochemistry and theology both at Cambridge and Oxford, he has
been in the forefront of the fight against the dogma of scientific reductionism. Yet throughout, he has maintained a spirit of humility, which Sir John
Templeton has insisted is a prerequisite of wisdom. On one occasion, Dr.
Peacocke responded to a widely read book, *Chance & Necessity* by French
biologist Jacques Monod, who argued that elements of chance and contin-
gency were so pervasive in evolutionary processes that any inferences about
direction or purpose were inadmissible. Arthur's reaction was to point out
that chance and necessity — apparent randomness and lawful necessity —
were just what would be needed to explore the full God-given potentialities
of living matter at the genetic level.

JOHN POLKINGHORNE

In 2002, the judges chose yet again a distinguished scientist, this time a
physicist and priest, Sir John Polkinghorne. In the April issue of the then-
new journal *Research News and Opportunities in Science and Theology* (now *Science and Theology News*), editor Dr. Karl Giberson wrote:

John C. Polkinghorne, mathematical physicist turned Anglican priest, has won the 2002 Templeton Prize. Polkinghorne, one of the most well-known figures in science and religion, is widely appreciated for his articulate search for connections between contemporary science and traditional Christian understandings. The announcement was made during a March 14 news conference at the Church Center for the United Nations in New York.

Polkinghorne's prominence stems in part from the impeccable scientific pedigree that he brings to the science-and-religion dialogue. He spent the bulk of a distinguished scientific career at the University of Cambridge as a professor of mathematical physics. Through his own work, which generated scores of scientific publications in leading journals, and the mentoring of graduate students, he made significant contributions to our modern understanding of the detailed structure of matter.

In 1979, Polkinghorne resigned his prestigious position as professor of mathematical physics at the University of Cambridge to pursue theological studies. He became a priest in 1982. Since then, his extensive writings and lectures have provided a compelling view of religion, as seen through the eyes of one trained as a scientist and who demands that the foundations of religion be more than "blind faith."

After serving for seven years as a parish priest, he was appointed president of Queens' College at the University of Cambridge.

In 1997, he was knighted by Queen Elizabeth II for distinguished service to science, religion, learning and medical ethics.

The impact of the life and work of Sir John Polkinghorne has been nothing short of stupendous. As Thomas Torrance, retired professor of Christian dogmatics at the University of Edinburgh, said in his nomination of the prizewinner: "Polkinghorne has not only destroyed the idea that the world-views of science and theology are opposed to one another, but he has opened up the road ahead for a new stage in conceptual integration, which cannot but make for immense progress in religion all over the world."

HOLMES ROLSTON III

The 2003 Prize was awarded to Rev. Dr. Holmes Rolston III, University Distinguished Professor of Philosophy at Colorado State University and an ordained minister in the Presbyterian Church. For thirty years, Dr. Rolston has been involved in research, writing, and lecturing on the religious imperative to respect nature, and his work has been a major factor in establishing the field of environmental ethics. He has become one of the world's leading advocates for protecting the earth's biodiversity and ecology in recognition of the intrinsic value of creation, including the ongoing evolutionary genesis in the natural world. In philosophical circles he is widely known as the "father of environmental ethics," and in theological circles he is known for his concept of a sacred, prolific, and "cruciform" creation. He gave the Gifford lectures in 1997 at the University of Edinburgh; the lectures were subsequently published as *Genes, Genesis and God* (1999).

GEORGE F. R. ELLIS

The 2004 Prize was awarded to George F. R. Ellis, a leading theoretical cosmologist renowned for his bold and innovative contributions to the dialogue between science and religion and whose social writings were condemned by government ministers in the former apartheid regime of his native South Africa. Dr. Ellis, a professor of applied mathematics at the University of Cape Town, specializes in general relativity theory, an area first broadly investigated by Einstein. He is considered to be among a handful of the world's leading relativistic cosmologists, including luminaries such as Stephen Hawking and Malcolm MacCallum. His most recent investigations question whether or not there was ever a start to the universe and, indeed, if there is only one universe or many.

In nominating Ellis for the Prize, Rev. Dr. William R. Stoeger, an astrophysicist with the Vatican Observatory Research Group, noted that Ellis' service to a broad spectrum of social, economic and ethnic groups in South Africa and elsewhere had sparked significant insights into the workings of the physical universe. "He has demonstrated how genuine religious and theological perspectives can help us understand the constitution and character of our universe in terms of 'kenosis,' self-sacrificing love," Stoeger wrote, adding that Ellis had shown, "that our universe seems to be particularly suited for fostering that attitude and practice, and to require it for its harmonious functioning at every level."

So, through the wisdom and foresight of Sir John Templeton, the world of the new millennium has been introduced to some of the keenest minds of our age. We look forward to many more thinkers of the same caliber joining their ranks.

CHAPTER 13

The John Templeton Foundation

A SECOND GREAT STEP in John Templeton's spiritual journey was made in 1987, when he established the John Templeton Foundation in Sewanee, Tennessee. Its primary purpose was to explore and encourage the relationship between science and religion, bringing together scientists, theologians, medical professionals, philosophers, philanthropists, and other scholars to plan programs and help disseminate the tremendous opportunities for new spiritual information through research.

The first meetings of the Foundation were small. There were the usual officers: John Templeton as chairman, his son Dr. John Templeton as president, his niece Ann Templeton Cameron as treasurer, and his nephew Harvey M. Templeton III as secretary. There were five trustees: Sir John, his wife Lady Irene Butler Templeton, his son Jack, and two others, Rev. Professor Thomas Torrance (Templeton Prize winner of 1978), and myself.

Recruitment of a staff for the organization began in the following year, when Frances Schapperle, former staff member of the Robert Wood Johnson Foundation, was hired as executive assistant. I first met Frances while I was doing some writing and research at the Center of Theological Inquiry in Princeton, New Jersey, in December 1988. She wanted to talk about the goals of the John Templeton Foundation and about Sir John, to get some idea of what it would be like to develop a set of programs almost "out of whole cloth," and what it would be like to work closely with a man known mostly as a world-class investor but becoming better known for his philanthropic activities and especially for his interest in progress in religion. I told her I thought the job would be challenging, not only because it would involve administering a very new kind of program, which was virtually without precedent, but also because John Templeton is a unique person who carries an enormous amount of information in his head. It would be her job to put his ideas and the many projects he is involved in down on paper. Sir John was involved in a great variety of philanthropic activities, especially in North America and Europe, but to my knowledge, only the Templeton Prize had an administrator, Rev. Wilbert Forker, assisted by Sir John's personal executive secretary, Mena Griffiths.

When Frances Schapperle came on board, she began to assemble a list of projects receiving support, which included the following:

- College Honor Roll for Character-Building Colleges;
- "Laws of Life" Essay Contest;
- Religious Editors Prize;
- Religious Heritage of America Awards Program;
- Templeton College, Oxford;
- Templeton United Kingdom Projects Trust; and
- Unity and the Association of Unity Churches.

The most time-honored is probably the Templeton United Kingdom Projects Trust, which has been administered by clergy at Windsor Castle since 1984. It has provided four awards yearly totaling £12,000 to honor British individuals and organizations that have made significant contributions to progress in religion in the United Kingdom.

Also included in Frances Schapperle's first annual report was a list of book projects underway, which included:

- *Who's Who in Theology and Science*, a directory of scholars in the science-religion field;
- *The God Who Would Be Known* by John Templeton and Robert Herrmann, published in 1989 and revised in 1998, and their second book, *Is God the Only Reality?* published in 1994;
- A "Laws of Life" textbook, which eventually became *Worldwide Laws of Life*;

- *Looking Forward: The Next Forty Years*, edited by John Templeton; and *Riches for the Mind and Spirit: John Marks Templeton's Treasury of Words to Help, Inspire and Live By.*

One of the early activities of the Foundation was the production of a set of bylaws. Sir John was determined to describe his goals for the Foundation as clearly as possible, recognizing that many foundations have strayed from their original goals because the founder's wishes were not made sufficiently specific. I became involved in this process, helping John organize his ideas about a theology of humility into a major statement for the bylaws. John put down his ideas in a series of one-sentence statements, which were designed to raise the awareness of the infinite size and all-encompassing nature of God, of the dynamic nature of His activity and the incredible variety of His ongoing creations, and of our response in humility as we recognize that we know almost nothing about this Unlimited Creative Spirit. These statements were then organized into paragraphs characterizing the theology of humility as: 1) centered in an infinite God; 2) creative, progressive; and 3) welcoming diversity.

In a section outlining some potential benefits of humility theology under the heading "Encouraging Progress," John involved a number of associates such as theologian and trustee Thomas Torrance in the process. Others were also added, including Bryant Kirkland, with whom John had been associated at the American Bible Society and at Princeton Theological Seminary, and Glenn Mosley, executive director of the Association of Unity Churches. Among later additions were Russell Stannard, professor of physics at the Open University in England, and former U.S. Secretary of the Treasury William Simon.

The annual board meeting was convened each year in early June in Sewanee or Monteagle, Tennessee. The meetings were large because all the family, as members of the Foundation, were invited to the members' meeting, which preceded the trustees' meeting. Here the purposes of the Foundation and its various programs were described by Sir John.

These gatherings were always heartwarming and quite fascinating, especially for someone like me who grew up in New York City and had little contact with small-town America, especially in its Southern version. The hospitality and genuine friendliness were striking, and the hilarity was delightful. But I especially remember the attention the family gave to the explanations Sir John provided about his vision for progress in spirituality. Here were educated people who could appreciate his concern and enthusiasm for the future growth of the human spirit.

THE HUMILITY THEOLOGY INFORMATION CENTER

Soon after the establishment of the bylaws, Sir John began to form an advisory board for the Foundation to function within the framework of what was first called a Center for Humility Theology. The center's research program was announced in the March 1992 issue of *Progress in Theology:*

> In recognition of the enormous impact that recent scientific research has had upon our knowledge of God's creation, the Center for Humility Theology has instituted a research program, which at present has three areas of concentration:
>   1. Utilization of scientific methods in understanding the work and purpose of the Creator.
>   2. Research on studying or stimulating progress in religion.
>   3. Research on the benefits of religion.
>   The John Templeton Foundation's resources are directed principally to operating its own program initiatives. The center's research programs involve a broad range of projects, which include:
>   1. A bibliographic survey of work by scientists on spiritual subjects.
>   2. A program to assess the extent of teaching of university and college courses on science and religion and to stimulate courses emphasizing progress in religion.
>   3. A training module on religion and psychiatry that illustrates the extent to which spiritual factors impact positively on clinical therapy.

4. Templeton lectures held in the United States and the United Kingdom, which explore the relationship between science and theology.

Sir John received a number of letters concerning the announcement. Amid the general enthusiasm was a concern that the Foundation was seeking to establish itself as the only institution interested in humbly seeking new spiritual information. In response to this idea, Sir John decided to change the name to the Humility Theology Information Center. His thoughts were published in the September 1993 issue of the newsletter:

In keeping with a spirit of self-examination and an eagerness to learn more about God, the Center for Humility Theology of the John Templeton Foundation has been given a new name. A few of our readers have expressed a concern that simply by designating ourselves a "Center" we are calling into question our own much-sought spirit of humility.

We appreciate that criticism, and we want all people who seek progress in the knowledge of God to be assured that our quest is open-ended and that our desire is to be free of any suggestion that we are the sole searchers for new ideas about God. The addition of the word "information" in our title is designed to emphasize the hopefully non-interpretive aspect of our center. We want to be a useful channel for information, but at the same time we wish to avoid the restrictive language and even dogmatic assertions that often accompany theological constructions. Our hope is to be a catalyst in the search for new knowledge of God, and we see humility theology as a potentially powerful tool in such explorations.

The Humility Theology Information Center, now simply referred to as the John Templeton Foundation Advisory Board, grew quickly and included scholars in the science and religion field from many branches of science, and a few from theology. Over the years the board has become quite diverse, with experts in comparative religion from both Harvard and Oxford, with academics of Indian extraction and the Muslim faith, and with philanthropists and journalists, publishers and political leaders as members.[1]

CHAPTER 14

Honors for Sir John Templeton

D ESPITE SIR JOHN'S DIFFIDENCE and humble spirit, or maybe because of it, society has found ways to honor this gentle man with the uncanny eye for financial investment but with an even greater vision of the spiritual future. I have mentioned his frequent appearances on *Wall Street Week*, and we can add that he has received twenty honorary degrees, as well as a very special retirement ceremony in 1985, at the end of thirty-nine years of service on the Board of Trustees of Princeton Theological Seminary. The plaque he was given simply but beautifully quoted John 1:6, "There was a man sent from God whose name was John."

Then, in 1987, he was inducted into the Imperial Society of Knights Bachelor by Queen Elizabeth II for his philanthropic work both in Britain and around the world.

John Templeton had been a British citizen since making his permanent home in the Bahamas in 1968, and so was eligible for knighthood. John Templeton has had a strong affinity for the British people, and a generous hand in their spiritual endeavors for many years, and that has not gone unnoticed. In addition to the Templeton United Kingdom Trust and the fact that the Templeton Prize has been annually presented by Prince Philip, it should also be mentioned that John has made a very significant contribution to Oxford University through Templeton College. When John had been a Rhodes scholar at Oxford, he had noted that there was no school of business at the university. So in later years, as a successful investor, he donated

$5 million to the Oxford Centre for Management Studies. Then in 1984, after the Centre received an additional commitment from John of $5 million over a five-year period, and an agreement from the university to allow the matriculation of twelve postgraduate students, the Centre became Templeton College. Today it is a full-fledged college of the University of Oxford.

Among other Templeton interests in Great Britain, two particularly stand out. A Templeton science and religion lecture program in London, cosponsored by the venerable Royal Society for Arts, Manufactures and Commerce (RSA), began as the result of a communication to Sir John from Christopher Lucas, director of the RSA, in the fall of 1991. The RSA has had a long and distinguished history of promoting cultural interchange in Great Britain and in the various other English-speaking countries, especially the United States. With a membership of 15,000, the RSA seemed a highly desirable venue for a series of lectures on science and religion. The membership is well educated and accustomed to dealing with controversial subjects, and John could foresee the development of an excellent schedule of lectures given the outstanding speakers available from two British academic groups, the Science and Religion Forum and another religion-science organization called Christians in Science.

The facilities, too, are excellent. The RSA has its offices and conference rooms in central London, just off the Strand on John Adams Street. The building has been restored beautifully, even to the extent of providing eating facilities in a large basement area of bricked arches and exposed cobblestone floors, which may date back to its waterfront warehousing days in the sixteenth century.

Sir John asked me to organize the lectures through the American Scientific Affiliation, and I in turn asked the British-based Science and Religion Forum to carry out the planning with the RSA on behalf of the Templeton Foundation. The lecture series was presented in the fall of 1992 and the following spring, with eight lectures in all. They were well attended and the discussions spirited. Five of the lectures were published in the *RSA Journal*, which is sent to the 15,000 fellows of the society.

A second Templeton program was later put together with the RSA by

Templeton trustee Professor Russell Stannard of the Open University. This program began a valuable discussion of religious education in English schools, a controversial subject area, with professional people and policy makers throughout Great Britain.

The aftermath of these and many other Foundation activities was another honor for Sir John, the presentation of the Benjamin Franklin medal. The occasion was a memorable one for all of us, and I described it in the March 1995 issue of *Progress in Theology*.

On November 30, 1994, Sir John Templeton received the Benjamin Franklin Medal of the Royal Society of Arts, Manufactures and Commerce (RSA). The presentation was made by HRH The Prince Philip, The Duke of Edinburgh, president of the society, at a ceremony held in the reception hall of St. James Palace, London.

My wife and I were privileged to be present at the ceremony, along with some one hundred others — officers and fellows of the RSA, Templeton Foundation staff and trustees, clergy and educators. Among the group were several lords and ladies, dukes and duchesses, and one Spanish cavalier. It was a delightful occasion, with Prince Philip adding his own special hospitality by circulating through the gathering just before the medal ceremony. Our small group introduced ourselves to him — though three were clergy from Windsor Castle whom he already knew well — and he asked me about my role in the Templeton Foundation. I tried to give a two-sentence description of humility theology, to which he listened patiently. Then, gesturing with his hands pointing in opposite directions, he said, "Scientists and theologians talk past each other." He obviously knows something of our problem!

The medal ceremony was short but quite moving. Sir John was being honored for his global philanthropy, especially in connection with the Templeton Prize for Progress in Religion and the Templeton U. K. Prizes, which are awarded to four British charitable and religious leaders and organizations each year. Also mentioned were Templeton College at Oxford and the two Templeton-sponsored lecture series at the RSA.

The Benjamin Franklin medal has an interesting history. It is an annual prize, awarded alternately to citizens of the United Kingdom and the United States who have forwarded the cause of British-American understanding. Previous recipients have included American architects Robert Venturi and Denise Scott Brown, who designed the most recent addition to the National Gallery in London; Sir David Attenborough; and Sam Wanamaker, the American actor who has forwarded the restoration of Shakespeare's Globe Theatre on the Thames waterfront. Earlier recipients were Alistair Cooke, J. William Fulbright, Prime Minister Harold Macmillan, and famed ballerina Dame Margot Fonteyn. The medal originated as a result of Benjamin Franklin's contribution to the RSA's work in the 1770s as chair of the RSA's Trade and Colonies Commission, which sought to help the British people realize the importance of treating the American colonies fairly.

Sir John's acceptance address, emphasizing the way in which Benjamin Franklin's ideals have become a strong focus of the Templeton Foundation's goals, was as follows:

> Cecil John Rhodes was the benefactor who enabled me to return to the United Kingdom, my ancestral home, from America, the land of my birth. I was born and raised in Franklin County (Tennessee), which is one of the fifty-six United States counties and cities named in honor of Benjamin Franklin.
>
> It is a joy indeed to follow humbly in the footsteps of Benjamin Franklin, who tried in many ways to help the young people of these two great nations to learn more about the noble virtues. Spiritual principles and strength of character produce lives that are both useful and happy. Both Cecil John Rhodes and Benjamin Franklin would approve, I think, of the programs of the Templeton Foundation and especially the new

college at Rhodes's own university, Templeton College, which teaches nothing but better business management.

It is a blessing indeed that the laws of the United Kingdom require every school to teach religious education. Really effective religious education can become a center for virtue, progress, prosperity, happiness, freedom, and spiritual growth. Such virtues will radiate automatically to all humanity.

Courses in religious education might be more productive if they focus less on history, rituals, and differences between religions and focus more on encouraging each student to develop his own list of virtues and spiritual principles, which can make his whole life more useful and happy. Many, many such laws of life can be discovered and learned, which are self-enforcing rather than depending on authority. By collecting strong scientific evidence, many of these laws can be convincing even to skeptics. Most important of all, laws collected in this way can avoid divisiveness, sectarianism, and regionality.

A few spiritual laws which can be supported by strong evidence are as follows:

1. Thanksgiving results in more to be thankful for.
2. The family that prays together, stays together.
3. It is more blessed to give than to receive.
4. We receive freely when we give freely.
5. It is better to love than to be loved.
6. You cannot be lonely while helping the lonely.
7. Agape given grows, agape hoarded dwindles.
8. Enthusiasm is contagious.
9. You are only as good as your word.
10. A loving person lives in a loving world.
11. Laugh and the world laughs with you; weep and you weep alone.
12. We tend to find what we look for, good or evil.
13. You can build your own heaven or hell here on earth.

14. We tend to become what we think.

15. It is better to praise than to criticize.

16. Crime does not pay.

17. If you do not know what you want to achieve with your life, you may not achieve much.

Can every religion on earth agree on these same virtues and vices? Probably every nation can agree and also every political party. So why not help every student to learn them? Why not have examinations and grades and credit toward graduation for learning and explaining the virtues? Probably Benjamin Franklin would have been enthusiastic about this idea.

It is my sense that religious education in our public secondary schools on both sides of the Atlantic is not so much absent as it is irrelevant. Perhaps Sir John Templeton's initiative is a way to bring moral-spiritual content, the result of any good theology, back into the mainstream of Western education and Western life.

᠁᠁

Another recent celebration in which Sir John Templeton has had a major part took place at Westminster Abbey in October 1995. The occasion was a service of dedication of the ancient cathedral after a dozen years of restoration work. Sir John had been a member of the committee, chaired by Prince Philip, which raised the funds to renovate the aging structure.

Sir John was honored as one of the major contributors during the thanksgiving and dedication service attended by Queen Elizabeth and Prince Philip. Along with Dr. Jack Templeton, Sir John's son, and Jack's two daughters, Heather and Jennifer, I again was privileged to attend the ceremony and report on it; my wife Betty was with me.

The renovations focused the Lady Chapel, especially on the new west window, which replaced a temporary clear glass window installed after the London bombings in World War II. Lord Catts, chairman of the Westminster Abbey Trust, said, "Your Majesty, on behalf of the trustees, I ask you to unveil this new west window of the Abbey's Lady Chapel, itself a gift of our fellow trustee Sir John Templeton, to mark the completion of the restoration." The Queen replied, "Mr. Dean, in thanksgiving for the restoration of our collegiate church, and in gratitude to all its benefactors and craftsmen, we commend this window to the care of the Dean and Chapter as a token of the completed work, and ask you to dedicate it."

The richly colored window contains over fifty panels of stained glass displaying the heraldic arms, ciphers, and initials of the trustees, donors, church officers, and representative craftsmen, all gathered around the sovereign's arm in the center. Sir John Templeton's panel, with his coat of arms and his name spelled out, is at the center of the lower set of panels, just below the three-panel depiction of the Queen's coat of arms.

In 1992, Sir John was honored with a festschrift, a collection of articles by some of his most respected friends and colleagues, with a foreword written by His Royal Highness, the Duke of Edinburgh. Prince Philip wrote:

29 November 1992

Dear Sir John,

The world is full of experts and specialists, but it is given to few to be pluralists; those exceptional people who not only comprehend the great issues, but whose questing minds can go straight to the heart of the matter. Your highly successful business career and the wide scope of your interests bear witness to both the clarity and the originality of your thoughts. You have backed this up with a truly magnificent generosity to the many causes close to your heart.

It is not the passionate revolutionaries who improve the world; the only genuine progress is made by those who have a clearer vision and a greater ability to see through the tangled web of humbug and convention. Your great contribution to human civilization has been to encourage people to concentrate on the things that really matter and to appraise both conventional as well as unconventional ideas for their true worth.

No one person can change the world by themselves, but each one of us can strive to leave the world a slightly better place. Many do strive, but in your long life you have succeeded in making this world a better place both for present and future generations.

Yours sincerely,
Philip
Buckingham Palace

These were warm words for John Templeton, who has indeed been a great encourager, believing that we all have God-given abilities to develop and use, and, as Prince Philip implies, the aggregate of our efforts will leave the world a better place.

One of John's favorite passages of scripture is from Luke's gospel, from the second part of Jesus' Sermon on the Mount.

> But alas for you who are rich: you are having your consolation now.
> Alas for you who have your fill now: you shall go hungry.
> Alas for you who laugh now: you shall mourn and weep.
> Alas for you when the world speaks well of you!
> This was the way their ancestors treated the false prophets.

> But I say this to you who are listening: Love your enemies, do good to those who hate you, bless those who curse you, pray for those who treat you badly. To the man who slaps you on the cheek, present the other cheek too; to the man who takes your cloak from you, do not refuse your tunic. Give to everyone who asks you, and do not ask for your property back from the man who robs you. Treat others as you would like them to treat you. If you love those who love you, what thanks can you expect? Even sinners lend to sinners to get back the same amount. Instead, love your enemies and do good, and lend without any hope of return. You will have a great reward, and you will be sons of the Most

High, for he himself is kind to the ungrateful and the wicked.
(Luke 6:24–35)

Based upon this passage, what Sir John Templeton would perhaps add to
Prince Philip's words is the special place of both humility and love in our
dealings with each other. It is a passage that John Marks Templeton has made
foundational in his own life.

CHAPTER 15

The Growth of the Vision

THE STAFF OF THE JOHN TEMPLETON FOUNDATION

I N 1988, Francis Schapperle, the lone staff member of the John Templeton Foundation, began her work in an office in the garden house of Dr. John Templeton's home in Bryn Mawr, Pennsylvania. Francis arrived with excellent credentials from the University of Pennsylvania and the Robert Wood Johnson Foundation, but the job before her was a daunting one. One of the most demanding parts of the job was the large amount of travel as she divided her time between Sir John's home in Lyford Cay, Nassau, and the Bryn Mawr office. But the most challenging aspect was the responsibility for the large number of projects with which Sir John was engaged and the variety of his interests as a world philanthropist. His projects in those early years already spanned the globe — most notably in the variety of winners of the Templeton Prize for Progress Toward Research or Discoveries about Spiritual Realities but also in prizes and donations on five continents.

By 1992, the number of major projects supported by the Foundation grew to twenty; by 1997 it had reached sixty-five; and in 2004, almost 250 projects. Francis found great support with the heavy workload from Judith Marchand, a former University of Pennsylvania Foundation staff member who joined the Templeton Foundation in 1991. Since then the office has moved to Radnor Corporate Center, a large complex in another part of suburban Philadelphia, and by 2004, the number of staff had grown to twenty-eight.

Sir John hoped this new group of experts would enhance the future of his vision of achieving new spiritual information through scientific research. Foremost in this thinking was the promise of the new executive director and senior vice president, Dr. Charles Harper, who came to the Foundation in September 1996. He was recruited from a large number of candidates to replace Francis Schapperle, who moved to California because of a family relocation and who continued to oversee several of the Foundation's larger programs until recently. Charles Harper's employment came as a result of Sir John's unusual recruitment strategy. A Rhodes scholar himself, Sir John contacted all the younger Rhodes scholars to inquire of their interest in the executive director position. Dr. Harper's wife, a Rhodes scholar, received one of the letters; thus began the contact that would bring Dr. Harper on board.

Charles Harper was eminently suited for the job. He was trained in both science and theology, earning a bachelor's degree in civil and geological engineering at Princeton, a doctorate of philosophy in cosmology and planetary science at Balliol College, and a diploma of theology from Balliol College and Wycliffe Hall at Oxford. Before coming to the Foundation he was a research scientist at Harvard University and a research fellow with the National Aeronautics and Space Administration in Houston.

Dr. Harper has published more than fifty papers and abstracts in scientific journals and he brings to the Foundation an unusual level of tireless energy, not unlike Sir John.

Another new senior staff member, and interim director of the Foundation before Harper took the position, was Rev. Dr. Bryant Kirkland, the former, much beloved, minister of the Fifth Avenue Presbyterian Church in New York City. Mentioned previously as an early trustee of the Foundation, he stepped down to take the staff position in 1996. He brought great sagacity, warmth, and commitment to the job. Dr. Kirkland was educated at Wheaton College and Princeton Seminary and had been president of the American Bible Society and president of the board of trustees of Princeton Theological Seminary. Sadly, he died Easter Sunday, April 23, 2000.

The rest of the Radnor senior staff now include the veteran Judith

Marchand, now vice president of administration and special programs; Dr. Arthur Schwartz, vice president of research programs in the human sciences; Dr. Paul Wason, director of science and religion programs; Pamela Thompson, vice president of communications; Valerie Martin, controller; Mary Ann Meyers, senior fellow overseeing the Humble Approach Initiative; and Lynn Glodek, office manager and conference coordinator. Most recently, the Foundation has added two new senior staff: Dr. Barnaby Marsh is the director of venture philanthropy and new programs development, aiding in the development of new sources of support for research for new spiritual information; and Dr. Dennis Cheek, vice president for venture philanthropy and managing director, heads up a new division of the Foundation that is called Templeton Venture Philanthropy Associates.

In Lyford Cay in Nassau, Sir John has two very able assistants: Mena Griffiths, vice president of Sir John's First Trust Bank, who has been with John for twenty-eight years; and Irish-born Mary Walker, who has assisted Sir John for twenty-six years. Also in the Lyford Cay office was Rev. Wilbert Forker, formerly an officer of the World Council of Churches, who was the director of the Templeton Prize program with the assistance of Mena Griffiths until his retirement in 2000.

Those of us who have been fortunate to be trustees of the John Templeton Foundation have had the privilege of meeting many of these staff people, especially at the annual trustees' meetings in Sewanee, Tennessee, each summer.

Further evidence of Sir John's careful forward-thinking approach to the development of the programs to multiply our knowledge of spiritual realities comes from the way he has planned the structure of the Foundation. Because he thinks that the goal of a one-hundredfold increase in spiritual information may take as much as a century, he has sought to insure that the aims he has set forth will be achieved over this lengthy period. He has pointed out that the history of large foundations reveals frequent departures from the intent of the founder. Indeed, as he says, "Even foundation managers who are conscientious and diligent may stray far away from donor intent a few generations after the death of the donor."

In addition, laws may be passed that make it difficult to fulfill the donor's intent. Accordingly, Sir John has established large charity foundations not in one, but rather in three nations. The foundations were created when Sir John turned 80 and are located in the Cayman Islands and The Turks and Caicos as well as in Tennessee. The governing documents require future foundation managers to find legal ways to shift assets to different nations when necessary to preserve donor intent. In addition, the documents require independent audits, at least every five years, and change in corporation executives if donor intent has not been properly observed.

In Tennessee, the incorporated home of the John Templeton Foundation, are two principal officers, Ann Templeton Cameron, secretary, and Harvey Templeton III, treasurer. They are the children of Harvey and Jewel Templeton of Winchester, Tennessee. Sir John wishes to insure continued family involvement, which he believes is a key factor in maintaining donor intent.

In addition, Sir John has emphasized that the Foundation focus should be on prevention rather than on alleviation of human miseries such as sickness, poverty, ignorance, and war. The bylaws also specify that the investment of foundation funds will be worldwide, and a variety of selections and investment experts will manage the three foundations' assets. The performance of these experts will be monitored according to global investment standards.

The Advisory Board

During the first year of the Foundation's existence, Sir John began to develop a board of advisors to aid in the formulation of programs and, in some cases, to participate in programs themselves. Because of Sir John's concern for good science as the backbone of a spiritual research program, many of the advisors chosen were working scientists with a commitment to integrate their science into the spiritual dimension of their lives. Many advisors are or were connected with organizations that have this integration as a major goal, including the American Scientific Affiliation, the Center for Theology and the Natural Sciences, the Chicago Center for Religion and

Science (now the Zygon Center), the Christian Medical and Dental Society, the British organization called Christians in Science, the European Society for the Study of Science and Theology, the Institute for Religion in an Age of Science, and two additional British organizations, the Science and Religion Forum and the Union of Ordained Scientists.

All of the major scientific disciplines have been represented on the advisory board by such distinguished scholars as Owen Gingerich, a Harvard astronomer, historian of science, and Smithsonian fellow; Princeton physicist Freeman Dyson of the Institute for Advanced Study; Nobel laureate Sir John Eccles, then a neurophysiologist at the Max Planck Institute, Heidelberg; and Nobel laureate Charles Townes, a physicist at the University of California, Berkeley. Also well-known are Herbert Benson, a Harvard Medical School professor and president of the Mind-Body Institute; and V. Elving Anderson, professor of genetics at the University of Minnesota and former president of the Society of Sigma Xi, the national research honorary society.

In addition, the board — past and present — has included several individuals holding degrees in both science and theology, including physicist Robert Russell of the Center for Theology and the Natural Sciences, who is also an ordained minister in the Church of Christ; Ian Barbour, professor of physics and professor of religion at Carleton College; and Michael Heller, Roman Catholic priest, cosmologist, professor of philosophy at the Pontifical Academy of Theology in Cracow, Poland, and adjunct member of the Vatican Observatory staff.

Other early members included the late Karl Schmitz-Moormann, first president of the European Society for the Study of Science and Theology, a theologian who spent a lifetime studying the paleontological and theological work of Pierre Teilhard de Chardin. British biochemist Arthur Peacocke and physicist John Polkinghorne are longtime advisors, and both are recent Templeton Prize winners. Others who have been advisors include Elizabeth Peale Allen, daughter of Sir John's longtime friend the late Norman Vincent Peale; Francisco Ayala of the University of California, Irvine, biologist and former president of the American Association for the Advancement of

Science; theologian Diana Eck of Harvard Divinity School; publisher Kenneth Giniger; the late psychiatrist David Larson of the International Center for the Integration of Health and Spirituality; Islamic scholar Seyyed Nasr of George Washington University; and philanthropist Laurence Rockefeller.

At first the advisory board met each spring and fall in the United States for North American advisors and in late spring in London for the advisors from the United Kingdom, the Continent, and Australia. Since 1995, under the guidance of Foundation Executive Director Charles Harper, the board has often held small workshops or large two-day meetings prior to the regular board meeting to review scientific progress and uncover promising new research directions in various areas of science especially relevant to theology. These meetings bring together key scholars in topical areas such as altruism and love, research on Islam and science, or purpose and biology, to explore the potential for further research and to help with program design. In addition, individual advisors consult with the Foundation on the various programs.[1]

MAIN OBJECTIVES OF THE JOHN TEMPLETON FOUNDATION

Sir John Templeton began to set out the current objectives of the Foundation in December 1996. These generally took the form of broad statements of purpose, and it will be my goal in this chapter to describe the way in which these objectives are being interpreted and are being implemented by the Foundation staff. As usual, Sir John's vision is vast and far-reaching in scope, and the present chapter can only hope to anticipate a few of the developments that will result from his plans.

1. The first objective was to encourage progress in obtaining new spiritual information that rivals the progress that has been made in obtaining medical and other scientific information.

When the National Institutes of Health began its major extramural program in support of medical and biological research forty years ago, no one could have predicted what researchers would learn about the human body

Sir John Templeton with his dog Spotless, 1996.

Bryant Kirkland and Frances Schapperle, 1996.

John Templeton Foundation executives at a board of advisors meeting, 1997. (*l to r*): John M. Templeton Jr., Charles L. Harper Jr., and Sir John Templeton.

(*l to r*): John C. Polkinghorne, John M. Templeton Jr., and HRH The Duke of Edinburgh at the 2002 Templeton Prize ceremony at Buckingham Palace.

TEMPLETON PRIZE

Sir John Templeton and Holmes Rolston III, 2003 Templeton Prize winner.

Sir John reading *The Humble Approach.*

Templeton Library, Sewanee, Tennessee.

Sir John on the cover of *Publishers Weekly* magazine launching Templeton Foundation Press, December 1996.

Sir John and Joanna Hill, director of Templeton Foundation Press, 1996.

Templeton Foundations staff, Radnor, Pennsylvania, 2001. (*l to r*): Front: Patricia Hotz, Paul Wason, Sharon Sizgorich, Carol Miller, Andrea Blane, Susan Shipe, Pamela Lairdieson, Mary Anne Meyers, Judith Marchand, Sir John Templeton, Karyl Wittlinger, Kevin Stehm, Stephanie Stair, Patricia Vergilio, Lynn Glodek, Linda Kelly. Back: Patricia Laird, Ruth Macauley-Barrett, Joanna Hill, Margaret Brennan, Pamela Thompson, Charles Harper, Laura Barrett, Alexander Rementer, Jim Rementer, Rozanne Tarlecky, Arthur Schwartz.

John Templeton Foundation members gathering, 2001. (*l to r*): Row 1: Mary Ann Meyers, Joanna Hill, Sir John Templeton, Anne D. Zimmerman, Harvey M. Templeton III, Karyl J. Wittlinger, David Myers, Lauren Templeton, Wendy Brooks. Row 2: Clara Stephens, Peggy Veljkovic, Amy Butler, Pamela Thompson, Harold Koenig, Renee Dawn Stirling, Russell Stannard, Mrs. Watson, Gail Zimmerman, Charles Harper. Row 3: Eleanor Folk, Robert Herrmann, Donald Munro, Glenn Mosley, Pamela Lairdieson, Frances Schapperle, Tom Watson, Mary Walker. Row 4: Christopher W. Templeton, Bobby Singleton, Martha Templeton, Sonny Templeton, Josephine Templeton, Robert Handly Cameron, Leigh Cameron, Ann Cameron, Douglas Cameron, John Barrow, Dererk Griffiths, Mena Griffiths. Row 5: Rebecca M. Templeton, Handly Templeton, David Lubinski, Mrs. Lubinski, John M. Templeton Jr., Jennifer Templeton, Speed Baranco, Virginia Templeton, Judith Marchand, Heather Dill, Jeffery Dill.

John M. Templeton Jr.
president of the John
Templeton Foundation
and Templeton
Foundation Press.

Great-grandson John Templeton Dill and John Marks Templeton, 2004.

and about the diagnosis and treatment of disease. Indeed, entirely new areas of interdisciplinary research have appeared, including:

- Human genetic research with the goal of sequencing the entire human genome and the beginning of treatment of a broad range of human genetic diseases;
- Brain research including the goal of developing means for treatment of degenerative brain disease by brain tissue transplantation and regeneration;
- Immunological studies of tissue transplantation leading to effective means of heart, liver, and other organ transplantation; and
- Neuroendocrinology research elucidating the interaction of the hormonal and nervous systems in promoting recovery from and resistance to disease.

In the case of brain research, the results of recent brain developmental studies indicate that the brain, heretofore thought to be static and unchanging, is actually an active, dynamic, ever-changing structure, which even in adulthood responds to new experiences and new learning patterns. The current viewpoint is that the brain is remarkably plastic in character, responsive to stimuli by generating new neuronal networks, and even capable of regenerating old networks such as those lost in Parkinson's disease.

Sir John argues that significant research support for the acquisition of new spiritual information could be even more beneficial. Here are just a few examples of the thousands of questions that might be addressed.

- HUMAN EVOLUTION. Studies have shown that late Neanderthals and early Homo sapiens had definite ideas of a hereafter, which were reflected in their burial practices and cave drawings. Further research might clarify the fundamental nature of this spiritual understanding, and the importance of the spiritual to being human.
- GENETIC BASIS FOR WELL-BEING. Dr. Herbert Benson has analyzed the nature of some spiritual factors in healing and has proposed that we are hardwired for wellness. Research could be carried out to study wellness as a genetic trait or group of traits.
- BRAIN CAPACITY. Neural science research is uncovering new insights

into human and other animal cognition. Research of the biochemical basis of genius and creativity, especially in the cases of the great mystics and the Nobel laureates, might be revealing and suggest ways to unlock the potential of the brain.

- NEUROENDOCRINE RELATIONSHIPS. Research into spiritual activities (e.g., prayer, meditation, and especially thanksgiving) to ascertain various hormone release actions — endorphins and other "pleasure" agents — might establish a basis for spiritual experience as an alternative to various psychoactive drugs (e.g., cocaine and heroin) currently ravaging society.

- VIOLENCE AS A SOCIAL PROBLEM. Research into genetic and neurological bases for antisocial behavior is an area of political sensitivity, but scientifically rigorous research might arrive at much-needed understanding and possible therapies.

2.The Foundation's second objective was to encourage the idea that no human has yet known one percent of God, the basic Reality, but that we can learn more about God in many ways through rigorous scientific research.

This second objective is closely aligned to the first, but the emphasis now shifts to the recognition that we are pitifully ignorant of the fundamental Reality that is God, and that doors are now open to explore many new avenues in our pursuit of spiritual information. Some of our approaches may involve careful statistical studies, as in the attempt to correlate spirituality and health. Other approaches may involve psychological studies, as in some research on the laws of life.

The initial plan is to concentrate on a few representative areas, such as through major research programs to support research on forgiveness or on unlimited love, encouraging the development both of new perspectives on a subject and refined methods of investigation, and in the process delineating the kinds of approaches and demonstrating the multitude of questions that can be asked within any one approach. Sir John sees the involvement of the university scientific community for this effort as possibly crucial. Leading scientists may be asked to propose research methodologies and to provide expert review of proposals.

3. The third objective was to encourage the expenditure by a growing network of funders of at least one-tenth as much on obtaining spiritual information as is spent on all scientific research. This is an ambitious goal. The world spends approximately one billion dollars a day now on scientific research. To even begin to achieve support at one-tenth this level will require the recruitment of enormous funding from many sources. The pursuit of spiritual information needs to capture the imagination of opinion makers and scientific planners throughout the world.

Partners in the Templeton Foundation-sponsored programs might be found among the nation's traditional science supporters if the work planned is rigorous and peer-reviewed, and if the initial studies mentioned above demonstrate the richness this kind of research can add to our understanding of reality. The National Institutes of Health, especially through the Human Genome Initiative, the National Institute for Mental Health, and the National Institute on Aging, could become strong allies in this research area. The new office of Alternative Medicine at NIH could find studies of spirituality and health an attractive fruitful focus for research support. Again, if the value of this work is sufficiently demonstrated, current private foundations and aspiring philanthropists may well focus some of their support on the study of spiritual matters.

4. Another Foundation objective was to study the possibility that the visible and tangible are only tiny manifestations of the vast timeless and limitless Reality. Here, current research in physics and cosmology, as described by scientists such as Paul Davies and Robert Russell, reveals that reality is vastly greater and more mysterious than we had thought. In a book titled *How Large is God?* edited by Sir John, several contributors lend support to the vastness and infinitude of that reality. My own chapter, entitled "How Large Is God? How Deep Is Reality?" testifies to the fleeting nature of scientific reality. In the conclusion to that chapter I wrote:

We have seen that science has gone through a healthy re-evalua-
tion of its understanding of the nature of truth over the past two
decades. No longer would most scientists claim that their theories
represent anything more than approximations of the structures of
reality. We have looked also at some of the current research in
physics and chemistry and found that our goal of simplification
and unification has been thwarted by drastic limitations in our
capacity to provide experiential verification and by undreamt of
levels of complexity in the systems under study.

The present situation in the sciences seems to shout for cau-
tion in our statements of what is, and how it came to be. What
seems abundantly clear is that reality is much deeper and more
profound than we had thought. Clerk Maxwell appears to have
been "on the mark" when he suggested that appropriateness and
tenability of scientific theories might best be evaluated by
whether they measured up as far as possible to the "riches of creation." If we are attempting to think the Creator's thoughts, our
thoughts must surely be only the simplest inklings of what really
lies behind this vast universe and its awesome Creator.[2]

5. Sir John's next objective is to study the probability that nothing exists
separate from God and that we may be tiny temporary manifestations of
God just as a wave of the ocean is not separate from the ocean but is only a
tiny temporary manifestation of that ocean.

This concept was elaborated as the first point in the original description
of humility theology in the Foundation bylaws. Sir John first introduced
the idea of a progression from biological life to the sphere of the human
intellect and then to the sphere of the spirit.

Perhaps this heralds a new quality, the sphere of the spirit. God
may be creating not only the infinitely large but also the infinitely
small; not only the outward but also the inward; not only the
tangible but also the intangible. Thoughts, mind, soul, wisdom,
love, originality, inspiration, and enthusiasm may be partial

manifestations of a Creator who is omniscient, omnipotent, eternal, and infinite. The things that we see, hear, and touch may be only appearances. They may be only manifestations of underlying forces, including spiritual forces that may persist throughout all the transience of physical existence. Perhaps the spiritual world, and the benevolent Creator whom it reflects, may be the only reality.

Presumably, the sphere of the spirit may enclose not only this planet but the entire universe, and so God is all of nature, inseparable from it, and yet exceeds it. Perhaps it is mankind's own ego that leads us to think that we are at the center of a vast universe of being which subsists in an eternal and infinite reality that some call God. Maybe all of nature is only a transient wave on the ocean of all that God eternally is. Maybe time, space, and energy provide no limit to the Being that is God. Likewise, the fundamental parameters of the universe — the speed of light, the force of gravitation, the weak and strong nuclear forces, and electromagnetism — would seem to pose no limits to the Being that is God.

Experiments such as the famous double-slit experiment, the possible significance of which we described in *The God Who Would Be Known*, suggest that there is indeed a wholeness about the universe, an interconnectedness, a higher kind of order.

Can the Foundation find ways to further encourage scientific studies of wholeness, perhaps supporting further studies of cooperativity in reaction systems and new approaches to interference phenomena?

6. The next goal is to study evidence that God is creative and purposeful and that humanity's role may be as an agent of progress for God's purposes.

The fundamental nature and benefits of purpose have been a focus of Sir John's thinking for many years, and Charles Harper and Paul Wason have made the search for varieties of evidence of universal purposes a primary goal.

The 1994 volume *Evidence of Purpose*, edited by Sir John, was intended to encourage more scientific research about design and purpose in the universe. In his introduction to the book, he notes that in the last several decades the number of scientists raising philosophical and spiritual questions as a result of recent scientific discoveries has multiplied.

> There is here no knockdown argument for design and purpose, but certainly there are strong hints of ultimate realities beyond the cosmos, just as Owen Gingerich says in his chapter. One of the strongest hints, in our opinion, relates to the new understanding of the creativity of the cosmos, its capacity for so-called self-organization. For, following the big bang, a most astounding story of creativity unfolds throughout time, from the void of space to galaxies, planets, crystals, life, and people. Science has heretofore been ruled by the Newtonian and thermodynamic paradigms, viewing the universe as either an unchanging and static machine, or as a process moving inexorably toward degeneration and decay.
>
> But current science leads us to look for a new paradigm, a universe fraught with creativity in the direction of cooperative and organizational processes. The gradual growth of complexity has been noted through the history of science, but it was given powerful support through the theory of biological evolution proposed by Charles Darwin and Alfred Russel Wallace. Subsequent developments in cosmological science have demonstrated that the increased complexity and diversity inherent in biological evolution have also been characteristic of the entire universe from its origin. Indeed, there appears to be a continuity of organization into novel and increasingly complex structures and relationships throughout the spectrum of transitions from stardust to thinking man. How did these changes come about? What processes are involved?
>
> The new studies of nonlinear thermodynamics provide insights into such creativity, and further studies of evolutionary processes may add more data about this remarkably creative phenomenon.

Then, in 2000, Professor John Haught of Georgetown University published a book entitled *Science and Religion in Search of Cosmic Purpose*. This
was a collection of papers originally presented at a landmark conference,
"Cosmology and Teleology," in Seattle in 1997. The conference was cosponsored by the Georgetown Center for the Study of Science and Religion and
the American Association for the Advancement of Science (AAAS) Dialogue
on Science, Ethics and Religion. The Templeton Foundation was a major
encourager in the development of the AAAS program and provided funding
for the Seattle conference.

The Cosmology and Fine Tuning Program

In 1999, the Cosmology and Fine Tuning Program of the Templeton Foundation was begun as an interdisciplinary exploration to answer the question: "Are there evidences of universal purposes in the cosmos?" The
program offered $1 million for twenty grants for high-level research by sci-
entists, philosophers, mathematicians, and theologians, with emphasis on
cross-disciplinary research among academicians in the world's major
research universities. Charles Harper worked with Max Tegmark, a physicist
at the University of Pennsylvania, and John Barrow, a mathematician at
Cambridge University, in crafting the program. The fine-tuning aspect of
the program considers the fact that the universe appears to be governed by
fundamental constants that are restricted to very narrow limits. Changing
these constants even slightly would render the universe uninhabitable, at
least by creatures comprehensible to humans. One possible conclusion could
be that the universe was designed for life — for us. But many of the grant
recipients are looking at other possibilities as well for cosmic purpose.

Another direction in understanding purpose was explored in a Temple-
ton-sponsored conference at Stanford University in October 2000. Stanford
Professor William Hurlbut of the university's human biology program pre-
pared the agenda with the cooperation of Charles Harper and Paul Wason.
This time the focus was on human evolution; the topic, "Becoming Human:
The Evolutionary Origins of Spiritual, Religious and Mental Awareness."

Much new research in a range of disciplines has been generating new understanding of what it is to be human and how we evolved. The plan was to explore how these new approaches could be expanded to investigate the origins, development, and significance of the spiritual and religious elements of nature, including evolving human nature.

Yet another workshop on purpose was convened in March 2001 at Duke University, in conjunction with the spring meeting of the Templeton Foundation advisory board. This workshop was entitled "Trends in Evolution and the Question of Teleonomic Purpose." Its goal was to explore the potential for a major program to support research into macro-directionalities in evolution and the question of teleonomic purpose. Teleonomy refers to questions around whether and how the laws of nature can be interpreted in terms of goal-directedness with respect to their role in the evolution of life.

The Biology of Purpose: What Are the Purposes of Life?

These workshops demonstrated that there were many promising areas for research into the nature of purpose in the living world, so a multiphase research program has been developed by Drs. Wason and Harper that will provide $5 million for support of research projects and for the organization of several groups of consultants to guide the research effort. The program is entitled "What Are the Purposes of Life?" and it has the following goals:

    a. to provide empirical scientific documentation that will help people understand the importance of purpose in their lives.

    b. to deepen our understanding of divine or cosmic purpose by making use of major developments in various fields of biology, especially human biology.

    c. to aid in the development of an expanding rather than a reductionist view of life.

    d. to creatively expand the range of disciplines participating in scientific research for new spiritual information. Important contributions are anticipated from the often-slighted disciplines of ethology, primatology, paleoanthropology, prehistoric archeology, rock art studies, and linguistics.

    e. to provide a solid understanding of teleology as a precursor for future programs on human purpose and meaning, including programs like those Dr. Arthur Schwartz is developing under the human sciences program area of the Foundation.

f. to develop a core group of scholars to become a community of discourse in the area of purpose in the living world.

g. to cooperate with the cosmology and fine-tuning program through the sharing of data, ideas, and personnel, and through the exploration of links between cosmology, biology, and the study of humanity.

Deeper Reality Research Program

Finally, over the past several years Charles Harper has been developing a related program directed toward research into the most fundamental aspects of reality. This $2.3 million program, the Deeper Reality Research Program, will support three levels of research rewards, create cross-disciplinary links, develop presentation materials and databases, and involve top research scientists in studies of conceptually expansive ways of understanding the world. The expectation is that such studies will ultimately connect science with concepts of divinity. Expected research areas include quantum information theory, quantum chaos, game theory and ethics, emergence of order, timetabling, consilience, the nature of mathematics, the limits of knowledge, aesthetics, the theology of artificial intelligence, and the theology of extraterrestrials.

Several conferences and workshops have already been convened in connection with the Science and Ultimate Reality Program, an aspect of the Deeper Reality Research Program. A landmark conference honoring John Archibald Wheeler, pioneer philosopher-physicist, on the occasion of his 90th birthday, was convened in March 2002 at Princeton University. Charles Harper's remarks at the November 2001 advisory board meeting of the Templeton Foundation introduced us to the vision of this remarkable conference, which was given the title "Science and Ultimate Reality: Celebrating the Vision of John Archibald Wheeler and Taking It Forward into a New Century of Discovery."

Harper said in part:

Professor John Archibald Wheeler, now in his 90th birthday year, is widely recognized as one of the most outstanding visionary leaders in physics. A student of quantum mechanics pioneer Niels Bohr and a teacher of the astonishing Richard Feynman, Wheeler's long and exemplary career is celebrated for its rigor in teaching and research and also for its bold intellectual adventurousness. His lineage of students and research colleagues have pioneered many and varied fruitful explorations in physics, now reaching to several generations of influence — including the students of his students' students.

The Science and Ultimate Reality project celebrates the vitality of Wheeler's approach to future-oriented scientific exploration by commissioning leading research physicists and cosmologists to consider in depth how new major advances in physics might be developed over the coming decades. Most especially, the project is focused on large-scale challenges for gaining new insights into the deep nature of the physical world. The entire project, consisting of a thirty-chapter book covering five different topical areas and an associated conference, is being developed by the following program oversight committee members, including three Nobel laureates in physics: Freeman Dyson, chair, Institute for Advanced Study; Max Tegmark, deputy chair, University of Pennsylvania; John Barrow, University of Cambridge; George Ellis, University of Cape Town; Robert Laughlin, Stanford University; Charles Misner, University of Maryland; William Phillips, National Institute of Standards and Technology (USA); and Charles Townes, University of California at Berkeley.

A special feature of the symposium was an opportunity to participate in a listserv hosted by the Metanexus Institute, moderated by Templeton laureate Professor Paul Davies, at that time associated with Macquarie University, the University of Queensland, and Imperial College, London. The conference was cosponsored by Peter Gruber, a longtime advisor to the

Foundation and the donor of a major prize awarded annually for new research into cosmology. The award is called the Peter Gruber Foundation Cosmology Prize.

Also taking place at Princeton, on the Monday following the March 2002 symposium, was a workshop entitled "Is There a Teleonomic Moral Fabric to the Universe?" which was hosted by Dr. Martin Nowak, director of the theoretical biology program at Princeton's Institute for Advanced Study. Co-chaired by Dr. Jeffrey Schloss of Westmont College and Dr. Stephen Post of Case Western Reserve University in cooperation with Drs. Harper and Wason, the workshop was designed to explore innovative directions in mathematical modeling to investigate a possible moral fabric of the universe. The concept statement introducing the workshop says in part:

> This workshop is meant as a first step toward one or more future possible research sponsorship programs. These programs could be in the field of theoretical mathematical biology, or could draw on mathematical modeling traditions of several fields, and would focus on developing new scientific insights into the possible moral fabric of the universe. What is the nature of goodness, its natural rootedness, and does it have a universal or cosmological significance? We expect that approaches would include a broad portfolio of topics including the nature of altruism, unconditional love, the moral sense, the religious sense, the spiritual quest, the sense of justice, compassion, and fairness.
>
> Also important is the human hunger for wholeness, significance, meaning, and righteousness. For success, such programs likely would require an active interdisciplinary component to draw in contributions from a range of sources not normally connected with quantitative studies, including a range of philosophical and theological scholarship. We would like to use the time together to identify major problems and areas of study which should be given priority in future research agendas as well as more practical issues like how we might truly bring together the range

of expertise needed — keeping in mind that the distinctive feature of this work would be the perspectives and tools of mathematical modeling.

Also within the purview of the Deeper Reality Research Program is initial thinking on the possibility of an interdisciplinary program on the topic of "emergence." Discussion at the March 2002 advisory board meeting was lead by Templeton advisor Dr. Philip Clayton, professor of philosophy at California State University, Sonoma, and director of Science and Spiritual Quest II at the Center for Theology and the Natural Sciences, Berkeley, California. Part of Clayton's description of the emergence research initiative appears below:

> The emergence paradigm deserves to be the focus of a major research program by the John Templeton Foundation for three reasons. First, it expresses the need to move beyond the epistemology of reductionism, which has been so damaging to the science-religion partnership in the modern period. However, unlike "holism," which scientists by and large view with suspicion as foreign to the spirit of scientific inquiry, emergent phenomena are fully amenable to study by scientific techniques. The biophysicist Harold Morowitz, formerly of Yale University, has identified no fewer than twenty-eight levels of emergence in the natural world. Recent scientific articles by physicists, chemists, biologists, and neuroscientists make profitable use of the emergence concept in constructing actual explanations within science.
>
> Second, the emergence paradigm is ideally suited to expressing how religious or spiritual knowledge can arise out of the natural world. If the empirical evolution of the cosmos gradually produces life, awareness, consciousness, and culture over the course of its history, then it becomes natural to ask why it could not move on to produce spiritual knowledge of the Divine. No other concept allows, indeed requires, so smooth a transition from the

beauty and regularity of physical law to the most lofty thoughts and aspirations of the human soul.

Third, and finally, emergence cannot fully be grasped within any existing field or theory. It therefore suggests the importance of *meta*-physical reflection in order for one to comprehend it. This means that discussions of emergence naturally shade over to discussions of metaphysical and theological topics. Emergence thus becomes a natural bridge between the world of nature and the kingdom of God.

7. The Foundation's next goal is to encourage rigorous study by scientific methods of some of the laws of life and to apply those proving valid to character-building courses in universities and colleges. In this way, education in moral development might be allowed to go forward in secular institutions that are prohibited from using the teachings of ancient scripture.

Forgiveness Research Program

The first request for proposals for research on the laws of life focused on the phenomenon of forgiveness. The program was directed by Dr. Everett Worthington, a professor of psychology at Virginia Commonwealth University and an expert in research on religion in counseling. The June 1997 draft of the announcement read:

> The John Templeton Foundation seeks to stimulate progress in science, particularly by encouraging the appreciation of an open, humble, and empirical approach to developing new aspects of spiritual and moral understanding. Through this request for proposals (RFP) we seek to sponsor innovative, methodologically rigorous scientific research in the area of forgiveness; enhance the scientific understanding of moral and spiritual principles; and stimulate the growth of new understanding in this area of research. The Foundation is open to considerations of a wide range of approaches and methodologies relevant to the study of

forgiveness in many contexts. Extensive information on the founder's vision and publications and on the mission and activities of the John Templeton Foundation may be found on the John Templeton Foundation's Web page (www.templeton.org).

SCOPE OF THE PROPOSED RESEARCH: Examples of areas of interest include: studies of individual health and happiness; studies relating to the health and stability of marriages, families, neighborhoods and communities; studies relating to the development of character in children and youth; studies relating to racial and ethnic conflict, as well as studies relating to the role of forgiveness in business, legal, political, and historical contexts. Research projects should involve empirical examinations rather than philosophical or ethical or theological investigations, except in relation to the development of testable hypotheses or models involving human subjects. (In exemplary cases, proposals for innovative primate studies will be considered.) Applications from a broad range of disciplines are sought, and interdisciplinary collaboration is strongly encouraged.

Research focusing on the development of habits of forgiveness as a *spiritual discipline* and the appreciation of forgiveness as a *spiritual principle* are especially encouraged. Researchers are also encouraged to investigate biological aspects of forgiveness as well as proposing projects posing critical challenges to forgiveness as applied in particular circumstances.

Objectivity and analytical rigor is stressed. Investigators involved in advocacy must be particularly exacting in their methodological design in order to avoid biasing their research findings.

When this research initiative was developing, Templeton Foundation Press published Sir John's book on the laws of life, *Worldwide Laws of Life: 200 Eternal Spiritual Principles.* The book included a number of laws of life on the theme of forgiveness (see Appendix J).

The response to the RFP on forgiveness research was overwhelming. The Foundation had set aside $4 million for this first effort, and the review committee found quality proposals totaling $8 million. Everett Worthington subsequently assembled a committee of prominent national figures to aid in the procurement of additional support from sources outside the Foundation. This had been one of Sir John's philanthropic goals from the outset. Ultimately, a total of $7 million was raised for this project. In October 2003, a major conference on forgiveness research was convened in Atlanta, Georgia. Forty investigators presented the results of their research into the nature and efficacy of forgiveness.

Research on Unlimited Love

A second major development in the study of the laws of life was organized in 2001 under the direction of Stephen Post, a bioethicist in the Case Western Reserve University School of Medicine. The focus this time was on unlimited love, a research area for which Post is eminently suited. He has a background of studies at the University of Chicago Divinity School in philosophical ethics and religion. He also has a long-term involvement in the study of neurology and dementia, with a focus on Alzheimer's disease. Initial funding of $4 million from the Templeton Foundation has created the Institute for Research on Unlimited Love, with Stephen Post as president.

The plans of the Institute are as follows:

- fund high-level scientific research on altruistic and unlimited love;
- develop a sustained dialogue between religion and science on the meaning and significance of unlimited love through publications and conferences;
- disseminate the real story of unlimited love as it is manifested in the helping behaviors of those whose lives are devoted to giving to others;
- enhance the practical manifestations of unlimited love across the full spectrum of human experience, including family life, education, leadership, community service, religion, and the professions, by providing conference opportunities and awards for innovative scholars and practitioners.

In its first year, the institute sent out a request for proposals for research on unlimited love to leading scientists throughout the United States. There were 320 letters of interest received and in December 2002 the institute awarded $1.7 million in research grants for twenty-one research projects. Topics included volunteerism, organ donations, rescue work, and other examples of selfless altruism, compassion, and service. Information released by the institute explains: "Though it is generally assumed that altruism is a good thing, scant hard scientific evidence exists to support that notion, or precisely how or why it is good. Whereas negative human behavior — such as spousal abuse, childhood neglect, and anger — has been examined through innumerable studies, few studies have investigated the benefits of love, especially unlimited love, which the institute describes as altruistic affirmation and care for all humanity without exception."

The research will explore a vast range of human activity that falls under that category and attempt to establish a body of evidence that will advance the institute's stated mission of "helping all persons better understand their capacities for participation in unlimited love as the ultimate purpose of their lives." One of the more interesting aspects of the funded projects will be the sophistication of how such human phenomena as religion and spirituality will be examined using the scrutiny of pure science.

The twenty-one projects span a startling array of subject matter. Though at first glance some of the projects seem distant from the concept of unlimited love, each offers the promise of valuable insights.

One study, for example, will examine the valor of 9/11 rescuers. Another will peer into the mystery of autism in an attempt to discern whether empathetic deficits lie in the mind or behavior of autistics, or both. Still another study hopes to determine if divine or human love provides a curative or protective defense against the effects of military post-traumatic stress disorder. And another will research Paleolithic hunter-gatherer societies in a test of competing theories on the origin of human activities that fall outside the parameters of nepotism and strict reciprocity.

Other projects include the neurobiology of parental love, the relationship of brain hormones and social bonding, the nature of love outside one's social group, organ donors, volunteerism in faith-based service organizations, civic engagement of African-American adolescents and their parents, and a study of why chimpanzees display "consolation behavior" — reassuring physical contact — to distressed fellow chimps.

The grants represent dramatic and steady progress of the not-for-profit institute since its founding in 2001 with a $4 million dollar grant from the John Templeton Foundation, one of the world's foremost benefactors and advocates for rigorous, open-minded, and empirically focused investigations into the boundary between theology and science.

The newly funded projects are categorized into six areas:

- Human Development
- Public Health and Medicine
- Mechanisms by Which Altruistic Love Affects Health
- Other-Regarding Virtues
- Evolutionary Perspectives on Other-Regard
- The Sociological Study of Faith-Based Communities and Their Activities in Relation to the Spiritual Ideal of Unlimited Love

The broad scope of studies underscores the vast possibilities for this nascent yet growing movement among researchers. In 2003, for example, the institute provided $300,000 in matching funds to four ongoing studies of the Fetzer Institute's Science of Compassionate Love initiative.[3]

Additionally, the institute hosted an international, interfaith, and interdisciplinary conference — "The Works of Love: Scientific and Religious Perspectives on Altruism" — in the spring of 2003 at Villanova University in Pennsylvania, cosponsored by the Metanexus Institute on Religion and Science.

Besides the grants and the conference, the Institute for Research on Unlimited Love will also extend its work over the next few years by publishing and disseminating its findings, conducting a national essay competition for young people as a way to underscore the importance of compassionate love in their development, and providing opportunities for scholars in science and religion to develop book proposals that will be supported by the institute after competition review. The institute's first book, *Altruism and Altruistic Love: Science, Philosophy and Religion in Dialogue*, was published in June 2002 by Oxford University Press.

Templeton Foundation Press has published two others, *Unlimited Love: Altruism, Compassion, and Service* by Stephen Post, as well as *Research on Altruism and Love: An Annotated Bibliography of Major Studies in Psychology, Sociology, Evolutionary Biology, and Theology*, edited by Stephen Post along with Byron Johnson, Michael McCullough, and Jeffrey Schloss.

Sir John also looks to the possible development of academic courses utilizing the *Worldwide Laws of Life*, and welcomes research proposals from established scientists for evidence to verify or falsify any of these laws.

Spiritual Transformation Research Program

In 2000, Sir John Templeton approved funding in the amount of $3.3 million for a landmark research program to generate scientific research on the nature and benefits of spiritual transformation. At the core of the research program is a compelling question that Sir John Templeton raises in his book *Possibilities for Over One-Hundredfold More Spiritual Information*: "Can study of the nature of such changes offer another possibility for developing spiritual progress based on improved understanding of, and appreciation for, spiritually transforming experiences?" (p. 112)

The program is administered by the Metanexus Institute, under the leadership of University of Pennsylvania professor Solomon Katz. The Institute widely disseminated a call for proposals and received 471 Letters of Intent (LOI), the most LOI's received for any competitive research program funded by the Foundation. Sixty principal investigators were invited to submit full proposals, and after a rigorous review and ratings process, Metanexus Institute awarded twenty-four grants to a range of top-level scholars and researchers in a variety of academic fields and disciplines (including neuroscience, theology, sociology, medicine, and psychology).

Laws of Life Essay Contest

Another ongoing program of the Foundation, now under the direction of Ms. Peggy Veljkovic, is the laws of life essay contests. Focusing on teenagers, the program had grown by December 2003 to include 122 local programs with an estimated 100,000 participants. The program has also extended to fifty-four countries, including the United Kingdom, Canada, Argentina, Uganda, and New Zealand.

One of the largest U. S. programs is in Georgia, directed by Sir John's step-daughter-in-law, Amy Butler. In September 2003, 15,400 essays were submitted. Individual contests in Georgia are now administered by the various Rotary clubs.

Sir John is pleased with the reception given the laws of life approach to character building. He hopes that *Worldwide Laws of Life* will be extensively translated for use in Europe and Asia. As mentioned earlier, several translations have already been published.

8. Another objective of the Foundation is to encourage rigorous research by scientists about spiritual benefits to health and to extend these results to medical school educators.

Two major programs were launched, one carried on by the International Center for the Integration of Health and Spirituality (ICIHS, formerly NIHR) and the other by the Mind-Body Medical Institute of Harvard Medical School. The ICIHS developed a network of highly competent research fellows. The Mind-Body Medical Institute continues to develop a major network of researchers and is helping graduate programs in a number of major medical institutions.

Both ICIHS and the Mind-Body Institute have convened highly successful conferences of researchers and healthcare providers to emphasize the opportunities for a major impact on disease through spiritual outreach and engagement. These conferences give promise of developing into regular yearly series.

Medical school education will also be helped further by expanding the program of prizes for courses in medicine and religion currently being administered through Dr. Christina Puchalski at George Washington University School of Medicine.

9. Another objective was to extend the academic science-religion dialogue. Some of the programs in this outreach are discussed below.

The Science and Spiritual Quest Program

The Templeton program to encourage university and college courses in science and religion, which ended in 2002, broke new ground in establishing science and religion as valid subjects to be studied together in the academic arena. This eight-year program was the foundation for another program, also carried out by the Center for Theology and the Natural Sciences, entitled Science and Spiritual Quest. This program had its beginning in 1996, and focused on high-level scientists who were asked to share their interest and concerns about the deeper things of faith and spirit. Over a two-year period, some sixty leading scientists met together for advanced workshops. In June 1998, twenty-seven of them joined in a conference at the University of California, Berkeley, to address a broad range of questions about science and spirituality.

Some of the questions, concerns, and the impact of the conference included:

- Is there common ground in the practice and experience of science and religion?
- Does science offer evidence of a transcendent reality and purpose?
- Science and morality — is there a bridge?
- Reductionism vs. holism: multiple models of the spiritual quest.
- The distinctiveness of being human: how science informs the spiritual quest.

The SSQ conference drew massive press attention — over 90 million media impressions so far, including articles in *The New York Times, The Washington Post, Scientific American, Der Spiegel,* and a cover story in *Newsweek* ("Science Finds God"). The coverage was still continuing in September 2002, with articles about the conference appearing in both *Scientific American* and *Forbes ASAP*'s "big issue on convergence."

The Science and Spiritual Quest program was renewed for an additional four years under CTNS administration in 1999. The new program, denoted SSQII, again involved dialogue with leading scientists, and held major conferences in San Francisco, Boston, Paris, Israel, India, and Japan. Dr. Philip Clayton, philosopher from California State University, Sonoma, directs the program. Dr. Mark Richardson, theologian at the General Theological Seminary and director of SSQI, is co-director; and Dr. Robert Russell, director of CTNS, is senior advisor. An article in the September/October 1999 issue of *Progress in Theology* described plans for the new program and is reprinted below.

> In order to carry out this ambitious project, the staff of SSQII will work in conjunction with a variety of partners around the world, including the Interdisciplinary University of Paris and universities in Granada, India, and Japan. In a series of major public conferences, the scientists will share the results of their work in this field with other scholars, business and political leaders, and the public at large. Among the planned events are a Silicon Valley event for leading figures in the fields of computer science and information technology, a major Boston conference to be telecast to some one hundred universities across the United States, and a European conference at the UNESCO headquarters in Paris. SSQII also includes symposia in Jerusalem, Bangalore, and Tokyo, at which scientists from Western and Eastern religious traditions will engage in sustained dialogue on religious and spiritual questions, using their shared scientific expertise as a starting point and common thread.

The final SSQII conference took place in Bangalore, India, in January 2003. The four-day conference involved 12 sponsoring organizations, a dozen foreign speakers, and 36 Indian speakers addressing an audience that ranged between 250 and 400 people. Invited participants were drawn mainly from the Indian Institute of Science, from universities and institutes across India, and from the business and religious communities.

Among publications stemming from the SSQ program is the volume titled *Science and the Spiritual Quest: New Essays by Leading Scientists.*[4]

Humble Approach Initiative

In addition, a program to help university researchers in the arena of science and religion has also been initiated by the Foundation. Called the Humble Approach Initiative, it is also designed to bring top scientists together in small, intimate conferences to consider some of the wide-open possibilities that the joining of scientific and theological ideas makes possible. Partial funding will be solicited from outside agencies for organization of these consultations, which may occur at the rate of four or five a year over a five-year period. The ideas that may be addressed by these working groups are many and varied; they include:

- Complexity and Purpose in the Universe
- "Laws of Life": The Mathematical Biology of Moral Behavior
- *Homo religiosus:* The Contribution of Neuroscience, Genetics, Anthropology, and Evolutionary Biology toward Understanding the Role and Significance of Human Spirituality
- The Evolution of the Brain and the Origins of Religion: An Inquiry into the Roots of Human Nature
- The Uses and Abuses of Scientific Reductionism: A Critical Issue for Science and Religion
- Truth and Beauty in the Universe: Is There a Purpose for Which It Exists?
- First International Congress on Forgiveness Research
- Neuroimmunology and the Faith Factor in Human Health
- Love and the Ultimate Nature of Reality
- Thinking about the Big Picture: The Hubble Deep Field and Our Evolving View of the Universe
- Being Thankful: Developing a Research Strategy for Understanding the Power of Gratitude
- Game Theory and Theological Metaphysics
- The Book of Nature: Old Theologies and New Perspectives for Enriching the Encounter of Evangelicalism with Science

The program was begun in the fall of 1998 under the direction of Templeton Foundation Senior Fellow Mary Ann Meyers. As described by the late Elizabeth Hall, staff writer for *Progress in Theology,*

> Each Humble Approach Initiative symposium project begins with identification of a topic that might lend itself to broad reflection on questions of meaning and value that grow out of advances in scientific knowledge. The general topic is subsequently developed through a series of questions designed to stimulate thinking about all aspects, angles, and approaches to the issue. A carefully selected group, representing a diversity of perspective and viewpoints, is then invited to submit brief papers addressing one or more of the broadly framed areas of inquiry. These papers are circulated to the entire group prior to its convening. Through oral presentations and extended discussion in a relaxed, collegial setting, the invited participants listen, probe, reflect, respond, and refine viewpoints. It is expected that an edited collection of essays, based on the original papers, will be published after each symposium.

The first program was convened in October 1998, and was entitled "Love and the Ultimate Nature of Reality: Cosmology, Freedom and the Theology of Kenosis." It was chaired by physicist John Polkinghorne, and brought eleven distinguished theologians, philosophers, and scientists to Queens' College in Cambridge to discuss the implications of the theological concept of kenosis, the self-emptying of Jesus Christ.

In November 1998, a second symposium took place, on the topic "Many Worlds: The New Universe and Its Theological Implications." The meeting was chaired by physicist Paul Davies. Since that time, there have been thirteen more symposia.[5]

The International Society for Science and Religion

Several years ago Sir John began to consider helping to form an international honorary society of scientists and theologians that would have a limited membership and be composed of the most prestigious scholars in the field of science and religion.

That vision came to fruition with an organizational meeting in Granada, Spain, in August 2003. Seventy individuals met to elect Sir John Polkinghorne as president of a new organization, to be called the International Society for Science and Religion. There were ninety scholars elected, with another sixty to be added to form the scholarly core of the society. An executive committee was formed to include John Polkinghorne, Frazer Watts as secretary, and as members, John Brooke and Malcolm Jeeves (UK), Ronald Cole-Turner (USA), George Ellis (South Africa), Bruno Guiderdoni (France), and Niels Henrik Gregersen (Denmark).

Though the current membership is primarily European and North American, the intent of the group is to expand the number of Asian, African, and South American members and to represent all the major scientific and religious traditions.

President Polkinghorne acknowledged with thanks the support of the Templeton Foundation in providing funds to cover the initial operating expenses but stated that the plan is to have the society be "absolutely free standing" in the future.

Metanexus Institute

The Foundation entered the Internet world in a substantial way in 1997 through the leadership of Dr. William Grassie, who was an award winner in the first year of the Science and Religion Course Program. The history of this highly successful partnership with the Foundation was recalled in an article in *Research News and Opportunities in Science and Religion* (now *Science and Theology News*) commemorating the third anniversary of the program.

> The Meta Lists on Science and Religion just marked its third birthday. The project began at an Internet Summit held under the auspices of the Dialogue on Science, Ethics, and Religion Project of the American Association for the Advancement of Science in May 1997. A dozen representatives of various organizations in the field met to discuss effective ways of harnessing the Internet for promoting the science and religion agenda. At that time, an Internet

search on the phrase "science and religion" resulted only in links to Scientology and Christian Science. Today, on the Internet, as on campuses across the world, science and religion is increasingly seen as a serious interdisciplinary and interfaith dialogue. Meta has helped in the mainstreaming of this intellectually challenging and spiritually exciting conversation. The plan was to create a moderated list-serve to facilitate the exchange of news, views, and information among the diverse organizations and individuals in the growing field of science and religion. At the 1997 meeting in Washington, D.C., William Grassie, then a professor of religion at Temple University and now director of the new Philadelphia Center for Religion and Science, offered to serve as the moderator and editor of this new e-mail distribution list. With technical and financial support from the John Templeton Foundation, Grassie was able to create a Web page, brochure, and publicity for the project. Seven organizations signed on as official sponsors.

Meta began publication on October 1, 1997, with a list of 650 subscribers taken from the Science and Religion Course Program. In three years, Meta had grown to over 3,000 subscribers in 56 different countries on what are now three separate lists. Metanews is an announcement list for events and opportunities. Metaviews is a venue for commentaries and book reviews with diverse contributors like Paul Davies, Holmes Rolston, Michael Ruse, William Dembski, George Ellis, Ursula Goodenough, and others. Meta-Reiterations is a high-volume, un-moderated discussion list that generates as many as twelve messages per day in an energetic debate. At last count, Meta had published 531 installments, distributing 624,000 pieces of e-mail, thereby becoming the source for the most up-to-date news and views on science and religion circulated almost instantaneously and cost-effectively via the Internet around the world.

Meta continues to explore the cutting-edge of computer technology, having recently videotaped and made available on the Web a two-day symposium at the University of Pennsylvania called "Extended Life, Eternal Life." The gathering brought together leading scientists, philosophers, and theologians to discuss the new technologies and trends in the medicine of life extension. "We may not be immortalized in our lifetime," notes Grassie, "but this fascinating conference has been immortalized on the Web and can be viewed twenty-four hours a day, seven days a week on demand on an Internet browser near you."

The Counterbalance Foundation has also become a major participant by creating a related content-rich resource site on science and religion with the URL http://www.counterbalance.org. Plans exist for further improvements and expansion to these Meta sites with new Internet services for the advancement of the constructive engagement of science and religion.

Dr. Grassie is himself a member of the Religious Society of Friends (Quakers) and feels this relates to his role as editor and moderator of Meta.

Grassie's organization, since formalized as the Metanexus Institute on Religion and Science, has expanded its role to include support of several additional Foundation initiatives. The first was the convening of several high-level advanced summer workshops within the Science and Religion Course Program. The 2001 program, entitled "Interpreting Evolution: Scientific and Religious Perspectives," attracted over one hundred faculty to Haverford College near Philadelphia.

In the same year, Metanexus assumed leadership of the Foundation's Local Societies Initiative, designed to encourage the building of networks of dialogue groups in science and religion worldwide. In the first year, thirty-five academic groups received grants of $15,000 for support of a three-year program. An inaugural meeting of the recipients was convened in June 2002 to consider the topic "Interpretation Does Matter." Twenty-four groups were represented, including society members from Canada, Denmark, France, Germany, India, Korea, the Netherlands, Pakistan, Russia, and the

United States. In September 2002, Metanexus reported that the fifth round of applications had resulted in the addition of six additional grantees, bringing the total to forty-two representing fourteen countries around the globe.

Templeton Research Lectures

The year 2001 also marked the beginning of another program, The Templeton Research Lectures, entitled "The Constructive Engagement of Science and Religion." The primary aim of the lectures is to promote the constructive engagement and original research between the physical, biological, and human sciences and those modes of inquiry and understanding generally found within the domains of theology, religious studies, and philosophy. These high-level lectures were presented at the University of California at Santa Barbara and at Columbia University in 2001; Stanford University and Bar Ilan University in 2002; and University of California — Los Angeles and University of Montreal in 2003.

10. The Foundation also seeks to enhance education in virtue, ethics, and good character development.

The "Laws of Life" essay contests mentioned previously represent a significant beginning in education for character development. Likewise, the Templeton Honor Roll for Character-Building Colleges, which began in 1989 and has to date highlighted more than 350 colleges and universities with significant character-building programs, has played an important part.

In addition, in 1999, Templeton Foundation Press published a guidebook entitled *Colleges That Encourage Character Development*, edited by Foundation staff, which provides extensive curricular information in addition to the Templeton Honor Roll.

Power of Purpose

Is purpose woven into the very fabric of the universe? Does the belief that one's life has a purpose produce a power that transforms daily living? What role, if any, might particular religious traditions play in championing a vision of purpose adequate for our time? What are the potential public policy benefits of fostering purpose in retirement or during adolescence? These are some of the perennial and timeless questions that essayists will address by participating in the Power of Purpose Awards Competition. A total of $500,000 in prize monies will be awarded to writers who submit an essay that advances humanity's understanding of one of life's most important, complex, and mysterious realities — the power of purpose.

11. Sir John also plans to provide more yearly honors and prizes at the level of the Pulitzer Prize for the production of positive and inspirational programs and articles in the media. Some say the media — especially television — has become increasingly negative, antireligious, and focused on violence. Significant prizes for uplifting and inspirational programs will be very important.

Past awards have been directed to religious editors and to Christian television producers. Another goal is to extend such prizes to religious radio broadcasters and movie critics. In the long run, helping journalism schools in leading universities to give faculty awards for teaching positive journalism may have a beneficial impact.

Within this framework, Sir John has initiated a program of support for journalists and other media people for articles and programs illustrating that prosperity, progress, and peace result in those nations that encourage freedom in enterprise, competition, information, communication, travel, religion, and research.

The Foundation has addressed this goal with another academic course program, called the Visions of Freedom project, which began in 1998 and was based on the following five theses:

- Freedom is a complex, multifaceted topic. The goal of guiding students in the development of a nuanced understanding of freedom and its attendant responsibilities is worthy and commendable. It almost unavoidably calls for interdisciplinary approaches in course teaching.
- The topic of freedom readily lends itself to some form of coalescence of several domains of scholarship, including political history; the history of ideas/intellectual history; economic history and the history of

economic thought; legal/constitutional history; educational history; moral philosophy; political philosophy; religion, theology, and religious freedom; and the role of freedom in art and literature.

- Debate and dialogue are especially appropriate modes of teaching on the topic of freedom. A healthy, open, pedagogically creative environment is most likely to be achieved when the teaching team encompasses a wide diversity of opinion, especially on the political spectrum, and is able to demonstrate a high standard of orderly collegial debate.

- Quality in teaching a course on freedom and responsibility is enhanced when considerations of philosophical views are illuminated by careful surveys of empirical evidence, whenever relevant.

- The development of an international teaching project will provide a stimulus for curricular development and, most importantly, for the nurturing of a large and diverse community of scholars with broad interdisciplinary expertise suitable for teaching the topic of freedom eventually without the need for a special program of support.

Some major features of the program are:

- To launch courses at some ten distinguished institutions to provide a range of models of excellence;

- To establish a worldwide prize competition overseen by distinguished scholars;

- To establish common "core texts" to allow for a worldwide student examination prize competition; and

- To organize a parallel workshop program to be called the Templeton Institute for the Advanced Study of Freedom to support high quality faculty development.

The Foundation previously supported the Templeton Honor Roll for Education in a Free Society, which served to highlight individuals and institutions that most exemplify the ideals of education in freedom. An awards luncheon in Washington, D.C., attended by Milton Friedman, Gertrude Himmelfarb, and William Bennett as honored guests, drew a large audience of governmental and media people.

12. John Templeton also hopes to encourage a spirit of humility within all the great religions. Three programs of the Foundation address this objective directly. The 1997 winner of the Templeton Prize for Progress in Religion, the late Pandurang Athavale, is a good example of a humble man of the Hindu faith who emphasizes that God is in every human being regardless of caste or economic status. His ministry has transformed a significant part of Indian society. His testimony and the Foundation's recognition through the Templeton Prize is one more example of how all religions should "sit down together."

In addition, the Foundation's Science and Spiritual Quest program, described earlier, seeks to bring scientists of different religious persuasions together for mutual sharing and understanding.

Finally, the Foundation's Science and Religion Course Program has left a legacy of encouragement for faculty at universities and colleges who emphasize Judaism, Islam, Buddhism, and other Eastern religions to participate in the program.

13. Another goal of importance to Sir John as he established the Foundation was to encourage awareness of spiritual information through the establishment of new publications and a new publishing organization.

Templeton Foundation Press

The Press's beginnings were described in a *Progress in Theology* article:

> On December 10, 1996, Sir John Templeton, John M. Templeton Jr., MD, and the trustees of the John Templeton Foundation announced the inauguration of the Templeton Foundation Press, which will publish books in the areas of religion and science, moral education, and the scientific verification of basic spiritual principles.
>
> "Templeton Foundation Press is dedicated to the same principles as the Templeton Foundation and the Templeton Prize for Progress in Religion," said Sir John Templeton on the launch of the publishing venture held in New York City. "This new branch

of the Foundation presents us with another venue for supporting ongoing exploration of the vital connections between religion and scientific research. The books that will be published under the imprint will promote a deeper understanding of the influence of spirituality, beliefs, and values on human health, happiness, and prosperity."

In 1996, Joanna Hill was named director of publications, a new position for Templeton Foundation, Inc. Prior to her appointment, Hill had a diverse background in publishing, having worked at the North Carolina, Texas, and Louisiana State University presses. Upon accepting the position, Hill said, "Sir John's vision offers exciting possibilities for publishing. I see us doing a combination of trade and scholarly books that focus on spirituality, science and religion, health and healing, and character building. The scientific/religious interests of the John Templeton Foundation will be reflected in the list; in fact, some of the manuscripts will come as a result of grants and funding provided to scholars by the Foundation."

The Foundation had already co-published or sponsored more than two dozen books on diverse topics, including science and religion. Some of these publications are: *Discovering the Laws of Life, The Humble Approach, Is God the Only Reality?* and *The God Who Would Be Known,* all by Sir John Templeton. Other titles include *Who's Who in Theology and Science, 1996 Edition* and *Looking Forward: The Next Forty Years,* edited by Templeton.

Since that time, the Press has expanded its operations and offerings. The 2004 catalog carries descriptions of sixty-two titles, most of which are also offered as e-books. After the success of its first book, *Worldwide Laws of Life: 200 Eternal Spiritual Principles* by Sir John, the Press has continued publishing approximately twelve to fifteen books each year. In 2002, they brought out the paperback edition of *The Hand of God,* edited by Michael Reagan, which contains awe-inspiring Hubble Telescope photographs juxtaposed to inspirational quotations from scientists, theologians, and others writers. The Press is also becoming a publisher of significance in the field of spirituality and health, with six recent titles by Harold Koenig.

In 2001, the Press set up the new online Science and Religion Bookstore to provide a full and diverse listing of books in science and religion from many publishers. Readers can search the site by category, author, title, or publisher, and buy selections through a secure e-commerce site. Books are sent from the distributor within twenty-four hours.

Many of the Press's books, particularly inspirational books, have been widely translated and sold internationally. They have been translated into such languages as Spanish, Chinese, Korean, Bulgarian, Russian, German, Italian, Croatian, and Slovenian. In addition to sales representation in the U.S., the Press has set up distribution for its books in the U.K, Europe, Canada, and Australia. As Hill points out, "Our goal is to take cutting-edge ideas and distribute them to a broad audience. We work to be flexible, limited only by our own imagination."

Among the books Sir John has written are three books directly relevant to the objective of expanding spiritual information through establishing the Templeton Foundation Press. One is *Wisdom from World Religions*, and a second is *Golden Nuggets from Sir John Templeton*. The third book is *Why Are We Created?*.

Science and Theology News

Another publication effort of the Foundation, *Progress in Theology*, an eight-page newsletter, was originally published quarterly but was expanded to six new issues and two readers' supplements in 1998. In 2000, *Progress in Theology* was replaced by an international newspaper, *Research News and Opportunities in Science and Theology*. In 2003, the title of this monthly newsletter was changed to *Science and Theology News*. The masthead states:

> The John Templeton Foundation encourages the application of the proven methods of scientific discovery to the study of spiritual realities. Science has provided us with vast quantities of information about forces, matter, the processes of life and other tangible parts of nature. The rapid pace of science in the 20th century increased our knowledge of such things more than one hundred-

fold. There are other spiritual realities, however, such as love, creativity, cosmic and human purpose, that are also real but are invisible and intangible. Despite the importance of such things, we have very little information about them. The Templeton Foundation supports research projects with the goal of motivating humanity to acquire spiritual information at the same rapid pace as other scientific knowledge.

Science and Spirit magazine

An international, interdisciplinary magazine that provides information about the fields of science, religion, and spirituality originated in 1990 as a newsletter and is now published six times a year in a magazine format. The articles focus on the work of the Foundation, its sponsored organizations and programs, and the societies and professional organizations working to expand research in these disciplines.

Also planned is the next edition (the third) of *Resources in Theology and Science*, an international bibliographic compilation of organizations, events, media access, and scholars working in the interdisciplinary field of science and religion, this time in a Web page format.

14. Finally, the thirty-year-old prize program originally titled the Templeton Prize for Progress in Religion has been revised and more clearly focused to optimize impact and to emphasize the interrelationship between "progress," "research," and "discovery." Accordingly, the prize program has been renamed the Templeton Prize for Progress Toward Research or Discoveries about Spiritual Realities (www.templetonprize.org).

The prize brochure states the following in regard to purpose and objectives:

PURPOSE
How might humankind's spiritual information and advancement increase by more than a hundredfold? This is the challenge presented by the Templeton Prize. Just as knowledge in science, med-

icine, cosmology, and other disciplines has grown exponentially during the past century, the Templeton Prize honors and encourages the many entrepreneurs trying various ways for discoveries and breakthroughs to expand human perceptions of divinity and to help in the acceleration of divine creativity.

Their various methods, particularly through scientific research, serve to supplement the wonderful ancient scriptures and traditions of all the world's religions. Many honors and titles and prizes have been given for many centuries and will be given in the future for good works, reconciliation, saintliness, or for relief of poverty and sickness. But these very worthy endeavors are not the purpose of the Templeton Prize.

Instead, this award is intended to encourage the concept that resources and manpower are needed to accelerate progress in spiritual discoveries, which can help humans to learn over a hundredfold more about divinity.

We hope that by learning about the lives of the awardees, millions of people will be uplifted and inspired toward research and more discoveries about aspects of divinity. The Prize is intended to help people see the infinity of the Universal Spirit still creating the galaxies and all living things and the variety of ways in which the Creator is revealing himself to different people. We hope all religions may become more dynamic and inspirational. The Templeton Prize is awarded annually to a living person. The Templeton Prize does not encourage syncretism but rather an understanding of the benefits of diversity. It seeks to focus attention on a wide variety of endeavors toward discoveries or spiritual realities research. It does not seek a unity of denominations nor a unity of world religions; but rather it seeks to encourage understanding of the benefits of diversity. There is no limitation of race, creed, gender, or geographical background.

OBJECTIVE

Progress is needed in spiritual discovery as in all other dimensions of human experience and endeavor. Progress in religion needs to be accelerated as rapidly as progress in other disciplines. A wider universe demands deeper awareness of the aspects of the Creator and of spiritual resources available for humankind, of the infinity of God, and of the divine knowledge and understanding still to be claimed.

The Templeton Prize serves to stimulate this quest for deeper understanding and pioneering breakthroughs in religious concepts and knowledge by calling attention annually to achievements in this area. It is hoped that there will result from this enterprise expanded spiritual awareness on the part of humankind, a wider understanding of the purpose of life, heightened quality of devotion and love, and a greater emphasis on the kind of research and discovery that brings human perceptions more into concert with the divine will.

CRITERIA

The judges consider a nominee's contribution to progress made either during the year prior to his/her selection or during his/her career. The qualities sought in awarding the Prize are: *freshness, creativity, innovation,* and *effectiveness.* Such contributions may involve new concepts of divinity, new organizations, new and effective ways of communicating God's wisdom and infinite love, creation of new schools of thought, creation of new structures of understanding the relationship of the Creator to His ongoing creation of the universe, to the physical sciences, the life sciences, and the human sciences, and the old releasing of new and vital impulses into old religious structures and forms.

AWARD

As of December 2003, the Prize award is a sum in the amount of £795,000.

CHAPTER 16

Conclusion

I N THIS BOOK I have tried to do justice to the story of a man of extraordinary insights and abilities, a humble Tennessee boy who grew, through wise parenting and remarkable determination, to become an outstanding student at Yale, a Rhodes scholar at Oxford, and a pioneering investment counselor in New York, where his success won him the appellation "The wizard of Wall Street."

One might have thought that as his very substantial fortune accumulated, he would have retired to a well-deserved rest, but not John Templeton. From early in life, he had become convinced that there was also another kind of wealth to be sought after, and in later years it has become the focus of his very considerable energies and investments.

In his many years of service to church and community, in his leadership in several presidents' associations, and especially during his thirty-nine years as a wise advisor on the board of Princeton Theological Seminary, which benefited greatly from his financial advice, he gradually came to realize that our view of God is truncated and distorted by our own narrow perceptions and the intrusion of personal ego. For John, the view of God is so vast and incomprehensible that we should be humbled by the realization of "how little we know and how eager to learn." To encourage this attitude, he initiated not only the Templeton Prize but an entire philanthropic infrastructure involved in a multitude of projects and initiatives to support the expansion — largely through the sciences — of our view of the vastness of the creation and its infinite and unlimited Creator.

Yet his view still retains the personal touch, the conviction that God's love is for all his creatures and for all time. John Templeton's vision of the future is a world alive to the realization that we are all spiritual beings; that we have been fashioned out of what appears material but is, in reality, more accurately described by science as a unique conjunction of wave patterns, material substance in appearance but spiritual beings in reality. If this is our true nature, he says, then perhaps the most important thing we could ever know is the extent of and the meaning of our spiritual selves and our relationship to the Creator God of the universe. Given the enormous success of the scientific approach thus far in our probing of this universe, Sir John's call to focus one-tenth of all research expenditures on the spiritual dimension would seem to be the best investment recommendation ever made.

This vision of his has not come about by happenstance. John Templeton's life has been marked by a special combination of spiritual influences: prayer, a God-motivated discipline, love of all people, and a humble and thankful spirit.

John Templeton's disciplined life has long been based on an assurance that God rewards the worker whose motivation is to serve the high calling of spiritual blessing for all of mankind. Whether in the role of investment counselor or seminary trustee or foundation executive, John has displayed a tireless commitment to this goal. Anyone who has worked with him marvels at his incredibly tight schedule and his refusal to waste a precious moment. He always carries something in his pocket to read or review in case there is a free minute. Yet he will always make time if you need his advice or counsel.

Perhaps John's most salient desire — to love all people — produces the most powerful influence of his life. Out of this deeply spiritual motivation comes a humble attitude toward his fellow man and a reasonable appraisal of his own remarkable talents. And this attitude, as emphasized in this book, leads to that most remarkable goal, a humble theology. As John's vision has revealed it, humility toward God is the key to our spiritual blessing. As we recognize how little we know of the Creator of this enormous and intricate universe, the opportunity presents itself to explore our knowledge of God and our spiritual future in a new and powerful way. This is what John Templeton cherishes for our future.

He has gathered a veritable host of scientists, theologians, philosophers, writers, and fellow investors as staff and advisors as he seeks to reach his goal of one-hundredfold more spiritual information. The benefits, he believes, will far outweigh even the amazing growth in science and technology that has so affected our physical lives. The practical, reasoned, empirical approaches being carried out with the help of these colleagues to achieve this goal are also the theme of this book.

ON A PERSONAL NOTE

In a book about a remarkable man, I am pleased to add a final remark congratulating him and his family on an occasion of considerable joy and thankfulness: Sir John's granddaughter, Heather Templeton Dill, presented Sir John with his first great grandson, John Templeton Dill, born November 28, 2002, weighing in at 7 lbs 10 oz.

Awards, Accomplishments, and Career of John Marks Templeton

1967–1973	President of the Board of Trustees of Princeton Theological Seminary
1973	Founded the Templeton Prizes for Progress in Religion
1979	Recipient of the Churchman of the Year Award from the Religious Heritage of America
1981	International Churchman of the Year Award
1981	Ecumenical Patriarch's Honorary Order of Mount Athos
1983–1985	Member, Templeton College Council
1984	Free Enterprise Award, Palm Beach Atlantic College
1984	Founded Templeton UK Project Trust
1987	Knight Order of the British Empire
1987	Centennial Medal of the New York Mayflower Society
1991	*USA Today* Award for Excellence in Investment Management
1991–1996	Member of the Board of Trustees, Westminster Abbey Trust
1993	Royal Society of the Arts Benjamin Franklin Award
1993	Lifetime Achievement Award from the Layman's National Bible Association
1994	*Wall Street Week* Hall of Fame Award
1995	National Business Hall of Fame Award from the Junior Achievement Association

1997   The Abraham Lincoln Award presented by the Union
        League of Philadelphia
1998   Mutual Funds Lifetime Achievement Award
2003   William E. Simon Philanthropic Leadership Prize

COLLEGES AND DEGREES

Yale University: June 1934 Bachelor of Arts
University of Oxford (Balliol College): June 1936 M.A. (Rhodes Scholar)
Beaver College: June 1965 Honorary Doctor of Laws
Wilson College: May 1974 Honorary Doctor of Literature
Buena Vista College: May 1979 Honorary Doctor of Divinity
Marquette University: May 1980 Honorary Doctor of Laws
Maryville College: May 1984 Honorary Doctor of Laws
University of the South: May 1984 Honorary Doctor of Civil Law
Florida Southern College: February 1990 Honorary Doctor of Literature
Manhattan College: May 1990 Honorary Doctor of Literature
Babson College: May 1992 Honorary Doctor of Laws
University of Rochester: May 1992 Honorary Doctor of Laws
Rhodes College: May 1992 Honorary Doctor of Laws
University of Dubuque: September 1992 Honorary Doctor of Humane
    Letters
Jamestown College: May 1993 Honorary Doctor of Laws
Louisiana College: May 1993 Honorary Doctor of Laws
Campbell College: September 1993 Honorary Doctor of Humane Letters
Moravian College: May 1994 Honorary Doctor of Laws
Stonehill College: May 1995 Honorary Doctor of Philosophy
Furman University: November 1995 Honorary Doctor of Humanities
Notre Dame University: May 1996 Honorary Doctor of Laws
Methodist College of North Carolina: April 1997 Honorary Doctor
    of Laws

On-going Templeton Prize Programs

£795,000	Templeton Prize for Progress toward Research or Discoveries about Spiritual Realities
$3,500	Templeton Religion Story of the Year
$50,000	Epiphany Prize
SF5,000	Templeton European Religion Writer of the Year
SF10,000	Templeton European Film Award
$4,200	Reporter of the Year Award
$1,000	Martin E. P. Seligman Award for Positive Psychology

Buildings and Scholarships

Templeton Building, Nassau

Templeton Hall, Princeton Theological Seminary

Templeton College, Oxford

Templeton Library, Sewanee, Tennessee

Memorial Plaques, Henry VII Chapel, Westminster Abbey

John M. Templeton Scholarship Endowment Fund, Princeton Theological Seminary (funded by the Barra Foundation)

John Templeton Scholarship, Zeta Psi Fraternity, Yale University

Templeton Scholarship, University of the South

Judith Folk Templeton Memorial Scholarship, Princeton Theological Seminary

Books by John Marks Templeton

AUTHOR

Is Progress Speeding Up? Our Multiplying Multitudes of Blessings
This book is a thought-provoking documentation of human progress in the last century. In spite of the pessimism that prevails in the media, people are better fed, better clothed, better housed, and better educated than at any previous time. Loaded with statistics, charts, and photographs that illustrate this perspective, the book covers many aspects of modern life. It

is a reassuring and uplifting view of the state of the world and where it is going.

Golden Nuggets
This inspiring collection of sayings by Sir John Templeton provides a welcoming book for a person seeking deeper meaning in life. Filled with practical and uplifting advice, it is based on a lifetime of experience. For young or old, rich or poor, this wisdom will find many applications in one's life.

Worldwide Laws of Life: 200 Eternal Spiritual Principles
This treasury of wisdom is drawn from major sacred scriptures of the world and various schools of philosophical thought, as well as from scientists, artists, historians, and others. Its aim is to assist people of all ages to learn more about the universal truths of life that transcend modern times or particular cultures.

Is God the Only Reality? Science Points to a Deeper Meaning of the Universe
(with Robert L. Herrmann)
Reviewing the latest findings in fields from particle physics to archaeology, the book leads the reader to see how mysterious the universe is, even to the very science that seeks to reduce it to a few simple principles. Far from concluding that religion and science are in opposition, the book shows how these two fields of inquiry are intimately linked, and how much they can offer to one another.

Discovering the Laws of Life
Two hundred "laws of life" come not only from the experiences of one of the world's most prominent businessmen, but also from the scriptures of the great spiritual traditions. This collection can serve as inspiration to the reader or form the basis for a study group.

The Templeton Plan: 21 Steps to Personal Success and Real Happiness
(as described to James Ellison)
John Templeton shares the secrets of his phenomenal success in twenty-one principles that provide readers with solid guidelines for prosperity and happiness. He emphasizes truthfulness, perseverance, thrift, enthusiasm, humility, and altruism—qualities that can help everyone discover and develop his or her individual abilities.

The God Who Would Be Known: Revelations of the Divine in Contemporary Science
(with Robert L. Herrmann)
"This is a book about signals of transcendence," the authors write, "about points to the Infinite that are coming to us not from mystics but instead through the most recent findings of science." Positive in tone, this outstanding work seeks to preserve the mystery and wonder of our universe and emphasizes the potential blessings intended for us by God.

Riches for the Mind and Spirit
This book contains a collection of John Templeton's favorite inspirational passages from the Bible, from philosophers and poets, and from other writers.

The Humble Approach: Scientists Discover God
For generations the discoveries of science tended to challenge the very existence of God. John Templeton makes a striking argument for just the opposite point of view. He goes to the writings of many of the world's leading scientific thinkers—as diverse as Albert Einstein and Teilhard de Chardin—and discovers them in awe of the universe, perceiving the hand of Divine mystery at work.

Global Investing: The Templeton Way
(as told to Norman Berryessa and Eric Kirzner)
Readers will learn how to protect their money by following a strategy of global investing that both maximizes potential and minimizes risk factors.

Agape Love: A Tradition Found in Eight World Religions
Agape, or altruistic love, challenges the spiritual person to "love your enemies" or to "love without thought of return." It is love that flows out to others in the form of compassion, tenderness, and charitable giving.

Story of a Clam: A Fable of Discovery and Enlightenment
(with Rebekah Alezander Dunlap)
This book is a magical tale of how egotism clouds our understanding and misdirects us to think that we are the center of the universe, yet through exciting events we can come to experience that true joy, creativity, and love exist within us all.

Why Are We Created? Increasing Our Understanding of Humanity's Purpose on Earth
(with Rebekah Alezander Dunlap)
A compilation of questions designed to encourage thoughtfulness, observation, and research toward understanding how to live a more useful, fulfilling life. Accompanying commentary is provided from a wide range of sources: scripture, Mother Teresa, Albert Einstein, Edward O. Wilson, Emanuel Swedenborg, Emmet Fox, and others.

Pure Unlimited Love:
An External Creative Force and Blessing Taught by All Religions
An exploration of the process of understanding and expressing unconditional love — also called agape love. Is it an action, universal energy, or a creative principle? If we understand it, can its expression ever be realized or is it simply a divine attribute? These and other questions are addressed in an inspirational, philosophical, yet practical way.

Wisdom from World Religions: Pathways toward Heaven on Earth
The teachings of the world's major religions come to life through engaging stories and anecdotes. There are readings from Buddhism, Christianity, Confucianism, Hinduism, Islam, Jainism, Persian, Native American, Sikhism, Taoism, Zen, and Zoroastrianism. This is a book whose contents can be read, considered, studied, absorbed, and practiced, as a way of expanding spiritual understanding.

Possibilities for Over One Hundredfold More Spiritual Information:
The Humble Approach in Theology and Science
Sir John Templeton examines ways in which our energies may be applied to the pursuit of spiritual information, opening our minds to the possibilities of altruistic love for all peoples; new knowledge of the Divine and a greater sense of our place in the universe may be avenues to manifold blessings.

Editor

Spiritual Evolution: Scientists Discuss Their Beliefs
(with Kenneth Seeman Giniger)
These personal essays by esteemed scientists describe their spiritual journeys. They share their experiences of reconciling scientific and religious perspectives.

How Large is God? The Voices of Scientists and Theologians
Addressing this question, these essays reveal how very little we know about God and fundamental spiritual principles. Recent scientific research has shown that the universe is staggering in size and intricacy, and some scientists are now suggesting that our concept of God is much too small.

Evidence of Purpose: Scientists Discover the Creator
In this volume, respected scientists describe new developments in their fields and the relationship with theological views of the universe.

Looking Forward: The Next Forty Years
Ten experts discuss future trends in their fields and explain why they recommend an optimistic outlook. In communications, education, the economy, and more, change is in the forecast—change for the better.

Worldwide Worship: Prayers, Songs, and Poetry
This book is composed of unique selections of prayers, hymns, and poems from many world religions, drawn from classical and religious texts. These works celebrate the universal principles found in the human mind, and attempt to bridge the gaps between religions, cultures, and peoples of the world.

Overview of Financial Career

John Marks Templeton graduated in economics from Yale University in 1934 as president of Phi Beta Kappa and from Oxford University in law in 1936 as a Rhodes scholar.

In 1940, at 30 Rockefeller Plaza in New York City, Towne, Templeton and Dobbrow, Inc. was formed to provide private investment counsel for wealthy people, colleges, charities, and pension funds. The major method was to search out worldwide those securities whose prices were lowest temporarily in relation to appraisals by security analysts of their intrinsic value. By merger in 1942 with the older investment counsel firm Vance, Chapin & Co., the name was changed to Templeton, Dobbrow and Vance, Inc., with Templeton as 80 percent owner and clients' assets managed of about $30 million.

In 1950 our first mutual funds, Templeton Growth Fund, was formed by a $7 million public offering by White Weld & Co. and managed by Templeton Investment Management, Inc. One by one a variety of mutual funds were formed to be distributed nationally by Templeton Damroth Corporation.

Templeton Damroth Corporation and Templeton Dobbrow & Vance, Inc. were sold to the Richardson family of North Carolina in 1962 and are now operated as the Lexington Funds. John Templeton chose the Lyford Cay Club in the Bahamas as his permanent home. John W. Galbraith began to distribute Templeton Growth Fund Ltd. in 1964, and one by one many other Templeton Funds, and moved from New Jersey to St. Petersburg, Florida.

In 1980, Templeton opened an office in Fort Lauderdale with Thomas L. Hansberger as manager to begin again serving private clients, owned 80 percent by John Marks Templeton. In 1985, Templeton, Galbraith and Hansberger, Inc., were formed to combine the offices in the Bahamas, St. Petersburg, and Fort Lauderdale. In 1987 Cosgrove and Co. of London sold to the public worldwide 25 percent of the shares of Templeton, Galbraith and Hansberger that became listed on the London Stock Exchange.

Board of Advisors of the John Templeton Foundation, 2000–2003

ELIZABETH PEALE ALLEN is vice chairman of the Peale Center for Christian Living in Pawling, New York. She is chairman of the board of the Positive Thinking Foundation.

V. ELVING ANDERSON, PhD, professor emeritus of genetics and cell biology at the University of Minnesota, has been president of Sigma Xi, the Scientific Research Society. A diplomate of the American Board of Medical Genetics, Dr. Anderson's research in human genetics has explored the influence of genetics upon behavior, mental retardation, epilepsy, and breast cancer.

IAN G. BARBOUR, PhD, is professor emeritus in physics and religion at Carleton College in Northfield, Minnesota. In addition to serving as a Gifford Lecturer in 1989-91, he has written several books addressing the interface of religion and science including *Religion in an Age of Science* and *Ethics in an Age of Technology*. Both publications were recognized with the AAR Annual Book Award. Dr. Barbour was the recipient of the 1999 Templeton Prize.

GREGORY BENFORD, PhD, is professor of physics at the University of California, Irvine. He specializes in plasma physics theory and was presented with the Lord Prize in 1995 for achievements in the sciences. Dr. Benford has served as an advisor to NASA, the U.S. Department of Energy, and the White House Council on Space Policy. He has received two Nebula awards for science fiction writing. In 1992, Dr. Benford received the United Nations Medal in Literature. He is the author of nearly 130 research papers in his field and several books, including *Timescape*(1980), *Deep Time* (1999), and *Cosm* (1999).

HERBERT BENSON, MD, is associate professor of medicine at the Mind/Body Medical Institute, Harvard Medical School, and president of the Mind/ Body Medical Institute at the Beth Israel Deaconess Medical Center. He is the author or coauthor of more than 150 scientific publications and six books and the recipient of numerous national and international awards. Dr. Benson is a pioneer in behavioral medicine, mind/body studies, and spirituality and healing. His work serves as a bridge between medicine and religion, East and West, mind and body, and belief and science.

PETER L. BENSON, PHD, is president of Search Institute, a not-for-profit research and educational organization dedicated to positive child and adolescent development. Under his leadership, the institute has developed a theoretical and research-based model for mobilizing the engagement of citizens and communities in creating the ecologies and relationships crucial for successful development. Dr. Benson currently serves as the first visiting scholar at the William T. Grant Foundation in New York City, is the author of twelve books on child and adolescent development, and is the general editor of the new Search Institute Series on Developmentally Attentive Community and Society. He has been a recipient of the William James Award from the American Psychological Association.

DOROTHY F. CHAPPELL, PHD, dean of natural and social sciences at Wheaton College, also served for five years as academic dean at Gordon College and as a trustee of Wheaton College. Dr. Chappell is an accomplished teacher, mentor, and faculty leader who served as chair of the biology department, vice chair of the faculty, and chair of the faculty personnel committee at Wheaton. She completed her BS in biology at Longwood College in Virginia, MS in biology at the University of Virginia, and PhD in botany at Miami University in Ohio. Dr. Chappell is the recipient of several National Science Foundation grants and of a Fulbright Scholar grant that enabled her to do research at Massey University in New Zealand. Dr. Chappell has served as president of the American Scientific Affiliation, and also holds membership in the American Association for the Advancement of Science, American Association of University Women, American Institute of Biological Sciences, Botanical Society of America, Fulbright Association, Psychological Society of America, and Sigma Xi.

PHILIP CLAYTON, PHD, holds a doctorate in both philosophy and religious studies from Yale University. He has taught at Haverford College and at Williams College and until 2001 was professor and chair of philosophy at the California State University, Sonoma. Clayton is a past winner of the Templeton Book Prize for best monograph in the field of science and religion and a winner of the first annual Templeton Research Prize. Dr. Clayton is the author of *The Problem of God in Modern Thought* (Eerdmans, 2000); *God and Contemporary Science* (Edinburgh University Press, 1997); and *Explanation from Physics to Theology: An Essay in Rationality and Religion* (Yale University Press, 1989). Dr. Clayton was principal investigator of the Science and the Spiritual Quest project (SSQ) at the Center for Theology and the Natural Sciences in Berkeley, California. SSQ has brought together over one hundred top scientists from around the world to explore the connections between science, ethics, religion, and spirituality. SSQ-sponsored events have been held at Silicon Valley, Harvard University, the UNESCO World Headquarters in Paris, Jerusalem, Bangalore, and Tokyo.

RONALD COLE-TURNER, MDIV, PHD, is H. Parker Sharp Professor of Theology and Ethics at Pittsburgh Theological Seminary. He is a member of the advisory board of the American Association for the Advancement of Sciences, Program of Dialogue between Science and Religion. He is chair of the United Church of Christ Working Group on Faith, Science, and Technology and chair of the Task Force on Genetic Engineering for the United Church of Christ. Dr. Cole-Turner has written extensively on the relationship between religion and genetics. He is the author of *Beyond Cloning: Religion and the Remaking of Humanity* and coauthor of *Pastoral Genetics: Theology and Care at the Beginning of Life*.

FRANCIS S. COLLINS, MD, PHD, is physician and director of the National Human Genome Research Institute, NIH. Dr. Collins oversaw a thirteen-year project that completed the mapping and sequencing of all human DNA in April 2003. Dr. Collins received his PhD in physical chemistry at Yale University and his medical degree from the University of North Carolina. After completing his residency in internal medicine, Dr. Collins returned to Yale for a fellowship in human genes. With the research team of Lap-Chee Tsui and Jack Riordan, Dr. Collins identified the gene for cystic fibrosis in 1989, the neurofibromatosis gene in 1990, and the gene for Huntington's disease in 1993. Dr. Collins's accomplishments have been recognized by his election to the Institute of Medicine and the National Academy of Sciences, and he has received numerous national and international awards.

GEORGE V. COYNE, SJ, PHD, is the director of the Vatican Observatory (Specola Vaticana), headquartered at Castel Gandolfo (Rome, Italy), and the director of a research branch at the University of Arizona. Father Coyne received his PhD in astronomy from Georgetown University in 1962 and the Licentiate in Theology from Woodstock College, Maryland, in 1966. Since 1966, he has been associated with astronomy programs at the University of Arizona, serving from 1976 to 1980 in the administration of the astronomical observatories there. His research interests have ranged from the study of the lunar surface before the NASA Ranger and Apollo programs to the birth of stars. He has pioneered a special technique, polarimetry, as a powerful tool in astronomical research. Fr. Coyne has published more than one hundred articles in reviewed scientific journals and has edited numerous books. Alongside his scientific research, he explores the history and philosophy of science and the relationship between science and religion.

WILLIAM DAMON, PHD, is a professor of education and the director of the Center on Adolescence at Stanford University. He is also senior fellow at the Hoover Institution on War, Revolution, and Peace. Dr. Damon has written widely on moral commitment at all ages of human life. His books include *The Moral Child* (1990); *Some Do Care: Contemporary Lives of Moral Commitment* (1992); *Greater Expectations: Overcoming the Culture on Indulgence in our Homes and Schools* (1995); *The Youth Charter: How Communities Can Raise Standards for All Our Children* (1997); *Good Work: When Ethics and Excellence Meet* (2001); and *Noble Purpose: The Joy of Living a Meaningful Life* (2003). Dr. Damon is editor-in-chief of *New Directions for Child and Adolescent Development* and editor of *The Handbook of Child Psychology* (1998). He has received numerous awards and grants and has been elected to membership in the National Academy of Education.

FREEMAN J. DYSON is a professor of physics at the Institute for Advanced Study, Princeton, New Jersey. He has received numerous honors and been widely published for his work in physics and ethics in science with regard to arms control. Mr. Dyson is a fellow of the Royal Society of London and a

1985 Gifford lecturer. He received the Phi Beta Kappa Award in Science in 1988 for his book *Infinite in All Directions*. Mr. Dyson was the recipient of the 2000 Templeton Prize for Progress in Religion.

LINDON J. EAVES, PhD, is distinguished professor of human genetics and psychiatry at the Virginia Commonwealth University School of Medicine. He directs the Virginia Institute for Psychiatric and Behavioral Genetics. Dr. Eaves is a priest of the Episcopal Church. He has published extensive research involving genetic studies of human behavior, and has also published on the interface between religion and science.

ROBERT A. EMMONS, PhD, is a professor of psychology at the University of California, Davis. Dr. Emmons received his doctorate in personality and social ecology from the University of Illinois at Urbana-Champaign. He is the author of nearly eighty original publications in peer-reviewed journals or chapters in edited volumes, including the books *The Psychology of Ultimate Concern: Motivation and Spirituality in Personality* and *Words of Gratitude for Mind, Body, and Soul*. Professor Emmons is associate editor for the *Journal of Personality and Social Psychology* and a consulting editor for the *International Journal for the Psychology of Religion*. He is president-elect of The American Psychological Association's Division of the Psychology of Religion. His research focuses on psychology and spirituality of gratitude and thankfulness, personal goals, purpose, psychological and physical well-being.

KITTY FERGUSON studied at the Juilliard School of Music in New York City and for many years was a professional musician. After a period of residence at Cambridge University in England, she chose to devote herself full-time to writing about a second lifelong interest, science. As an independent scholar and lecturer, she has written several outstanding books, including *Black Holes in Spacetime* (for young adults); *Stephen Hawking: Quest for a Theory of Everything*; *The Fire in the Equations: Science, Religion, and the Search for God*; *Prisons of Light: Black Holes*; *Measuring the Universe*; and *Tycho Brahe and Johannes Kepler, The Strange Partnership that Changed Our Concept of the Heavens*. She has been a part of many workshops, panels, and lecture series, written for *Astronomy* magazine, contributed a chapter to Russell Stannard's *God for the Twenty-First Century*, and served as a consultant for Stephen Hawking's *The Universe in a Nutshell*.

FOSTER FRIESS is chairman and founder of Friess Associates, a firm that manages approximately $7 billion in equities, including the Brandywine Mutual Funds. A graduate of the University of Wisconsin in 1958, he is past president of the Council for National Policy, which networks leaders in the United States committed to a strong national defense, traditional values, and the free enterprise system. He also founded the Life Enrichment Foundation, whose giving is focused on replicating proven, faith-based, inner-city entrepreneurial ministries.

LINDA K. GEORGE, PHD, is a professor of sociology, psychology, and psychiatry at Duke University. Associate director of the Duke University Center for the Study of Aging and Human Development and of the Duke University Center for the Study of Religion, Aging, and Health, Dr. George is the past president of the Gerontological Society of America and is the author of seven books and nearly two hundred journal articles and chapters. Her research interests include spirituality and health, as well as the effects of stress and social support on health.

THOMAS GILLESPIE, PHD, is the president of Princeton Theological Seminary. An alumnus of Princeton Seminary, he earned his Doctor of Philosophy degree in New Testament studies from the Claremont Graduate School. Dr. Gillespie is a member of the Presbytery of New Brunswick, the Association of Governing Boards Advisory Council of Presidents, and is a trustee of the Interdenominational Theological Center in Atlanta, Georgia. He is the author of the book *The First Theologians: A Study in Early Christian Prophecy*.

OWEN GINGERICH, PHD, is a professor of astronomy and of the history of science at the Harvard-Smithsonian Center for Astrophysics in Cambridge, Massachusetts. He is a member of the American Philosophical Society, the American Academy of Arts and Sciences, and the International Academy of the History of the Sciences. Professor Gingerich has published over five hundred technical or educational articles and reviews. His most recent book is *The Book Nobody Read*.

KENNETH S. GINIGER is president of the K. S. Giniger Company, Inc., publishers. He has published several of Sir John Templeton's books and co-edited *Spiritual Evolution* with him. He is chairman emeritus of the National Bible Association.

WILLIAM GRASSIE, PhD, is founder and executive director of the Metanexus Institute on Religion and Science. Dr. Grassie also serves as the editor of the institute's online magazine and discussion forum. He received his doctorate in religion from Temple University and his BA from Middlebury College. Prior to graduate school, Dr. Grassie worked for ten years in religious-based social service and advocacy organizations in Washington, D.C.; Jerusalem, Israel; Berlin, Germany; and Philadelphia, Pennsylvania. He has taught in a variety of positions at Temple University, Swarthmore College, and the University of Pennsylvania. Dr. Grassie is the recipient of a number of academic awards and grants from the American Friends Service Committee, the Roothbert Fellowship, and the John Templeton Foundation.

PETER GRUBER is president and principal of Globalvest Management Company, L. P., a U. S.-based and SEC-registered investment advisor. He has been in the investment business for more than forty years. During his Wall Street years, he gained significant experience in all areas of the securities industry, including trading, research, underwriting, and investment management. For a number of years, he was also actively engaged in corporate reorganizations. Since 1977, he has been investing globally, for private clients and his own account, though more focused in the securities market of Latin America and other emerging markets. Globalvest was founded to offer investment management and advisory services to qualified investors, pension funds, and other institutions. It is headquartered in St. Thomas, U. S. Virgin Islands, with offices in Rio de Janeiro, Brazil, and has more than $1 billion under management.

JOHN F. HAUGHT, PhD, is the Landegger Distinguished Professor at Georgetown University and member of the theology faculty. Dr. Haught is the founding director of its Center for the Study of Science and Religion. He is the author of more than fifty articles and book chapters and has published ten books, including: *The Promise of Nature: Ecology and Cosmic Purpose* (1993); and *Science and Religion: From Conflict to Conversation* (1995); and his latest volume, *God After Darwin: A Theology of Evolution* (1999). Dr. Haught is the editor of a new book of essays, *Science and Religion in Search of Cosmic Purpose* (2001), published by Georgetown University Press.

PHILIP HEFNER, PHD, is professor of systematic theology, Lutheran School of Theology at Chicago. He earned his doctoral degree with distinction from the University of Chicago and has taught at Lutheran seminaries his entire career. He currently serves as co-director of the Chicago Center for Religion and Science and is former editor-in-chief of *Zygon: Journal of Religion and Science*. His most recent book is *The Human Factor: Evolution, Culture, and Religion*.

ROBERT L. HERRMANN, PHD, taught medical school biochemistry for twenty-two years, during which time he developed a keen interest in interrelating science and religion. In 1981, he left medical education to become executive director of the American Scientific Affiliation, and a member of the chemistry faculty at Gordon College. While at ASA, he met fellow member, John Templeton, and they have since cooperated in writing several books, including *The God Who Would Be Known, Is God the Only Reality?* and Sir John's biography. Dr. Herrmann is currently on the staff at Gordon College in Wenham, Massachusetts, where he directs several projects for the John Templeton Foundation.

WILLIAM H. HURLBUT, MD, is a consulting professor in the Program in Human Biology at Stanford University and a member of the President's Council on Bioethics. His main areas of interest involve ethical issues associated with advancing technology and the integration of the philosophy of biology with Christian theology. Dr. Hurlbut has been working with the Center for Security and International Cooperation on a project formulating policy on chemical and biological warfare and with NASA on projects in astrobiology.

DEBORAH IRBY, a member of the board of regents at Harris-Manchester College at Oxford University in Oxford, England, attended Trinity University in San Antonio, Texas, on a four-year academic scholarship, receiving a BA in sociology in 1977. After graduation, Debbie W. Irby taught junior high school science for twelve years and actively participated in all aspects of local science fairs. In 1995, she and her husband, Stuart C. Irby Jr., created the Soli Deo Gloria Foundation, a private foundation serving to promote and implement John Templeton Foundation's Laws of Life Essay Contest in Mississippi, prison reform, and bicycling as a secondary means of transportation. She is a member of Covenant Presbyterian Church in Jackson,

Mississippi, where she and her husband played an instrumental role in the formation of the Covenant School for the Arts.

CHARLES E. JOHNSON is president and chief executive officer of Templeton Worldwide, Inc., and Franklin Institutional Service Corporation. He is senior vice-president and director of Franklin Resource, Inc., the parent company of the Templeton organization. Johnson also serves as a director and/or officer of many of the various Franklin and Templeton mutual funds and subsidiaries. He received an MBA from the Harvard University Graduate School of Business and is a certified public accountant.

CHRISTOPHER B. KAISER, PhD, professor of historical and systematic theology at Western Theological Seminary, Holland, Michigan, has published in the field of historical studies in theology and science and on the relation of science, theology, and society.

HAROLD G. KOENIG, MD, is professor of psychiatry and behavioral sciences and associate professor of medicine at Duke University Medical Center. Dr. Koenig is the director and founder of the Center for the Study of Religion/Spirituality and Health at that institution. He has published extensively in the fields of mental health, geriatrics, and religion, with over 160 scientific peer-reviewed articles, 40 book chapters, and 18 books. He is editor of the *International Journal of Psychiatry in Medicine*, and is founder and editor-in-chief of *Science and Theology News*.

DAVID B. LARSON, MD, was president of The International Center for the Integration of Health and Spirituality (ICIHS). Dr. Larson was adjunct professor of psychiatry and behavioral sciences at Duke University Medical Center and at Northwestern University Medical School, as well as adjunct professor of preventive medicine and biometrics at the Uniformed Services University of the Health Sciences in Bethesda, Maryland. Prominent among Dr. Larson's research interests was the influence of religious and spiritual commitment on physical, mental, and social health status and care.

RICHARD M. LERNER, PhD, is Bergstrom Chair in Applied Developmental Science and the director of the Applied Developmental Science Institute in the Eliot-Pearson Department of Child Development at Tufts University. In 1971, he received his PhD in developmental psychology from the City University of New York. Dr. Lerner has been on the faculty of Michigan State

University, Pennsylvania State University, and Boston College, where he was the Anita L. Brennan Professor of Education and the director of the Center for Child, Family, and Community Partnerships. During the 1994–95 academic year, Dr. Lerner held the Tyner Eminent Scholar Chair in the Human Sciences at Florida State University. He was a fellow at the Center for Advanced Study in the Behavioral Sciences, and is a fellow of the American Association of the Advancement of Science, the American Psychological Association, and the American Psychological Society. Dr. Lerner is the recipient of numerous awards, including the New England Psychological Association (NEPA) Distinguished Scholar Award in 2002 and Faculty Fellow at Tufts University College of Citizenship and Public Service for 2002–2004. The author or editor of fifty-five books and more than four hundred scholarly articles and chapters, he was the founding editor of the *Journal of Research on Adolescence and of Applied Developmental Science*.

MARTIN E. MARTY, PHD, is founding president and George B. Caldwell Senior Scholar at Park Ridge Center for the Study of Health, Faith, and Ethics in Chicago. He has received the National Medal for Humanities, the Medal of the American Academy for Arts and Sciences, and the National Book Award. As a prolific author who has written or edited over fifty books on religious subjects, his foremost field of expertise is religious history. Dr. Marty is the editor of *Second Opinion*, a journal providing a forum for interface of health, faith, and ethics.

DALE A. MATTHEWS, MD, practices general internal medicine in Washington, D.C. and teaches at Georgetown University School of Medicine. He conducts research and lectures nationally and internationally on the doctor-patient relationship and the psychological and spiritual dimensions of medicine, including the role of faith, religion, and prayer in clinical care and healing. He is the author of *The Faith Factor: Proof of the Healing Power of Prayer* (1998).

SANFORD N. MCDONNELL is former chairman and chief executive officer of McDonnell Douglas Corporation, one of America's foremost aerospace companies. Educated at Princeton University, the University of Colorado, and Washington University, he holds degrees in economics, mechanical engineering, and applied mechanics. A fellow of the American Institute of Aeronautics and Astronautics, he has received numerous professional and civic awards. Mr. McDonnell is chairman of CHARACTERplus, a character education program in the public schools of Greater St. Louis. He is chairman of the board of the Character Education Partnership, Inc., Washington, D.C. Mr. McDonnell was the first president of the foundation for the Malcolm Baldrige National Quality Award, and is a past national president of the Boy Scouts of America.

ERNAN MCMULLIN, PHD, is director emeritus of the Program in History and Philosophy of Science at the University of Notre Dame. He also held the John Cardinal O'Hara Chair of Philosophy. Dr. McMullin received his BS in physics as well as his BD in theology from Maynooth College, Ireland. He earned his doctorate in philosophy at the University of Louvain. Dr. McMullin is a fellow of the American Academy of Arts and Sciences, the International Academy of the History of Science, and the American Association for the Advancement of Science. He is author or editor of nine books and more than two hundred journal articles, book chapters, encyclopedia entries, and other scholarly pieces. Dr. McMullin served as president of all four of the leading philosophy associations in the United States: the American Philosophical Association, Central Division; the Philosophy of Science Association; the Metaphysical Society of America; and the American Catholic Philosophical Association, which also awarded him the Aquinas Medal.

ADAM MEYERSON is the president of The Philanthropy Roundtable, a national association of six hundred individual donors, foundation trustees and staff, and corporate giving officers. The mission of The Philanthropy Roundtable is to foster excellence in philanthropy, to help donors achieve their philanthropic intent, and to help donors strengthen America as a land of freedom, opportunity, and personal responsibility. Meyerson was editor-in-chief of *Policy Review*, Heritage Foundation's magazine, from 1983 to 1998, and was an editorial writer for the *Wall Street Journal*. Meyerson graduated summa cum laude and Phi Beta Kappa from Yale University.

GARY D. MOORE is counselor to ethical and religious investors with twenty years of Wall Street experience including service as senior vice president of investment for Paine-Webber. Moore founded Gary Moore & Co., a company dedicated to providing counsel to ethical and religious investors. He currently counsels some of America's best-known churches and banks. He is also a commentator on the political economy for UPI National Radio. He is the author of numerous books including *The Christian Guide to Wise Investing*, *Spiritual Investments: Wall Street Wisdom from the Career of Sir John Templeton*, and *Faithful Finances 101: From the Poverty of Fear and Greed to the Riches of Spiritual Investing*.

GLENN R. MOSLEY, MScADM, PHD, is president and CEO of the Association of Unity Churches. His ministry began in 1957, and he has traveled extensively, speaking in Unity and non-Unity churches. He frequently serves as a visiting professor for colleges and universities and conducts workshops on interpersonal communications, life and death transitions, and integrative healing modalities. He has authored or coauthored a number of books on these topics. He is a trustee of the John Templeton Foundation.

NANCEY MURPHY, PHD, is professor of Christian philosophy at Fuller Theological Seminary, Pasadena, California. Dr. Murphy is on the board of directors of the Center for Theology and the Natural Sciences. Her books include: *Theology in the Age of Scientific Reasoning*; *On the Moral Nature of the Universe: Theology, Cosmology, and Ethics* (with G. F. R. Ellis); and *Anglo-American Postmodernity: Philosophical Perspectives on Science, Religion, and Ethics*. She is a 1999 recipient of the CTNS Outstanding Books in Theology and Natural Sciences Award. Dr. Murphy is an ordained minister in the Church of the Brethren.

DAVID G. MYERS, PHD, is the John Dirk Werkman Professor of Psychology at Hope College, Holland, Michigan. Dr. Myers has published twelve books including two best-selling psychology textbooks. He is the recipient of the Gordon Allport Prize for his National Science Foundation-funded experiments on group influence. His trade books include *The Pursuit of Happiness: Who is Happy — and Why*, *The American Paradox: Spiritual Hunger in an Age of Plenty*, and *Intuition: Its Powers and Perils*. Dr. Myers is a trustee of the John Templeton Foundation.

PRIYAMVADA NATARAJAN, PHD, is assistant professor of astrophysics at Yale University. Dr. Natarajan completed her undergraduate studies at MIT, obtained her PhD from the University of Cambridge in 1998, and is a research fellow at Trinity College, Cambridge. Her research interests span a range of topics in astrophysical cosmology. She also spent two years in the MIT Program in Science, Technology, and Society pursuing studies in the history and philosophy of science. Dr. Natarajan is currently a member of the advisory panel for the Dialogue on Science, Ethics, and Religion of the American Association for the Advancement of Science (AAAS), and has an abiding intellectual interest in understanding issues in spirituality and science.

AYUB K. OMMAYA, MD, is a professor of neurosurgery at Georgetown and George Washington Universities in Washington, D.C. He has received many honors, including: Harper Nelson Gold Medal, King Edward Medical College; Hunterian Professorship of the Royal College of Surgeons UK; James Wills Kirkaldy University Prize, Oxford University; Star of Achievement (Pakistan). Dr. Ommaya is a member of the Committee of Bioacoustics and Biomechanics of the U.S. National Research Committee and the National Academy of Science and a fellow of the Third World Academy of Science. He has authored over two hundred publications in neuroscience and biomechanics. He is the inventor of the CSF reservoir and is currently working on a book, *Evolution of Consciousness as Emotion.*

TED PETERS, PhD, is a professor of systematic theology at Pacific Lutheran Theological Seminary and the Graduate Theological Union in Berkeley, California. Dr. Peters formerly directed the Science and Religion Course Program at the Center for Theology and the Natural Sciences and the CTNS-Templeton Foundation University Lectures. Among his books, he is author of the 1997 Templeton Foundation award-winning book, *Playing God? Genetic Determinism and Human Freedom* (Routledge, 1997) and *Science, Theology and Ethics* (Ashgate, 2003). Dr. Peters is editor of *Evolution from Creation to New Creataion: The Controversy in Laboratory, Church, and Society* (Abingdon, 2003) and *Bridging Science Together* (Augsburg Fortress, 2003).

ROBERT POLLACK, PhD, is a professor of biological sciences, lecturer in psychiatry at the Center for Psychoanalytic Training and Research, and director of the Center for the Study of Science and Religion, all at Columbia University. He received the Alexander Hamilton Medal from Columbia University, and has held a Guggenheim fellowship. His *Signs of Life: The Language and Meanings of DNA* received the Lionel Trilling Award; his second book, *The Missing Moment: How the Unconscious Shapes Modern Science*, was released by Houghton Mifflin (1999); and his latest work, *The*

Faith of Biology and the Biology of Faith: Order, Meaning and Free Will in Modern Science, was published by Columbia University Press as the inaugural volume of a new series on science and religion. He is a member of the Century Association.

STEPHEN G. POST, PHD, is a professor of biomedical ethics at the School of Medicine, Case Western Reserve University. He serves on the National Ethics Advisory Panel of the Alzheimer's Disease and Related Disorders Association, and is ethics editor for the journal *Alzheimer Disease and Associated Disorders*, and is the editor-in-chief of the third edition of the *Encyclopedia of Bioethics*. He is the author of numerous books including *Human Nature and the Freedom of Pubic Religious Expression; Unlimited Love: Altruism, Compassion, and Service; The Moral Challenge of Alzheimer Disease*; and the editor of *Altruism and Altruistic Love and Research on Altruism and Love*. Dr. Post received his doctorate in religious ethics and moral philosophy from the University of Chicago Divinity School. In 1998 he received the annual award for outstanding public service from the Alzheimer's Association. Dr. Post is president of The Institute for Research on Unlimited Love.

V. S. RAMACHANDRAN, MD, PHD, director of the Center for Brain and Cognition, University of California at San Diego, holds academic positions at both the Salk Institute and the University of California, San Diego, and has published and lectured internationally on the subject of visual neuroscience. Among his notable publications, he was appointed editor-in-chief of a four-volume *Encyclopedia of Human Behavior* published by Academic Press.

RAVI RAVINDRA, PHD, is professor emeritus at Dalhousie University, Halifax, Canada. Born in India, Dr. Ravindra obtained his PhD in physics from the University of Toronto and has held post-doctoral fellowships in physics (University of Toronto), history and philosophy of science (Princeton University), and religion (Columbia University). He was a member of the Institute of Advanced Study in Princeton, a fellow of the Indian Institute of Advanced Study, Shimla, and was the founding director of the Threshold Award for Integrative Knowledge as well as chair of its international and interdisciplinary selection committees in 1979 and 1980. Dr. Ravindra is a member of the Board of Judges for the Templeton Prize program. He has published more than a hundred and twenty papers in scholarly and scientific journals as well as authored several acclaimed books. His most recent book is entitled *Krishnamurti: Two Birds in One Tree*.

MICHAEL J. REAGAN is president of Lionheart Books, Ltd., and former executive vice president and publisher of Turner Publishing, a division of Turner Broadcasting. While at Turner, he was responsible for developing the publishing company, which published over two hundred books, including a number of *New York Times* bestsellers: *Moon Shot* by Alan Shepherd and Deke Slaton, *Creating a New Civilization* by Heidi and Alvin Toffler, *Hoop Dreams* by Ben Joravsky, *Dinotopia* by James Gurney, and *The Native Americans*, edited by Alvin Josephy Jr. He recently produced two books for Templeton Foundation Press, *The Hand of God* and *Inside the Mind of God*.

LAURANCE S. ROCKEFELLER is a philanthropist, business executive, and conservationist. He has held various chairs and trustee appointments for a wide number of national, academic, and humanitarian organizations. He has been the recipient of many awards and medals for his conservation work and philanthropic interests, including the Congressional Gold Medal in 1991.

ROBERT J. RUSSELL, PHD, is founder and director of the Center for Theology and the Natural Sciences (CTNS) and professor-in-residence of theology and science at the Graduate Theological Union in Berkeley, California. He received his doctorate in physics from the University of California at Santa Cruz, and his specialized scientific interests include inflationary and quantum cosmology and philosophical foundations of quantum mechanics. Dr. Russell has coedited eight books on theology and science as a result of ongoing collaborative research between CTNS and the Vatican Observatory. He was a former judge for the Templeton Prize.

ALLAN SANDAGE, PHD, is a graduate of the University of Illinois who received his PhD in astronomy from the California Institute of Technology. Dr. Sandage began his career at Mount Wilson Observatory when he was chosen by Edgar Hubble to work as his personal assistant. He has achieved recognition for his work in stellar evolution, the composition of galaxies, and observational high-energy astrophysics. He is best known for his pathfinding work in observational cosmology, measuring the rate of expansion and the age of the universe. Dr. Sandage has received numerous honors for his work, including the Presidential Medal of Science, the Homewood Professor of Physics designation, the American Astronomical Society's Russell Prize, and the Swedish Academy of Science's Crawford Prize. He was at Johns Hopkins University (1986–87) and was senior visiting fellow at the Space Telescope Science Institute.

JEFFREY P. SCHLOSS, PHD, is a professor of biology at Westmont College. Dr. Schloss serves as director of biological programs for the Christian Environmental Association and is a science consultant for the Christian College Coalition Faculty Development Program in Faith and Learning. He has been a Danforth fellow, an AAAS fellow in science communication, and a fellow of the Discovery Institute. His dual research interests include ecophysiological adaptations and sociobiological theories of human altruism and religious faith.

JANE SIEBELS-KILNES, PHD, is CEO/CIO of Green Cay Asset Management, an investment firm that manages hedge funds investing in technology stocks, emerging markets, and global equities. The funds do not invest in tobacco, casino gambling, handguns, or hard liquor stocks, and they try to encourage companies doing "spiritual good" through positive screening. Dr. Siebels-Kilnes holds a doctorate in international economics from Hochschule St. Gallen, Switzerland, which was funded by a Rotary fellowship, a master's in international management from the American Graduate School of International Management, and a bachelor's degree in business administration from the University of Iowa. She is on the board of Opportunity International and is active in supporting Cambridge University. She has worked as head of European equity management at Union Bank of Switzerland, Zurich, as a Templeton portfolio manager/analyst, and as a portfolio manager for Storebrand International in Norway.

LAWRENCE E. SULLIVAN, PHD, a former director of the Harvard University Center for the Study of World Religions and a professor of religion. Dr. Sullivan received his PhD is the comparative history of religions from the University of Chicago under the direction of Victor Turner and Mircea Eliade, and later taught on the faculty there. His book, *Icanchu's Drum: An Orientation to Meaning in South American Religions*, received best book awards from the Association of American Publishers and the American Council of Learned Societies. He is associate editor of the 16-volume *Encyclopedia of Religion* published by Macmillan which received the Hawkins Prize and the Dartmouth Medal from the American Library Association for the best work in any category of publishing. He served as president of the American Academy of Religion.

TRINH XUAN THUAN, PHD, is a native of Hanoi, Vietnam. He obtained his BS in physics at the California Institute of Technology in 1970 and his PhD in astrophysics at Princeton University in 1974. Since 1976, he has been a professor of astronomy at the University of Virginia. He specializes in the study of galactic systems beyond the Milky Way and has written nearly two hundred articles on the formation of elements in the big bang and galaxy formation and evolution. Professor Trinh Xuan Thuan has written several books destined for the general public, in particular, *The Secret Melody* (Oxford University Press, 1994); *The Birth of the Universe* (Discoveries, HN Abrams, 1993); and *Chaos and Harmony* (Oxford University Press, 2000) — all best-sellers in France, in which he discusses the profound changes in world view brought about by modern scientific discoveries. His recent book, *The Quantum and the Lotus* (Crown), coauthored with French Buddhist monk Matthieu Ricard, also a bestseller in France, appeared in December 2001. In it, Professor Thuan explores the many remarkable connections between the ancient teachings of Buddhism and the findings of modern science.

CHARLES H. TOWNES, PHD, is a professor in the graduate school at the University of California, Berkeley, and a Nobel Prize recipient in physics. He has published articles about science and theology. Dr. Townes's research was primarily responsible for the development of the laser.

LYNN G. UNDERWOOD, PHD, is vice president of the Fetzer Institute, a nonprofit private foundation. She received her doctorate in epidemiology from Queen's University School of Medicine in the United Kingdom following medical studies at the University of Iowa School of Medicine. A veteran of ten years in the field of cancer epidemiology doing research into pathogenesis, prevention, and early decision, she co-edited *Measuring Success*, a text intended as a tool to help in study designs examining the interface between stress and health. Dr. Underwood has led the development of various workshops with NIH, NHLBI, and NIA, as well as Fetzer-sponsored funding initiatives. Her current research interests include investigating the role of various dimensions of religiousness and spirituality in living with disability.

J. WENTZEL VAN HUYSSTEEN, DTH, is James McCord Professor of Theology and Science at Princeton Theological Seminary. Dr. van Huyssteen specializes in the philosophy of science and religious epistemology. He has written many papers, and his influential books include *Duet or Duel? Theology and Science in a Postmodern World* (Trinity, 1998); *The Shaping of Rationality: Toward Interdisciplinarity in Theology and Science* (Eerdmans, 1999); and is an editor of the *Encyclopedia of Science and Religion* (2003). Dr. van Huyssteen is a member of the advisory board of the International Center for Fundamental Research in Modern Culture (St. Petersburg, Russia). Since 1992, he has served on the steering committee of the American Academy of Religion's Theology and Science Section and is the chair of the International Committee for the Assessment of Theological Research. He is also an ordained minister in the Dutch Reformed Church.

HOWARD J. VAN TILL, PHD, professor emeritus of physics and astronomy at Calvin College, Michigan, is a member of the American Astronomical Society and the American Scientific Affiliation. Dr. Van Till obtained his BS from Calvin College and his PhD in physics from Michigan State University. He is the author of numerous books, essays, and articles addressing creation and cosmology from a Christian perspective including *The Fourth Day* (Eerdmans, 1986) and editor/coauthor of *Science Held Hostage* (InterVarsity Press, 1988) and *Portraits of Creation* (Eerdmans, 1990). In 1999 he received the Faith and Learning Award from the Calvin Alumni Association.

JUDITH B. WATSON, a graduate of Wellesley College, has master's degrees from Case Western Reserve University in social work administration and in biomedical ethics. She practiced social work as a counselor and advocate for handicapped children and their parents. As a staff member of her church, she developed community awareness and outreach programs. Her current volunteer activities include membership on the vestry, executive, and rector search committees of her parish. In addition, she is a member and immediate past president of the board of Hanna Perkins Center, which provides lay child analyst training in the United States and abroad, school and therapy programs for children, and research and consultation in child development and education. Her work in bioethics focused on gerontology, especially late life and end-of-life healthcare choices.

RICHARD T. WATSON is senior partner of a law firm in Cleveland, Ohio, in the fields of tax, business, financial, and philanthropic planning for family groups and their related business enterprises. A graduate of Harvard College and Harvard Law School, he currently serves as a trustee of Case Western Reserve University and the Cleveland Museum of Arts, as well as chancellor of the Episcopal Diocese of Ohio. He is a member of Harvard University's Committee on University Resources and of the Visiting Committee of Harvard Divinity School.

EVERETT L. WORTHINGTON JR., PhD, is a professor of psychology at Virginia Commonwealth University and executive director of A Campaign for Forgiveness Research. Dr. Worthington conducts research in forgiveness and reconciliation, religious values within the family and psychological interventions, marital and family dynamics and counseling. He has published over one hundred and fifty articles and chapters and eighteen books in these areas.

ADRIAN WYARD is founder of the Counterbalance Foundation. Mr. Wyard studied computer science at Reading Tech in the United Kingdom and, after serving as the program manager for Microsoft Word, held various positions within that company, specializing in advanced functional and visual design. He holds several design patents. After leaving Microsoft, he formed the Counterbalance Foundation in 1996. The foundation promotes interdisciplinary education and specializes in the development of interactive teaching materials aimed at an undergraduate and popular audience. Mr. Wyard serves on the boards of the Center for Theology and the Natural Sciences, and Science and Spirit Resources, Inc.

EURASIA/AUSTRALIA

KAREN ARMSTRONG, PhD, spent seven years as a Roman Catholic nun, received her degree from Oxford University, taught modern literature at the University of London, and presently teaches at the Leo Baeck College for the Study of Judaism. She is one of the foremost British commentators on religious affairs. Dr. Armstrong is an honorary member of the Association of Muslim Social Scientists. Some of her books include: *Islam: A Short History*; *A History of God: The 4000-Year Quest of Judaism, Christianity and Islam*; *Jerusalem: One City, Three Faiths*; and *In the Beginning: A New Interpretation of Genesis*. She is also a regular contributor of reviews and articles in newspapers and journals.

M. A. ZAKI BADAWI, PhD, is principal of the Muslim College in London. He is chairman of the UK Imams and Mosques Council and the UK Muslim Law (Shariah) Council. He is a lecturer at Al-Azhar University, Cairo. Dr. Badawi frequently writes and broadcasts on Muslim affairs.

JOHN D. BARROW, DPhil, is professor of mathematical sciences and director of the Millennium Mathematics Project in the Department of Applied

Mathematical and Theoretical Physics at the University of Cambridge; he is a fellow of Clare Hall College. A leading researcher in cosmology and a well-known communicator of science, he has written over three hundred papers and thirteen books, including *Theories of Everything*, *Pi in the Sky*, *The Left Hand of Creation*, *The Origin of the Universe*, *The Anthropic Cosmological Principle*, *The World Within the World*, *Between Inner Space and Outer Space*, *The Artful Universe*, and *Impossibility: The Book of Nothing*. He received the Locker Award for Astronomy and the 1999 Kelvin Medal.

R. J. BERRY is a professor of genetics at University College London. He was previously the president of several ecological organizations and of the Research Scientists' Christian Fellowship (now Christians in Science). He is currently chairman of the Environmental Issues Network of CTBI. Professor Berry has lectured and published extensively about protection of the environment.

PAUL C. DAVIES, PHD, is professor of natural philosophy in the Australian Centre for Astrobiology at Macquarie University. His research has spanned the fields of cosmology, gravitation, and quantum field theory, with particular emphasis on black holes and the origin of the universe. He is currently working on the problem of the origin of life and the search for life on Mars. He is a well-known author, broadcaster, and public lecturer and has written over twenty-five books. Among his better-known works are *God and the New Physics*, *The Mind of God*, *About Time*, *The Fifth Miracle*, and *How to Build a Time Machine*. In recognition of his work as an author, he was elected as fellow of The Royal Society of Literature in 1999. His contributions to science have been recognized by numerous awards, including the 2002 Michael Faraday Prize by the Royal Society and the 2001 Kelvin Medal and Prize from the UK Institute of Physics. His most significant award was the 1995 Templeton Prize for Progress in Religion.

CELIA DEANE-DRUMMOND, PHD, is the director of the Centre for Religion and the Biosciences at Chester College. Dr. Deane-Drummond received a doctorate in plant physiology from Reading University. She has held post-doctoral fellowships at UBC (Canada) and Cambridge before accepting a teaching post in the botany department at Durham University. After receiving a doctorate in theology from Manchester University, Dr. Deane-Drummond took up a teaching post at Chester College. Her research has focused particularly on the interrelationship between Christian theology and the biological sciences, for which she received a personal chair in 2000. She has published numerous articles, chapters in books, and books in that field. She is coeditor of *Reordering Nature: Theology, Society and the New Genetics* as well as editor of *Brave New World: Theology, Ethics and the Human Genome*, published in 2003.

NOAH J. EFRON, PhD, is chairman of the Graduate Program for the History and Philosophy of Science at Bar Ilan University, where he specializes in Jewish attitudes towards nature and science. Dr. Efron received a grant from the John Templeton Foundation for research, writing, and publication of a book, *Golem, God and Man: Human and Divine in the Age of Biotechnology*, exploring the constructive interaction of science and religion, which he is presently writing. He has been a fellow at the Massachusetts Institute of Technology and at Harvard University. His book *Real Jews*, about religion in Israel, was published by Basic Books in 2003. Dr. Efron has been awarded grants from the National Endowment for the Humanities and the Mellon, Rothschild, and Thomas J. Watson Foundation, as well as the Israeli Academy for Higher Education. He is a founding member of the International Society for Science and Religion.

GEORGE F. R. ELLIS, PhD, is visiting lecturer and professor in cosmology, physics, and astronomy across the globe, including South Africa, England, Germany, Canada, Italy, and the United States. He received his PhD in applied mathematics and theoretical physics from St. John's College at Cambridge, is a fellow of the Royal Society of South Africa, and was president of the International Society of Relativity and Gravitation. Dr. Ellis is coauthor of *On the Moral Nature of the Universe: Theology, Cosmology, and Ethics* with Dr. Nancey Murphy, and has collaborated with Stephen Hawking on a number of publications, including *The Large Scale Structure of Space-Time*, and is the editor of *The Far-Future Universe: Eschatology from a Cosmic Perspective*. Professor Ellis was awarded the Star of South Africa Medal (nonmilitary) by President Nelson Mandela at the National Honours Ceremony held in Pretoria in June 1999. Dr. Ellis was the recipient of the 2004 Templeton Prize.

NIELS HENRIK GREGERSEN, PhD, is associate professor of systematic theology on the faculty of theology at the University of Aarhus and is an ordained minister of the Evangelical-Lutheran Church of Denmark. Dr.

Gregersen graduated from the Haderslev Cathedral School and the University of Copenhagen, where he earned his doctorate. For the past six years, in addition to teaching and writing, he has served as assistant pastor of the university's Church of St. John. The author of three books and more than fifty major articles, Dr. Gregersen serves as vice president of the European Society for the Study of Science and Theology and as a member of the Theological Commission of the Church of Denmark's Council on Inter-Church Relations. He has also been a leader in the Danish Forum for Science and Theology. Dr. Gregersen was awarded a Templeton Foundation research grant for exploring the constructive interaction of science and religion.

BRUNO GUIDERDONI, PhD, is an astrophysicist at the French National Center for Scientific Research (CNRS). His research field at the Paris Institute of Astrophysics is mainly related to galaxy formation. Since 1993, he has been in charge of the weekly TV show Knowing Islam of the state channel France 2. In his papers and lectures, he attempts to present the intellectual and spiritual aspects of Islam, to reflect upon the relation between science and the Islamic tradition, and to promote an interreligious dialogue.

MICHAEL HELLER, PhD, is professor of philosophy at the Pontifical Academy of Theology in Krakow, Poland, and is an adjunct member of the Vatican Observatory staff. A Roman Catholic priest, Dr. Heller was ordained in 1959. He graduated from Catholic University of Dublin, where he earned a master's degree in philosophy in 1965, and a doctorate in cosmology in 1966. After beginning his teaching career at the Institute of Theology in Tarnow, he joined the faculty of the Pontifical Academy of Theology in 1972 and was appointed to a full professorship in 1985. He twice held the Lemaitre Chair at Catholic University of Louvain, Belgium. Dr. Heller is an ordinary member of the Pontifical Academy of Sciences in Rome, a founding member of the International Society for Science and Religion, and a member of several other international societies. His current research is concerned with the singularity problem in relativistic cosmology and the application of noncommutative geometry to physics and cosmology. The list of his publications contains more than eight hundred entries, including nearly three hundred research papers in physics, cosmology, philosophy of science, and the history of science. He is also the author of more than twenty books, the most recent being Creative Tension: Essays on Science and Religion (2003), Is Physics an Art? (1998) and The Meaning of Life and of the Universe (2002).

PETER E. HODGSON, PHD, is head of the Nuclear Physics Theoretical Group, Nuclear Physics Laboratory, Oxford, and is a senior research fellow at Corpus Christi College. He has published widely on the subject of the future effect of nuclear energy applications as well as in the area of Christianity and science.

MAX JAMMER, PHD, is professor emeritus of physics and former president of Bar-Ilan University. Dr. Jammer earned his doctorate in experimental physics before attending Harvard University for postdoctoral research. He later received an appointment as lecturer at Harvard. Dr. Jammer cofounded the Institute for Philosophy of Science at Tel-Aviv University. He has served as president of the Association for the Advancement of Science in Israel. Dr. Jammer has received both the Monograph Prize of the American Academy of Arts and Sciences and the prestigious Israel Prize. His recent works include: *Concepts of Mass in Classical and Modern Physics* (1997); *Einstein and Religion* (1999); and *Concepts of Mass in Contemporary Physics and Philosophy* (2000). He is also the author of numerous scientific papers in professional journals. Dr. Jammer is a member of the New York Academy of Science and the Académie Internationale d'Histoire des Sciences (Paris).

MALCOLM JEEVES, PHD, research professor of psychology, University of St. Andrews, is president of the Royal Society of Edinburgh and was made Commander of the Order of the British Empire in 1992 for his services to science and to psychology in Britain. He established the department of psychology at St. Andrews University and his research interests center around cognitive psychology and neuropsychology.

ARGYRIS NICOLAIDIS, PHD, is professor of theoretical physics at the Aristotle University of Thessaloniki. His scientific work is centered on phenomenology of particle interactions, neutrino astrophysics, and extra dimensions of space. He received the Empirikion Award for Natural Sciences (1988) and was Fulbright Scholar of the Year in 1995. Dr. Nicolaidis is a member of the scientific council of NESTOR (Institute of Deep Sea Research and Technology and Astroparticle Neutrino Physics). He is the coordinator of the project Cosmos in Science and Religion and is the coorganizer of conferences and expositions on topics concerning the interface of science, philosophy, and religion.

STEPHEN ORCHARD, MA, PHD, is director of the Christian Education Movement and a minister of the United Reform Church. He previously served as an assistant general secretary of the British Council of Churches with responsibility for community affairs and on the ethics committee of SmithKline Beecham. His publications include *Our Commonwealth — A Christian View of Taxation* (1987). He is the editor of *REToday* and serves as a director and vice-chairman of the United Kingdom Temperance Alliance Ltd. Dr. Orchard is chairman of the United Reform Church History Society and of the British and Foreign School Society. He is also a governor of Westminster College, Cambridge, and the Cheshunt Foundation.

ARTHUR R. PEACOCKE, MBE, DD, DSc, is warden-emeritus of the Society of Ordained Scientists and honorable chaplain of Christ Church Cathedral, Oxford. He is also the former director of the Ian Ramsey Center for the Interdisciplinary Study of Religious Beliefs in Relation to the Sciences, including medicine. Rev. Dr. Peacocke has been the recipient of the Le Compte du Nouy Prize; his primary discipline is the physical chemistry of biological systems. A 1993 Gifford lecturer, he has pursued his dual calling through lectures, seminars, and writing, publishing *God and the New Biology*; *Theology for a Scientific Age*; *From DNA to DEAN*; *God and Science: A Quest for Christian Credibility*; and his latest book, *Paths from Science Towards God: The End of All Our Exploring*. Dr. Peacocke was the 2001 recipient of the Templeton Prize for Progress in Religion.

JOHN C. POLKINGHORNE, PHD, president emeritus of Queens' College, Cambridge, is a member of the Church of England Doctrine Committee and General Synod. Former professor of applied physics at Cambridge, he has published many papers on theoretical elementary particle physics. Among his science and religion books are *The God of Hope and the End of the world*; *Science and Theology: An Introduction*; *Faith, Science and Understanding*; and *Faith of a Physicist*. Rev. Polkinghorne was the recipient of the 2002 Templeton Prize.

F. RUSSELL STANNARD, PHD, is emeritus professor of physics at the Open University, United Kingdom. He was formerly vice-president of the Institute of Physics and trustee of the John Templeton Foundation. Professor Stannard has authored the popular Uncle Albert series, introducing modern physics to young children. Among his books on science and religion is *The God Experiment*, based on his Gifford lectures.

JEAN STAUNE, PHD, is assistant professor in philosophy of science in the MBA section of HEC Paris; he has several degrees from French universities and grandes ecoles in philosophy of science, human paleontology, computer science, mathematics, economy, and management. Dr. Staune is the founder and general secretary of the Interdisciplinary University of Paris (IUP), which has organized some of the most important meetings in science and religion in Europe. He is the director of the series of books Le temps des Sciences at Editions Fayard (Hachette Group). His current research concerns the meeting point between contemporary discoveries in physics, astronomy, mathematics, biology, neurology, and the probability of the existence of God.

KEITH WARD, PHD, is regius professor of divinity at the University of Oxford and was professor of history and philosophy of religion at King's College, London University. He is one of the country's foremost writers on comparative religion and Christian issues. His numerous books focus on a variety of theological issues, and among his works are *God: A Guide for the Perplexed; Images of Eternity; God, Chance and Necessity; Defending the Soul;* and his monumental comparative theology *Religion and Revelation.*

MICHAEL WELKER, DTHEOL, DPHIL, is chair for systematic theology at the University of Heidelberg, Germany. Dr. Welker was a professor at the universities of Tübingen and Munster before he took his chair position in 1991. Since 1996, he has also been the director of the Internationales Wissenschaftsforum der Universitat Heidelberg, a center for international and interdisciplinary research. He received a DTheol (Tübingen) and a DPhil (Heidelberg). Dr. Welker was a guest professor in North America (McMaster University, Princeton Theological Seminary, and Harvard Divinity School) and a senior consultant scholar at the Center of Theological Inquiry, Princeton. He is the author of about 180 articles in academic books and journals and the author, editor, or coeditor of 25 books.

ANTON ZEILINGER, PHD, is professor of physics, University of Vienna, Austria. Professor Zeilinger is currently director of the Institute of Experimental Physics at the University of Vienna. He is interested in the experimental and philosophical foundations of quantum physics. Dr. Zeilinger has held positions at the Massachusetts Institute of Technology, the Technical University of Munich, and the College de France, to name a few. His numerous honors include the Orden Pour le Mérite, the Visionary of the Year Prize 2001, the World Future Award 2001, and the Erwin Wenzl Prize.

JOSEPH ZYCINSKI, PHD, is professor of philosophy at the Catholic University of Lublin, Poland; chair of the relationship between science and religion; archbishop of Lublin; and grand chancellor of the Catholic University of Lublin. He has written more than 350 scholarly papers that have been published in *Zygon*; *British Journal for the Philosophy of Science*; *The Review of Metaphysics*; *Logos: A Journal of Catholic Thought and Culture*; and *Philosophy in Science, Cultures, and Faith*. He is the author of nearly forty books in philosophy of science, relativistic cosmology, history of the relationship between natural sciences, and Christian faith.

Trustees and Members of the John Templeton Foundation, 2000–2003

TRUSTEES

Sir John Templeton
John M. Templeton Jr.
John D. Barrow
Ann Cameron
Paul C. Davies
Heather E. Dill
George H. Gallup Jr.
Owen Gingerich
Robert L. Herrmann
Harold G. Koenig
Glenn R. Mosley
David G. Myers
Jennifer Templeton
Anne D. Zimmerman

MEMBERS

Baba Amte
Pandurangshastri Athavale
Ian G. Barbour
Connie Fillmore Bazzy
L. Charles Birch
John Blundell

Michael Bourdeaux
Wendy Brooks
Amy Van Hoose Butler
Ann Cameron
Douglas Cameron
Leigh Cameron
Robert Handly Cameron
Alejandro A. Chafuen
Paul C. Davies
Ramon P. Diaz
Heather E. Dill
Jeffrey S. Dill
Freeman J. Dyson
Edwin J. Feulner
Charles R. Fillmore
Wilhelmina Griffiths
Kyung-Chik Han
Robert L. Herrmann
Colin Humphreys
Stanley L. Jaki
Benjamin D. Juday
Jennifer "Jenna" Cameron Juday
Elizabeth Kernan
Josh Kernan

Avery Lloyd
W. David Lloyd
Chiara Lubich
Glenn R. Mosley
Donald W. Munro
Michael Novak
Arthur R. Peacocke
John C. Polkinghorne
Colin A. Russell
Anne Rymer
Pascal Salin
Eric Henry Sanders
Lise Shapiro Sanders
Cicely Saunders
Frances Schapperle
Roger Schutz-Marsauche
Jill Sideman
Richard Sideman
Robert A. Sirico
Marie E. Souder
F. Russell Stannard
Sigmund Sternberg
Renee Dawn Stirling
Christopher W. Templeton

Handly Templeton
Harvey M. Templeton Jr.
Harvey M. Templeton III
Jennifer A. Templeton
Jewel Templeton
Sir John M. Templeton
John M. Templeton Jr.
Josephine Templeton
Lauren Templeton
Leslie A. Templeton
Rebecca L. Templeton
Rebecca M. Templeton
Thomas F. Torrance
Stamps Transou
Mary P. Walker
Christian Watrin
Carl Friedrich von Weizsäcker
Linford G. Williams
Anne D. Zimmerman
Gail Zimmerman
Michael D. Zimmerman
Mitchell Dean Zimmerman
Rhonda Sue Zimmerman-
    Durdahl

Recipients of the Templeton Prize
for Progress in Religion

1973   Mother Teresa of Calcutta, founder of the Missionaries of Charity. She saw Christ in the "poorest of the poor" in what has become a worldwide ministry to the dying.

1974   Brother Roger, founder and prior of the Taizé Community in France. Taizé communes have appeared all over the world, bridging the gap between many denominations and languages.

1975   Sir Sarvepalli Radhakrishnan, who was president of India and an Oxford professor of Eastern religions and ethics. A strong proponent of religious idealism as the most hopeful political instrument for peace.

1976   His Eminence Leon Joseph Cardinal Suenens, who was archbishop of Malines-Brussels. A pioneer of charismatic renewal and a strong proponent of Christian unity.

1977   Chiara Lubich, founder of the Focolare Movement in Italy, which has become a worldwide network of more than a million people in communes and private homes engaged in spiritual renewal and ecumenism.

1978   The Very Rev. Dr. Thomas F. Torrance, who was moderator of the Church of Scotland. A leader in the new understanding of convergence of theology and science.

1979   The Rev. Nikkyo Niwano, founder of Rissho Kosei-Kai and the World Conference on Religion and Peace, Kyoto, Japan. A Buddhist world leader in efforts toward peace and understanding among religious groups.

1980   Dr. Ralph Wendell Burhoe, founder and former editor of *Zygon: Journal of Religion and Science*, Chicago, Illinois. A leading advocate on an intellectually credible synthesis of the religious and scientific traditions.

1981   Dame Cicely Saunders, originator of the modern hospice movement, England. Pioneer in the care of the terminally ill by emphasizing spiritual growth and modern methods of pain management.

1982   The Rev. Dr. Billy Graham, founder of the Billy Graham Evangelistic Association, Charlotte, North Carolina. He has preached the Christian gospel in more than fifty countries, brought diverse denominations together, and promoted respect for all peoples.

1983   Mr. Aleksandr Solzhenitsyn, Russia. Historical writer and novelist who has been an outspoken critic of totalitarianism and a strong proponent of spiritual awakening in the democracies as well.

1984   The Rev. Michael Bourdeaux, founder of Keston College, England, a research center for the study of religion in Communist countries. He has been a fearless supporter of Christians in Russia.

1985   Sir Alister Hardy, who was founder of the Sir Alister Hardy Research Centre at Oxford, England. An outstanding biologist, he also had a deep interest in man's spiritual nature. His work has demonstrated widespread religious experience in the British Isles.

1986   The Rev. Dr. James I. McCord, who was chancellor of the Center of Theological Inquiry, Princeton, New Jersey. A leader in spiritual education as president of Princeton Theological Seminary.

1987   The Rev. Dr. Stanley L. Jaki, OSB, professor of history and philosophy of science at Seton Hall University, New Jersey. His reinterpretation of the history of science provides a context for renewed belief in God in a scientific age.

1988   Dr. Inamullah Khan, secretary general of the World Muslim Congress, Karachi, Pakistan. Proponent of peace within and between the world religions.

1989   The Very Rev. The Lord MacLeod of the Iona Community, Scotland. A leader for spiritual renewal in the Church of Scotland.
        Jointly with
        Dr. Carl Friedrich von Weizsäcker of Starnberg, West Germany. Physicist and philosopher, a strong voice for dialogue between science and theology.

1990   Baba Amte, India. A learned Hindu scholar and philanthropist who has relieved the poverty of millions in rural India.
        Jointly with
        Dr. L. Charles Birch, Sydney, Australia. Molecular biologist and strong proponent of process theology and environmental stewardship.

1991   The Rt. Hon. The Lord Jakobovits, London. The chief rabbi of Great Britain and the Commonwealth, a leader in Jewish concern for medicine and especially medical ethics.

1992   The Rev. Dr. Kyung-Chik Han, Korea. Pioneer in helping the Presbyterian Church in Korea to become in only thirty years the largest Presbyterian denomination on Earth.

1993   Mr. Charles W. Colson, founder of Prison Fellowship, Washington, D.C. A strong Christian force for change in the American prison system.

1994   Dr. Michael Novak, historical and theological scholar at the American Enterprise Institute for Public Policy, Washington, D.C. A powerful voice for reemphasis of our rich religious and philosophical traditions.

1995   Dr. Paul C. Davies, currently professor of natural philosophy in the Australian Centre for Astrobiology at Macquarie University, Australia. He is a leading authority in expounding the idea of purpose in the universe and author of more than twenty books.

1996   Dr. William R. Bright, president and founder of Campus Crusade for Christ International, Orlando, Florida.

1997   Sri Pandurang Shastri Athavale, founder and leader of the Swadhyaya movement, a spiritual self-knowledge movement in India that has liberated millions from the shackles of poverty and moral dissipation.

1998   Sir Sigmund Sternberg, a Hungarian-born British philanthropist and businessman, has become an "interfaith ambassador," working to resolve conflicts within and between religions. He helped make the first papal visit to a synagogue possible.

1999   Dr. Ian G. Barbour, until his retirement professor of religion and professor of science, technology, and society at Carleton College, Northfield, Minnesota. Pioneer in the integration of science and religion.

2000   Mr. Freeman J. Dyson, physicist and professor emeritus of the Institute for Advanced Studies, Princeton, New Jersey.

2001   The Rev. Canon Dr. Arthur R. Peacocke, biochemist and warden-emeritus of the Society of Ordained Scientists and honorable chaplain of Church of Christ Cathedral, Oxford.

2002   The Rev. Dr. John C. Polkinghorne, FRS, president emeritus of Queens' College, Cambridge. Physicist and Anglican priest, former professor of applied physics at Cambridge.

2003   The Rev. Dr. Holmes Rolston III, university distinguished professor of philosophy at Colorado State University, a minister of the Presbyterian Church, and an environmental ethicist.

2004   Dr. George F. R. Ellis, professor of applied mathematics at the University of Cape Town and leading theoretical cosmologist, specializes in general relativity.

Examples of Programs
of the John Templeton Foundation

Study of the Therapeutic Effects of Intercessory
Prayer: A Replication and Expansion Study
Mind/Body Medical Institute
Project Director, Herbert Benson, MD
Funding for a scientifically rigorous replication of the original intercessory
prayer study performed by R. C. Byrd in 1988 which will now include the
relaxation response, a larger number of participants, the administering of
psychological and social questionnaires, and will take place over the course
of two years instead of one.

Pascal Centre Bibliographic Database
Pascal Centre, Redeemer College
Project Director, Dr. Jitse van der Meer
A database to stimulate worldwide research and teaching in the field of sci-
ence and religion by providing online access to comprehensive and contin-
ually updated bibliographic information.

Templeton Project for
Science and Religion in Schools
Millwood Education Trust
Project Director, Martin Rogers
The purpose of this project is to make a major impact on the teaching of
issues concerning science and religion in schools (11 to 18 years). The object
is to ensure that students in this age range are well informed, have a balanced view of the science and religion debate, and study both subjects with
open-minded humility.

Family Spiritual Values in the Transition from Adolescence to Young Adulthood

Medical College of Virginia

Project Director, Dr. Lindon J. Eaves

Research to analyze the protective role of family spiritual values in the healthy transition from adolescence to young adulthood. The study focuses on the interaction between genetic risk and environmental protection in the use and abuse of alcohol.

Templeton Research Lectures on the Constructive Engagement of Science and Religion

Philadelphia Center for Religion and Science

Project Director, William Grassie, PhD

Program to promote interdisciplinary research, dialogue, and publication on the constructive engagement of science and religion through the development of a high quality, distinguished lectureship program.

Science and Religion Local Societies Program

Philadelphia Center for Religion and Science

Project Director, William Grassie, PhD

Program to establish two hundred local societies in cities, colleges, universities, and in select large seminaries throughout the United States, Canada, the United Kingdom, Australia, and New Zealand.

Metanexus

Philadelphia Center for Religion and Science

Project Director, William Grassie, PhD

Support to improve and expand the operations, services, and outreach of Meta — an international moderated list server on science and religion.

Spiritual Transformation Research Program

Philadelphia Center for Religion and Science

Project Director, William Grassie, PhD

This grant outlines the goals, objectives, and structure for a research program designed to investigate the principles of spiritual transformation, to include multiple factors/themes of research.

ULTIMATE REALITY SYMPOSIUM AND BOOK PROJECT
Philadelphia Center for Religion and Science
Project Director, William Grassie, PhD
Support for the Wheeler Symposium on Science and Ultimate Reality on March 15–18, 2002. This conference commemorated John Archibald Wheeler's legacy of cosmological innovation and its future development in the growth of twenty-first-century science. The grant will also fund a book project of thirty world-class leaders in physics and cosmology and related metaphysical issues touching the field of science and religion in the topical area of research on ultimate reality.

EXPANSION GRANT
Philadelphia Center for Religion and Science
Project Director, William Grassie, PhD
PCRS will primarily serve the Foundation in expanded outreach of scholarly networking, program development, and implementation and management of select projects.

SCIENCE AND THEOLOGY NEWS
Research News Corporation, Inc.
Project Director, Harold Koenig, MD
A John Templeton Foundation newspaper publication that serves to stimulate communication, dialogue, and research in the field of science and theology.

SCIENCE & SPIRIT MAGAZINE: 1998–2002
Editor, Jennifer Derryberry
International, interdisciplinary magazine that provides information about the fields of science, religion, and spirituality. Articles focus on the work of the Foundation, its sponsored organizations and programs, and the societies and professional organizations working to expand research in these disciplines.

INSTITUTE FOR RESEARCH ON UNLIMITED LOVE
Project Director, Dr. Stephen G. Post
The Institute was founded to explore the area of study that Sir John Templeton named "Unlimited Love." By funding research into unlimited love and encouraging scholarship in this area, it is intended that this will become a new and respected field of study within the mainstream scientific community.

NATIONAL CONFERENCE ON RELIGION AND
SCIENCE/CENTER FOR COMPARATIVE RELIGIOUS STUDIES
Universitas Gadjah Mada
Project Director, Dr. Achmad Mursvidi
A three-year program leading to a National Conference on Religion and Science held in the fall of 2002 at Gadjah Mada University in Indonesia. The purpose of the conference was to initiate a new educational program in religion and science on a national level.

PERSPECTIVES AND DIMENSIONS OF GRATITUDE
University of California, Davis
Project Director, Robert A. Emmons, PhD
The goal of this research is to create and disseminate a large body of novel scientific data on the nature of gratitude, its causes, and its potential consequences for human health and well-being. The intention is to conduct at least ten studies over the course of three and one-half years.

FORGIVENESS, HUMILITY, AND GRATITUDE
IN RECENTLY MARRIED COUPLES: AN INTERVENTION
STUDY OF SOME IMPORTANT LAWS OF LIFE
Virginia Commonwealth University
Project Director, Everett L. Worthington Jr., PhD
Three-year forgiveness study on marriage examines psychological processes underlying responses to forgiveness-inducing interventions with 210 newly married couples.

POWER OF PURPOSE ESSAY CONTEST
Lionheart Books, Ltd.
Project Director, Michael Reagan
The Power of Purpose Essay Contest will solicit essays from a wide variety of people around the world who will write about the power of purpose, ranging from scientific, religious, and public policy perspectives to inspiring stories of life experience that illustrate the beneficial effects of constructive purpose. The emphasis will be on the idea of "noble" or "spiritual" purpose. Prizes amounting to $500,000 will be awarded and winning essays will be published in a leading news magazine.

Expanding the Pathway to Peace through Conflict: 2001–2004
Association of Unity Churches
Project Director, Rev. Glenn R. Mosley, PhD
This peacemaking project teaches community leaders how to embrace conflict as a pathway to peace. It offers clarity and cohesiveness throughout the church community.

2003 Templeton Prize for Progress Toward Research or Discoveries about Spiritual Realities
Davidson College
Project Director, Rev. Dr. Holmes Rolston III
Established in 1972, this annual award is presented to a person who has shown extraordinary originality in advancing humankind's understanding of God. Holmes Rolston III, professor of philosophy at Colorado State University, whose thirty years of research, writing, and lecturing on the religious imperative to respect nature have established the field of environmental ethics, has been named the 2003 Templeton Prize laureate. The prize, valued at more than one million dollars, was announced in March 2003 at a news conference at the Church Center for the United Nations in New York.

Maximize the Moment Program
Ethics Resource Center
Project Director, Dr. Patricia J. Harned
Two-year grant to provide weekly maxims-based announcement and discussion materials, introducing current issues, moral dilemmas, and discussion of ethical decision making in schools throughout the United States.

Is Capitalism Good for the Poor?
Foundation for Teaching Economics
Project Director, James R. Klauder
This project will create a set of classroom-ready materials and lesson plans for high school history, social studies, and economics teachers. This unit will give teachers a tool to help in their teaching about the values promoted by capitalism and about the innate fairness of capitalism.

RELIGION, POLITICAL ECONOMY, AND SOCIETY
Harvard University
Project Director, Prof. Robert J. Barro
Research project on the role of religion in the economic, political, and social development of nations and individuals.

EXPLORING THE TRENDS, PATTERNS AND PRINCIPLES OF SPIRITUAL GROWTH DURING THE COLLEGE YEARS
Higher Education Research Institute
Project Director, Alexander W. Astin
To establish a flagship research program to generate and strategically disseminate new spiritual information on the trends, patterns, and principles of spiritual growth during the college years.

WEB-BASED INTERACTIVE GLOBAL BUSINESS ETHICS CURRICULUM AND ANNUAL GLOBAL BUSINESS COMPETITION
Junior Achievement International
Project Director, Sam Taylor
Project for the development of a Web-based interactive global business ethics curriculum and annual global business ethics competition for Junior Achievement International. The ultimate goal of this two-part program is to encourage young people around the world to make conscientious, ethical business decisions by taking into consideration their responsibilities to their communities and to global society as a whole.

THE DEVELOPMENT OF PURPOSE IN THE LIVES OF YOUNG PEOPLE: A SCIENTIFIC EXAMINATION
Stanford University
Project Director, William Damon, PhD
This grant aims to discover how young people can acquire a sense of noble purpose in today's world. The study examines the social, cultural, and educational conditions that promote a sense of purpose, and will determine the extent to which these conditions are present or absent in today's world for diverse segments of the youth population.

PRIVATE SCHOOLS SERVING THE EDUCATIONAL NEEDS OF THE
POOR: A GLOBAL RESEARCH AND DISSEMINATION PROJECT
University of Newcastle
Project Director, James Tooley, PhD
This project aims to increase scholarly understanding and raise popular
awareness of the ways in which the educational needs and aspirations of the
poor in developing countries are served by free enterprise. The focus is on
the widespread but little understood phenomenon of private schools providing educational opportunities for the poor.

PROGRAM OF DIALOGUE ON SCIENCE, ETHICS, AND RELIGION
American Association for the Advancement of Science
Project Director, Dr. Audrey Chapman
Four-year program support that will include, in full or in part, outreach to
professional scientific organizations and societies; a public lecture series; a
series of research seminars on "What is life?"; a research seminar on order,
purpose, design, and directionality in nature; a public forum on intelligent
design; and a public conference on what it means to be human.

TEMPLETON/ASA LECTURE SERIES: 2001–2003
American Scientific Affiliation
Project Director, Donald W. Munroe, PhD
Two-year renewal support of the Templeton/ASA Lecture Series. The purpose of the series is to increase the value of the Templeton Science and Religion Course awards by enhancing the content of the local course, allowing
the course recipients to impact the whole college, university, or seminary
campus.

INTERNATIONAL SOCIETY FOR SCIENCE
AND RELIGION (ISSR) ADMINISTRATIVE OFFICE
Cambridge in America
Project Director, Kim McCann
Establishment of an International Society for Science and Religion (ISSR)
office. The society will foster and promote rigorous interdisciplinary
research and education relating to science and religion, conducted in an
international and multi-faith context.

SCIENCE AND THE SPIRITUAL QUEST II
Center for Theology and the Natural Sciences
Project Director, Dr. Philip Clayton
Support for a second major interdisciplinary conference outreach based on the proven success of the initial SSQ project. The SSQII program initiatives include: a) nine workshops involving sixty world renowned scientists; b) two major conferences, one in Boston and another in Paris; c) a one-day public event in the Silicon Valley with presentations by SSQI scientists; d) three international symposia held at major universities in Israel, India, and Japan; and e) publicity through news coverage and feature articles in magazines, books, and electronic media.

THE JOHN TEMPLETON OXFORD SEMINARS ON SCIENCE AND CHRISTIANITY: 2003–2005
Council for Christian Colleges and Universities
Project Director, Robert C. Andringa, PhD
Support for a second round of the John Templeton Oxford Seminars in Science and Christianity for 2003–2005, with a planning grant for 2002. The seminars will promote research and discussion on important issues regarding science and faith and will be held at Wycliffe Hall, Oxford, during the summers of 2003, 2004, and 2005.

IMPACT OF RELIGION AND SPIRITUALITY ON HEALTH SERVICE USE
Duke University Medical Center
Project Director, Harold Koenig, MD
Comprehensive four-year study to determine the impact of religion and spirituality on health service use during the year following hospitalization for acute medical illness. Research began August 1998. NIHR/ICIHS will assist with publicizing the results through press conferences, symposia at national meetings, and NIHR/ICIHS speakers bureau.

FIVE-YEAR POST-DOC RESEARCH FELLOWSHIP IN RELIGION/SPIRITUALITY AND HEALTH
Duke University Medical Center
Project Director, Harold Koenig, MD
Support for a five-year post-doctoral research fellowship program at Duke University Medical Center. During this time, Duke will train eight young

scientists to become leading researchers and academicians in the field of religion and health.

Spirituality and Medicine Curricular Awards, Compendium of Outstanding Curricula, and GWish Exhibit for AAMC Annual Meeting

George Washington Institute for Spirituality and Health
Project Director, Christine Puchalski, MD
Support for three programs at the new Institute for Spirituality and Health at George Washington University, including education in compassionate care, the John Templeton Spirituality and Medicine Curricular Awards, and a Compendum of Outstanding Curricula.

Spirituality and Health Education: Awards, Evaluation, and Development

George Washington Institute for Spirituality and Health
Project Director, Christine Puchalski, MD
This grant, a result of merging three existing GWish projects, will reinforce medical training/education in patient spirituality in residency programs via an awards program, formal evaluation of spirituality and health education programs, and the exploration of ethical guidelines for incorporating spirituality into patient care.

The Humble Approach Initiative

John Templeton Foundation
Project Director, Dr. Mary Ann Meyers
Approximately fifty high-level consultations on research in progress that are intended to facilitate conversation among scientists, theologians, and philosophers. Discussion topics will cover a wide range of subject areas, primarily in the natural and human sciences. As institutions and organizations are selected to carry out these consultations, new grants will be created and the Humble Approach Initiative Grant will be reduced by the awarded amount.

The Ultimate Reality Research Program

John Templeton Foundation
Project Director, Charles Harper, DPhil
Program to advance the core vision of Sir John Templeton through supporting highly innovative interdisciplinary research of a scientific nature

into the nature of Ultimate Reality and therefore to search for new insights into the being, purposes, and fullness of that Reality, uniting as far as is appropriately justifiable science and the spiritual quest.

RELIGION AND SPIRITUALITY FACTOR RESEARCH PROGRAM
John Templeton Foundation
Project Director, Charles Harper, DPhil
Program aimed at building the field of research in new spiritual information focused on the study of the benefits of religion. The Faith Factor Research Program seeks to capitalize on an outstanding current opportunity raised by the new "faith friendly" climate in U.S. government policy. The program builds on past investments of Sir John Templeton in building the concept of faith factor research through the support of Dr. David Larson and NIHR/ICIHS.

APPENDIX F

Examples of Symposia Funded by the John Templeton Foundation

PSYCHONEUROIMMUNOLOGY
AND THE "FAITH FACTOR" IN HUMAN HEALTH
Chaired by Harvey Jay Cohen, held at Duke University, Durham, North Carolina, in July 1999. Purpose: to reflect on the implications for science and religion of research that broadly links a faith factor with a range of other factors that promote longevity and physical well-being, and to focus, in particular, on one promising area that explores the ties between spirituality and the enhanced action of the human immune system.

COMPLEXITY, INFORMATION, AND DESIGN:
A CRITICAL APPRAISAL
Chaired by Paul Davies, held in Santa Fe, New Mexico, in October 1999. Purpose: to look at what kinds of metaphysical/theological questions can be specifically related to and linked with complexity research and whether key issues might be formulated in a way that summarizes the present state of knowledge and provides a road map for future investigations.

EVOLUTION, PURPOSE, AND MEANING
Chaired by Martin E. P. Seligman and Robert Wright, held in Lyford Cay, Nassau, Bahamas, in February 2000. Purpose: to consider the subject of purpose in relation to biological evolution, cultural evolution, and human psychology, and to ponder the meaning of the apparent arrow of life moving toward greater and greater complexity.

EXPANDING CONCEPTS OF GOD
Chaired by Lawrence E. Sullivan, held in Cambridge, Massachusetts, in April
2000. Purpose: to probe the mystery of a *Deus velatus* by examining God's
chosen modes of revelation of God's self to believing hearts and questing
minds throughout the world.

THE FAR-FUTURE UNIVERSE: ESCHATOLOGY
FROM A COSMIC PERSPECTIVE
Chaired by Martin J. Rees, held in Rome, Italy, in November 2000. Purpose:
to explore eschatology from a cosmic perspective.

SCIENCE AND THEOLOGICAL IMAGINATION
IN SCIENCE FICTION
Chaired by Stephen R. L. Clark, held in London, England, in June 2000. Purpose: to consider the broader issues raised by science fiction and to explore,
in particular, the relation of the genre to science and to theology.

KINDLING THE SCIENCE OF GRATITUDE
Chaired by Robert A. Emmons, held in Dallas, Texas, in October 2000. Purpose: to explore the subject of gratitude from the perspectives of anthropology, biology, moral philosophy, psychology, and theology.

MIND, BRAIN, AND PERSONHOOD: AN INQUIRY FROM
SCIENTIFIC AND THEOLOGICAL PERSPECTIVES
Chaired by Malcom A. Jeeves, held in San Diego, California, in January 2001.
Purpose: to consider the broader issues raised by recent neuroscience
research, in particular their impact on theological and philosophical concepts of human nature.

PANENTHEISM
Chaired by Philip Clayton and Arthur Peacocke, held at St. George's House,
Windsor Castle, England, in December 2001. Purpose: to consider what general frameworks for conceiving of the God-world relation may be consistent
both with biblical data and modern philosophical and scientific contexts.

THE SCIENCE OF NONLOCALITY AND EASTERN APPROACHES
TO EXPLORING ULTIMATE REALITY
Chaired by Bruno Guiderdoni, held in Jongny sur Vevey, Switzerland, in
June 2002. Purpose: to explore the implications of quantum nonlocality for
the character of physical reality, as well as the uses of the concept of com-

plimentarity in understanding the relationship between parts and wholes, the fundamental unity of creation from Eastern perspectives, and the search for meaning in modern science and mystical traditions.

Emergent Reality
Chaired by Paul Davies, held in Granada, Spain, in August 2002. Purpose: to search multiple layers of meaning, with exciting contradictions, for shards of an elusive reality in order to chart an emergentist's agenda.

Universe or Multiverse?
Chaired by Paul Davies, held at Stanford University in Palo Alto, California, in March 2003. Purpose: to examine the conjectures of multiverse theory that are so dramatically enlarging our cosmic perspective.

Spiritual Dimensions of Healing
Chaired by Sarah Coakley and Fraser Watts, held at Queens' College, Cambridge University, in January 2004. Purpose: to consider the broader issues raised by the possibility of a spiritual aspect to healing within the context of conventional medicine, in particular its impact on our worldview and the perception we have of our place in nature.

Books of Advisory Board Members
Published by Templeton Foundation Press

Damon, William. 2003. *Noble Purpose: The Joy of Living a Meaningful Life*.

Davies, Paul. 2004. *The Cosmic Blueprint: New Discoveries on Nature's Creative Ability to Order the Universe*.

Ellis, George F. R., ed. 2002. *The Far-Future Universe: Eschatology from a Cosmic Perspective*.

Emmons, Robert A. and Joanna Hill. 2001. *Words of Gratitude for Mind, Body, and Soul*.

Ferguson, Kitty. 2004. *The Fire in the Equations: Science, Religion, and the Search for God*.

Giniger, Kenneth Seeman and John Marks Templeton. 1998. *Spiritual Evolution: Scientists Discuss Their Beliefs*.

Heller, Michael. 2003. *Creative Tension: Essays on Science and Religion*.

Herrmann, Robert L., ed. 2000. *God, Science, and Humility: Ten Scientists Consider Humility Theology*.

Herrmann, Robert L., ed. 2001. *Expanding Humanity's Vision of God: New Thoughts on Science and Religion*.

Herrmann, Robert L. 2004. *Sir John Templeton: Supporting Scientific Research for Spiritual Discoveries*.

Herrmann, Robert L. and John Marks Templeton. 1994. *Is God the Only Reality? Science Points to a Deeper Meaning of the Universe*.

Herrmann, Robert L. and John Marks Templeton. 1998. *The God Who Would Be Known: Revelations of the Divine in Contemporary Science*.

Koenig, Harold G. 2002. *Purpose and Power in Retirement: New Opportunities for Meaning and Significance*.

Koenig, Harold G. 2002. *Spirituality in Patient Care: Why, How, When, and What*.

Koenig, Harold G. and Verna Benner Carson. 2002. *Parish Nursing: Stories of Service and Care*.

Koenig, Harold G. and Verna Benner Carson. 2004. *Spiritual Caregiving: Healthcare as a Ministry*.

Koenig, Harold G., Douglas M. Lawson with Malcolm McConnell. 2004. *Faith in the Future: Healthcare, Aging, and the Role of Religion*.

Koenig, Harold G. with Gregg Lewis. 2004. *The Healing Connection: The Story of a Physician's Search for the Link between Faith and Health*.

Moore, Gary. 1998. *Spiritual Investments: Wall Street Wisdom from the Career of Sir John Templeton*.

Moore, Gary. 2003. *Faithful Finances 101: From the Poverty of Fear and Greed to the Riches of Spiritual Investing*.

Mosley, Glenn and Joanna Hill. 2000. *The Power of Prayer around the World*.

Post, Stephen G. 2003. *Unlimited Love: Altruism, Compassion, and Service*.

Post, Stephen G., Byron Johnson, Michael E. McCullough, and Jeffrey Schloss. 2003. *Research on Altruism and Love: An Annotated Bibliography of Major Studies in Psychology, Sociology, Evolutionary Biology, and Theology*.

Reagan, Michael, ed. 2002. *The Hand of God: Thoughts and Images Reflecting the Spirit of the Universe*.

Reagan, Michael, ed. 2003. *Inside the Mind of God: Images and Words of Inner Space.*

Stannard, Russell, ed. 2000. *God for the 21st Century.*

Stannard, Russell. 2002. *www.Here-I-Am.*

Stannard, Russell. 2003. *Curious History of God.*

Worthington, Everett L. Jr., ed. 1998. *Dimensions of Forgiveness: Psychological Research & Theological Perspectives.*

1999 Science and Religion Course Competition and Workshops

The Center for Theology
and the Natural Sciences

presents

1999 SCIENCE & RELIGION
COURSE COMPETITION AND WORKSHOPS

The Center for Theology and the Natural Sciences announces the 1999 Science & Religion Course Program, which includes a course competition granting awards for outstanding courses in science and religion, and a series of workshops on science and religion, course development, and pedagogy. Funded by the John Templeton Foundation, the program will award up to 100 prizes for outstanding science and religion course proposals in colleges, universities, and seminaries. Each prize includes an award of US $10,000, to be divided evenly between the course instructor and the host institution. The preliminary application deadline for applicants is *December 1, 1998*, except for those applicants attending a winter workshop.

WINTER 1999 INTRODUCTORY WORKSHOPS		SUMMER 1999 ADVANCED WORKSHOPS	
Tallahassee, Florida	January 5–10	Berkeley, California	June 4–9
Berkeley, California	January 7–12	Chicago, Illinois	June 18–23
Oxford, England	January 8–13	Boston, Massachusetts	June 28–July 2
		Oxford, England	July 8–13
		Toronto, Canada	July 8–13

For more information on current and past programs, including details on regional activities, please visit the Templeton Foundation web site at:
www.templeton.org
For 1999 program information and application materials or workshop registration forms, please contact CTNS at:
Peter M.J. Hess, Ph.D., Competition Coordinator
Center for Theology and the Natural Sciences ▪ 2400 Ridge Road ▪ Berkeley, CA 94709
Phone: 510.665.8141 ▪ Fax: 510.665.1589 ▪ Email:SRcourse@ctns.org ▪ www.ctns.org

This program funded by the
JOHN TEMPLETON FOUNDATION

1999 Call for Exemplary Papers in Humility Theology

JOHN TEMPLETON FOUNDATION

1999

CALL FOR EXEMPLARY PAPERS IN HUMILITY THEOLOGY

To encourage scholarly research on matters of both spiritual and scientific significance, the John Templeton Foundation invites scholars to submit published papers on topics regarding the constructive interaction of:

- Theology and the natural sciences
- Religion and the medical sciences, or
- Religion and the behavioral sciences.

These papers must proceed from professional scholarship and display a spirit of intellectual humility, a respect for varied theological traditions, and an attitude of open-minded inquiry into the varied ways in which theology/religion and the empirical sciences can be mutually informative. Papers must have been published or accepted for publication in a peer-reviewed journal or similarly selective scholarly publication, be between 3,000 and 10,000 words in length, and be accompanied by a 600-word précis (in English, even if the paper is not).

Prizes ranging from $500 to $3000 will be awarded in November 1999.
The deadline for submission of papers is June 1, 1999.

For full details and application forms, please visit our web site, or write to:
Exemplary Papers Program Director
JOHN TEMPLETON FOUNDATION
P.O. Box 8322 ▪ Radnor, Pennsylvania 19087-8322 USA
www.templeton.org

Reference: PIT

Two Hundred Spiritual Principles
from *Wisdom from World Religions*

БY JOHN MARKS TEMPLETON

WEEK ONE

1. *When you rule your mind, you rule your world.* —Bill Provost
2. *Where there is no vision, the people perish.* —Proverbs 29:18
3. *Why were you created?* —John Marks Templeton
4. *Infinite in all directions.* —Freeman Dyson
5. *As you give, so shall you receive.* —Matthew 7:12 and Luke 6:31

WEEK TWO

1. *Your life becomes what you think.* —Marcus Aurelius
2. *Love given is love received.* —John Marks Templeton
3. *To be forgiven, you must first forgive.* —John Marks Templeton
4. *An attitude of gratitude creates blessings.* —John Marks Templeton
5. *You fear what you do not understand.* —Anonymous

WEEK THREE

1. *Nothing can bring you peace but yourself.* —Ralph Waldo Emerson
2. *Listen to learn.* —Alcoholics Anonymous
3. *Don't ever think you are wise enough.* —Proverbs 3:7
4. *Humility can lead to prayer as well as progress and brings you in tune with the infinite.* —John Marks Templeton
5. *Failing to plan is planning to fail.* —Benjamin Franklin

WEEK FOUR

1. *Beautiful thoughts build a beautiful soul.* —John Marks Templeton
2. *Progress depends on diligence and perseverance.* —John Marks Templeton
3. *Love thy neighbor as thyself.* —Matthew 19:19
4. *To be wronged is nothing unless you continue to remember it.* —Confucius
5. *Enthusiasm facilitates achievement.* —John Marks Templeton

WEEK FIVE

1. *By giving you grow.* —John Marks Templeton
2. *Does the word "religion" imply authority, whereas the word "spirituality" may imply progress?* —John Marks Templeton
3. *The family that prays together stays together.* —Common saying
4. *If at first you don't succeed, try, try again.* —William Edward Hickson
5. *See everyone in your own self and yourself in everyone.*
   —adapted from *Isha Upanishad*

WEEK SIX

1. *It is better to love than be loved.* —St. Francis of Assisi
2. *Thanksgiving leads to having more to give thanks for.* —John Marks Templeton
3. *You cannot be lonely if you help the lonely.* —John Marks Templeton
4. *You are sought after if you reflect love, joy, peace, patience, kindness, goodness, faithfulness, gentleness, and self-control.* —John Marks Templeton
5. *A smile breeds a smile.* —Ted Engstrom

WEEK SEVEN

1. *Great heroes are humble.* —John Marks Templeton
2. *Love given grows; love hoarded dwindles.* —John Marks Templeton
3. *Find good in everything.* —John Marks Templeton

4. *What the mind can conceive, it may achieve.* —Anonymous

5. *Be steadfast in prayer.* —Qur'an

WEEK EIGHT

1. *With God all things are possible.* —Matthew 19:26

2. *I shall allow no man to belittle my soul by making me hate him.*
   —Booker T. Washington

3. *Do your allotted task! Work excels idleness!* —Bhagavad Gita

4. *Enthusiasm is contagious.* —John Marks Templeton

5. *Small attempts repeated will complete any undertaking.* —Og Mandino

WEEK NINE

1. *Defeat isn't bitter if you don't swallow it.* —Ted Engstrom

2. *The unexamined life is not worth living.* —Socrates

3. *An honest man's word is as good as his bond.* —American proverb

4. *Tithing often brings prosperity and honor.* —John Marks Templeton

5. *Wisdom is more blessed than riches.* —John Marks Templeton

WEEK TEN

1. *If God is infinite, then nothing can be separate.* —John Marks Templeton

2. *Where there is a will, there is a way.* —Aesop

3. *Count your blessings and you will have an attitude of gratitude.*
   —John Marks Templeton

4. *We learn more by welcoming criticism than by rendering judgment.*
   —J. Jelinek

5. *What talents can you build?* —John Marks Templeton

WEEK ELEVEN

1. *You will find what you look for: good or evil, problems or solutions.*
   —John Marks Templeton
2. *Is creativity accelerating?* —John Marks Templeton
3. *The only way to have a friend is to be a friend.* —Ralph Waldo Emerson
4. *Your thinking greatly affects your life.* —John Marks Templeton
5. *Learning is a lifelong activity.* —John Marks Templeton

WEEK TWELVE

1. *Noble purpose creates fruitful lives.* —John Marks Templeton
2. *Birds of a feather flock together.* —Robert Burton
3. *Idle brains are the devil's workshop.* —H. G. Bohn
4. *You can make opposition work for you.* —Anonymous
5. *We are not punished for our anger; we are punished by our anger.*
   —Bhagavad Gita

WEEK THIRTEEN

1. *Life is filled with infinite possibilities.* —John Marks Templeton
2. *Thoughts are things.* —Charles Fillmore
3. *As within, so without.* —Hermetic principle
4. *Thanksgiving, not complaining, attracts people to you.*
   —John Marks Templeton
5. *If earth is a school, who are the teachers?* —John Marks Templeton

WEEK FOURTEEN

1. *The secret of a productive life can be sought and found.*
   —John Marks Templeton
2. *Happiness is always a by-product.* —John Marks Templeton
3. *The way to mend the bad world is to create the right world.*
   —Ralph Waldo Emerson
4. *It is better to praise than to criticize.* —John Marks Templeton
5. *Laughter is the best medicine.* —Norman Cousins

WEEK FIFTEEN

1. *Humility, like darkness, reveals the heavenly light.*
   —Henry David Thoreau
2. *Which entertainment is beneficial?* —John Marks Templeton
3. *If you do not know what you want to achieve with your life, you may not achieve much.* —John Marks Templeton
4. *More is wrought by prayer than this world dreams of.*
   —Alfred, Lord Tennyson
5. *Everyone and everything around you is your teacher.* —Ken Keyes

WEEK SIXTEEN

1. *Purpose and praise can increase productivity.* —John Marks Templeton
2. *The price of greatness is responsibility.* —Winston Churchill
3. *Good words are worth much and cost little.* —George Herbert
4. *You can never solve a problem on the same level as the problem.*
   —Emmet Fox
5. *What attitudes and endeavors can guide us toward experiencing "heaven on earth" as a way of life?* —John Marks Templeton

WEEK SEVENTEEN

1. *We receive freely when we give freely.* —Anonymous
2. *The truth will make you free.* —John 8:32
3. *Is progress, through competition to serve, a basic invisible reality?*
   —John Marks Templeton
4. *Habit is the best of servants, the worst of masters.* —J. Jelinek
5. *To discover new oceans you need the courage to lose sight of the shore.*
   —Anonymous

WEEK EIGHTEEN

1. *No one's education is ever complete.* —John Marks Templeton
2. *Cultivating a positive attitude can bring beneficial results in all areas of life.*
   —John Marks Templeton
3. *Forgiving uplifts the forgiver.* —John Marks Templeton
4. *The light of understanding dissolves the phantoms of fear.* —Ellie Harold
5. *Only one thing is more powerful than learning from experience,*
   and that is not learning from experience. —John Marks Templeton

WEEK NINETEEN

1. *Religion opens the door for science.* —Franklin Loehr
2. *Happiness comes from spiritual wealth, not material wealth.*
   —John Marks Templeton
3. *Religion is good for your health.* —Dale Matthews
4. *Progress requires change.* —John Marks Templeton
5. *Beneficial experiences often come through trial and self-discipline.*
   —Unknown

Week Twenty

1. *Are the visible and tangible only timeless manifestations of the vast timeless and limitless reality?* —John Marks Templeton
2. *To err is human, to forgive divine.* —Alexander Pope
3. *A good conscience is a continual feast.* —Robert Burton
4. *A good reputation is more valuable than money.* —Publilius Syrus
5. *The visible is the ladder up to the invisible; the temporal is but the scaffolding of the eternal.* —Henry Drummond

Week Twenty-One

1. *Our life is shaped by our mind; we become what we think.*
   —The *Dhammapada*
2. *Once a word is spoken, it cannot be recalled.* —Wentworth Roscommon
3. *You have the most powerful weapons on earth — love and prayer.*
   —John Marks Templeton
4. *Can egotism be a stumbling block to our growth?* —John Marks Templeton
5. *One of the greatest blessings to human beings is change, and the present acceleration of change in the world is an overflowing of this blessing.*
   —John Marks Templeton

Week Twenty-Two

1. *World progress needs entrepreneurs.* —John Marks Templeton
2. *As you are active in blessing others, they learn to bless others also.*
   —John Marks Templeton
3. *Expect the best and your positive outlook opens the door to opportunity.*
   —John Marks Templeton
4. *Anger and selfish desire are our greatest enemies.* —Bhagavad Gita
5. *The wise person looks within his heart and finds eternal peace.*
   —Hindu proverb

WEEK TWENTY-THREE

1. *Every discovery is a discovery of God.* —John Marks Templeton
2. *Live each day as a new beginning.* —John Marks Templeton
3. *Thanksgiving leads to giving and forgiving, and to spiritual growth.*
   —John Marks Templeton
4. *There is no difficulty that enough love will not conquer.* —Emmet Fox
5. *Self-control leads to success.* —John Marks Templeton

WEEK TWENTY-FOUR

1. *The tree is known by its fruits.* —English proverb
2. *Rid yourself of negative attitudes and beliefs and negative conditions will die of starvation.* —Russell W. Lake
3. *An hour wasted is never found again.* —John Marks Templeton
4. *To be upset over what you don't have is to waste what you do have.*
   —Ken Keyes
5. *Honesty is the best policy.* —Miguel de Cervantes

WEEK TWENTY-FIVE

1. *Your prayers can be answered by "yes," but also by "no," and by alternatives.* —Ruth Stafford Peale
2. *Healthy minds tend to cause healthy bodies.* —John Marks Templeton
3. *Give me beauty in the inward soul; and may the outward and inward man be at one.* —Plato
4. *Happiness has nothing to do with wealth and status, but is a matter of harmony.* —Lao Tzu
5. *Help yourself by helping others.* —John Marks Templeton

Week Twenty-Six

1. *You create your own reality.* —Jane Roberts
2. *A task takes as long as there is time to do it.* —Parkinson's Law
3. *It is a duty to cultivate kindness.* —*Sefer Hachinukh*
4. *Give credit and help to all who have helped you.*
   —John Marks Templeton
5. *Enthusiasm spells the difference between mediocrity and accomplishment.*
   —Norman Vincent Peale

Week Twenty-Seven

1. *You can build your own heaven or hell on earth.* —John Marks Templeton
2. *Science without religion is lame; religion without science is blind.*
   —Albert Einstein
3. *The unknown before us may be a million times greater than what we now know.* —John Marks Templeton
4. *Worry achieves nothing and wastes valuable time.*
   —John Marks Templeton
5. *Failure is an event, not a person.* —William D. Brown

Week Twenty-Eight

1. *Laugh and the world laughs with you; weep and you weep alone.*
   —Ella Wheeler Wilcox
2. *If nothing is ventured, nothing is gained.* —Sir John Heywood
3. *Honesty is the first chapter in the book of wisdom.* —Thomas Jefferson
4. *When you judge others, you do not define them, you define yourself.*
   —Wayne Dyer
5. *A soul without a high aim is like a ship without a rudder.*
   —Thomas Carlyle

WEEK TWENTY-NINE

1. *Joy provides assurance; envy brings loneliness.* —John Marks Templeton
2. *Forgiving builds your spiritual wealth.* —Rebekah Alezander
3. *Life is an attitude. Have a good one!* —Eric L. Lungaard
4. *Service is love made manifest.* —Maharishi Sadashiva Isham
5. *No man is free who is not master of himself.* —Epictetus

WEEK THIRTY

1. *It is by forgetting self that one finds self.* —St. Francis of Assisi
2. *Leave no stone unturned.* —Euripides
3. *What you focus on expands.* —Arnold Patent
4. *Change and improvement come from the inside out.* —Anonymous
5. *You choose the path you want to walk down.* —John Marks Templeton

WEEK THIRTY-ONE

1. *Destructive language tends to produce destructive results.*
   —John Marks Templeton
2. *Success feeds on itself and creates more success.* —John Marks Templeton
3. *Never put off until tomorrow what you can do today.* —Lord Chesterfield
4. *Invest yourself in your work.* —John Marks Templeton
5. *What good will this do?* —John Marks Templeton

WEEK THIRTY-TWO

1. *We can become bitter or better as a result of our experiences.*
   —Eric Butterworth
2. *Joy is not in things, but is in you.* —John Marks Templeton
3. *Retirement can begin a beneficial career.* —John Marks Templeton
4. *Happiness pursued, eludes; happiness given, returns.* —John Marks Templeton
5. *Thoughts of doubt and fear are pathways to failure.* —Brian Adams

Week Thirty-Three

1. *You shall know them by their fruits.* —Matthew 7:16
2. *Optimism has its roots in abiding goodness.* —Anonymous
3. *If you think you know it all, you are less likely to learn more.*
   —John Marks Templeton
4. *No person was ever honored for what he received. Honor has been the reward of what he gave.* —Calvin Coolidge
5. *The shadow of ignorance is fear.* —J. Jelinek

Week Thirty-Four

1. *Man must discipline himself by good thoughts, good words, good deeds.*
   —Zoroastrian scripture
2. *You are either part of the problem, or part of the solution.*
   —Eldridge Cleaver
3. *The borrower is a servant to the lender.* —Proverbs 22:7
4. *Whatever you have, you must use it or lose it.* —Henry Ford
5. *It is nice to be important, but it is more important to be nice.*
   —John Marks Templeton

Week Thirty-Five

1. *Those who seldom make mistakes, seldom make discoveries.*
   —John Marks Templeton
2. *The measure of a man's real character is what he would do if he would never be found out.* —Thomas Macaulay
3. *Change your mind to change your life.* —John Marks Templeton
4. *All aspects of creation are in an evolutionary process of progress and growth.*
   —Rebekah Alezander
5. *It is more blessed to give than to receive.* —Acts 20:35

WEEK THIRTY-SIX

1. *Purpose is the quality we choose to shape our lives around.*
   —Richard J. Leider
2. *The seven deadly sins are: pride, lust, sloth, envy, anger, covetousness and gluttony.* —St. Gregory
3. *Appearances are often deceiving.* —Aesop
4. *Zeal is the inward fire of the soul that urges you onward toward your goal.*
   —Charles Fillmore
5. *Minds are like parachutes — they only function when they are open.*
   —Dick Sutphen

WEEK THIRTY-SEVEN

1. *Out of the fullness of the heart the mouth speaks.* —English proverb
2. *The journey of a thousand miles must begin with a single step.* —Lao Tzu
3. *It is always darkest just before the day dawns.* —Thomas Fuller
4. *Love conquers all things.* —Virgil
5. *Count your blessings, name them one by one.* —Early hymn

WEEK THIRTY-EIGHT

1. *A merry heart makes a cheerful countenance.* —English proverb
2. *Everyone should keep in reserve an alternate plan for livelihood.*
   —John Marks Templeton
3. *If you are facing in the right direction, all you need to do is keep on walking.*
   —Buddhist proverb
4. *The unknown is not unknowable, and is vastly greater than the known.*
   —John Marks Templeton
5. *Humility opens the door to progress.* —John Marks Templeton

WEEK THIRTY-NINE

1. *Forgiveness benefits both the giver and the receiver.* —John Marks Templeton
2. *Your dreams can come true when you activate them.* —John Marks Templeton
3. *Work is love made visible.* —Kahlil Gibran
4. *For every effect, there is a cause.* —Hermetic principle
5. *Those who do good do well.* —John Marks Templeton

WEEK FORTY

1. *Focus on where you want to go instead of where you have been.*
   —John Marks Templeton
2. *Each of us can learn to be helpers in achieving God's purpose.*
   —John Marks Templeton
3. *Every useful life is a ministry.* —John Marks Templeton
4. *The more love we give, the more love we have left.* —John Marks Templeton
5. *Thanksgiving opens the door to spiritual growth.* —John Marks Templeton

Statement on Humility Theology

BY MARK RICHARDSON AND JUDITH MARCHAND
AS EDITED BY JOHN MARKS TEMPLETON ON DECEMBER 13, 1995

OBJECTIVES

An objective of Humility Theology is to encourage progress in spiritual information and research especially by interpreting diverse kinds of evidence from scientific investigations. Humility Theology, through inquiry into the observable world, presses toward information regarding matters of ultimacy.

Humility Theology encourages the idea that spiritual understanding and information continues to increase—human understanding should not be fixed and unchanging. Thus our knowledge is provisional; claims to possessing the full truth are unintentionally egotistical. Within this flux of time Humility Theology pursues evidence about spiritual information and Ultimate Reality (which some major religions call God), including design, purpose, love, and prayer. Time-honoured beliefs should be open to supplementation, improvement, or revision in view of continuous discoveries or unfolding of God's purposes.

The main purpose of the John Templeton Foundation is to encourage the top one-tenth of 1 percent of people and thereby encourage all people to think that progress in spiritual information is possible, desirable, can be done and will be done. Methods of statistics and of science may produce rapid progress in spiritual information as already produced in medicine and electronics. That progress in spiritual information can be enormously beneficial in accordance with God's purposes for all his children everywhere. As in other sciences the benefits are often unforeseen. More and more information (if verified by statistical or experimental evidence or other methods of science) can be recognized worldwide promptly after each discovery and thereby provide an increasing supplement to the wonderful revelations of all ancient scriptures and prophets, which have been so beneficial for thousands of years.

Spiritual information can be, should be, and will be rapidly increasing and accelerating. New information verified by statistics or experimental evidence or methods of science can be accepted worldwide quickly, as it is now in other sciences.

METHODS

Humility Theology interprets modern scientific developments in regard to what they might reveal about spiritual principles and the nature and the ways of God. In addition, where appropriate, it seeks to apply the hypothetical-deductive methods of the sciences to examination of spiritual data. Often this can be done by posing concepts in a testable mode, reflecting the provisionality, incomplete-ness, and fallibility of human utterances about spiritual reality.

Some methods of Humility Theology can be inferential. Reasonable concepts about unseen realities beyond our observation can be drawn from evidence based in those phenomena which are open to observation, experience, or analysis.

ATTITUDES

Humility Theology begins with the assumption that, because of our finitude in the face of the vastness of all reality, human knowledge about God, and about the world the scientist explores, should be regarded as very limited, and tentatively held.

Nevertheless, through the rigors of statistical, experimental, or other scientific methods of inquiry, there can be progress in our spiritual information. Toward this end, Humility Theology encourages an open-mindedness toward any new ideas, a respectful manner of engagement with those who hold different views, and a non-dogmatic style of presenting ideas.

Finally, Humility Theology encourages an attitude among theologians and scientists of respect for all religious traditions, openness to new theological insights based on the broadest possible range of human learning, testing and experience, and reverence toward God as the unlimited creative spirit and only Ultimate Reality. How little we know—how eager to learn.

POSTSCRIPT

The Templeton Foundations encourage progress in spiritual information and research. We have unlimited admiration for the wonderful benefits from all ancient scriptures, revelations, and prophets; but accelerating progress in spiritual information can result from experiments and research using methods of sciences.

We use the word *information* to include data history, principles, and concepts. We use the word *spiritual* to include those realities that lie beyond the visible, tangible, and temporary. We use the word *spiritual* to include love, joy, peace, patience, kindness, goodness, faithfulness, gentleness, self-control, self-sacrifice, honesty, reliability, humility, curiosity, purpose, creativity, progress, ethics, giving, forgiving, and thanksgiving.

Humility Theology Questions

Hoping to stimulate pondering and research by people of diverse cultures, a few of the following humility questions are repeated but in diverse wording.

1. Maybe in only a century or two, can humans discover information that is over one hundred times more spiritual? For example, in only the twentieth century, information has increased over one hundredfold in electronics, medicine, etc., by science research.

2. Can total information continue to double every three years, so that in thirty years one thousand times as much will be available and in sixty years a million times as much?

3. If things visible to humans only one millennium ago are only a tiny part of what has since been discovered, does this indicate that things visible are only a few temporary outward manifestations of fundamental reality?

4. Maybe no human has yet known even 1 percent of Unlimited Mind, which some call God. After humans gain one hundred times as much spiritual information, will we still know only 1 percent of reality?

5. If human information has multiplied over one hundredfold in only two centuries, will that progress accelerate, so that in year 2200, information will be over ten thousand times as great as in 1800?

6. Can science research increase over one hundredfold earthlings' information about reality, timeless and limitless, which some call God?

7. What evidence indicates that progress will continue to accelerate? In what areas are there evidences that creativity is accelerating? How can we help?

8. Is it likely that by accelerating progress, over half of what is taught as science today will become obsolete in only one century?

9. Is science research, which has flourished for only the latest 1 percent of 1 percent of human history, still in its infancy? In less than four centuries, have human perceptions expanded over a hundredfold?

10. Will accelerating discoveries continue to reveal multitudes of new mysteries?

11. What evidence indicates that the invisible can be over one hundred times larger and more varied than the visible?

12. Is the visible only a tiny, temporary manifestation of reality? Does 99 percent of science study not reality but human perceptions of reality? Do multiplying discoveries indicate that reality is more basic, complex, and vast than things tangible or visible?

13. Now that sciences have shown that realities can be vastly more numerous than the material world alone, is it egotistical to cling to the idea that reality means visible and tangible materials?

14. Do the discoveries by science just since Galileo about realities not previously comprehended by humans resemble the discoveries about realities that followed the development of eyes by the first creature?

15. Are we egotistical to ignore the mathematicians, who have recently suggested that reality can have as many as eleven dimensions rather than the three dimensions plus time, which were familiar to the prophets and to Isaac Newton and Albert Einstein?

16. When billions of dollars are spent searching for life elsewhere in the cosmos, is it egotistical to think that intelligences cannot exist unless they are comprehensible by us? Does our tiny comprehension cause us to think egotistically that we are not possibly swimming in a multitude of other intelligences? What are the chances that varieties of creatures already exist not yet comprehensible by us, even in our own vicinity?

17. Would we benefit by redefining reality to mean fundamentals instead of appearances? Can scientists study reality or only those few human perceptions of reality?

18. If we do not understand why matter exists or light or gravity, could that mean that reality is vastly more complex than humans yet comprehend, just as our ancestors did not comprehend television, germs, atoms, or galaxies?

19. Could living creatures on earth only ten million years ago conceive of present human intelligence? Has recent science research already taught

humans that reality is over one hundred times more complex and vast than humans perceived just two centuries ago?

20. In the next two centuries, can human perception of reality be multiplied over one hundredfold more? Is there evidence that human perceptions of reality are accelerating? Why? How?

21. Can human perceptions of reality be as meager as a clam's perceptions of humans?

22. Is it egotistical to think that what humans cannot yet perceive or measure is not real? Is egotism a common failing that has always caused many species to think that reality and intelligence are limited to what that species can conceive? Do most sciences serve to enlarge human perception of basic reality?

23. If science can study only human perceptions rather than reality, should we use the word "reality" to mean the total of appearances plus fundamentals?

24. Should we use the word "God" to mean something less than totality?

25. If God means totality, then what can be separate from God? Or do we want the word "God" to mean only part of the whole, somewhat like a king who can live separately from his subjects?

26. If sciences try to study total reality, then are science's methods for discovering more about God? Can the word "God" be defined as "basic reality"?

27. Do atheists believe there is no king, or do they believe there are no fundamentals behind appearances, which are often shown to be fleeting or partial? Could an egotistical ocean wave claim there is no ocean?

28. Does humility help humans to comprehend that humans are only tiny, temporary parts of reality, parts of a limitless, timeless Creator whom some call God?

29. Is it possible that research in genetics or other sciences can accelerate the progress of human intelligence?

30. Now that cosmology has convinced us that our sun is only one of more than a billion billion other stars, can we still egotistically imagine ourselves to be the ultimate purpose of the cosmos?

31. If each branch of science is showing that creation is vastly wider and more complex than comprehended two millennia ago or even just one century ago, does this reveal a vastly more worshipful Creator?

32. Can human concepts of God expand even more rapidly than science reveals reality?

33. Is all science research further information about the nature and vastness of God?

34. If God is not smaller than all of reality, then are most sciences discovering more about God? Are such sciences methods of theology to be welcomed by every person seeking God?

35. Can all the wonderfully beneficial ancient scriptures be supplemented over one hundredfold partly by science research for spiritual information and verification?

36. If the word *reality* no longer means a small land area on one planet, is it egotistical to think that reality cannot be vastly greater than now comprehended? If ancient peoples could imagine God usually as a spirit separate from reality, are we now egotistical to think that God can be in any way smaller or more limited than total reality?

37. Are scientists egotistical if they think that love and prayer and worship may not be a greater part of reality than visible materials?

38. Can all religions learn to be so humble as to be enthusiastic rather than resistant to new spiritual information, especially through science research, to supplement the wonderful ancient scriptures? Can most scientists become humble enough not to limit themselves to things visible or tangible but also to include various research about vastly greater spiritual realities in which we live and move and have our being?

39. Were many major religions held back by an unconscious concept that God is somehow separate from reality, a sort of wise old king?

40. Have human concepts of God always been too small? Or too anthropomorphic?

41. Has human ego caused people to imagine a God in human terms?

42. Is God larger than a single race or planet? What is the increasing evidence?

43. What additional evidence has been found that God may be timeless and unlimited? Omnipresent? Increasingly creative?

44. Will this comprehension of a larger, greater Creator continue? Why will comprehension continue to speed up?

45. Can each species think the universe was very finely tuned to produce that species because its perceptions are limited to only those parts of reality which affect that species, just as the anthropic principle might

mislead humans to think egotistically that the universe was designed for a single species on one tiny planet? Is it likely that earthlings are the ultimate?

46. Is human consciousness only a tiny, recent manifestation of a vast creative consciousness that could be called God?

47. Should we be enthusiastic and diligent to discover more about God?

48. Should this cause us to worship a God even more awesome than comprehended by the ancients? Why would anyone prefer to worship a God who can be described in human terms rather than a God who is unlimited and timeless?

49. Should we listen carefully, thoughtfully, and gratefully to everyone's concepts of God and God's purpose for humanity?

50. By devoting one-tenth of all science research funding to the discovery of new spiritual information, can the benefits be even greater than from all other science research? Maybe science research for spiritual information should be over one-tenth of all research, which now exceeds one billion dollars daily.

51. Is it egotistical to think that humans can ever comprehend all of reality or of God or of His nature or of His methods or purposes?

52. Do we now comprehend over one hundred times as much about God's creativity as humans understood just one thousand years ago?

53. Is God the only reality?

54. Can anything ever be separate from God? What are the advantages of perceiving God to be separate from basic reality?

55. Is God all of you and you a tiny part of Him?

56. Does humility theology mean more questions than answers?

57. Should all religions teach "How little we know and how eager to learn"?

58. Are there some laws from the great religions for happy and fruitful life that can be tested by science research and studied and researched in schools worldwide?

59. If humility is the mother of invention, could progress accelerate if religions encouraged enthusiasm for research more than creed, ritual, bureaucracy, or authority? Should humility ask for evidences and research to supplement or clarify belief or faith?

60. Is creativity reduced by excessive bureaucracy but accelerated by open minds and by free competition?

61. For accelerating creativity, do we need dogma and ritual or humble, searching, open minds? Is God's creativity accelerating, and can we become helpers in this acceleration?

62. Is the ability of humans yet to understand God just as tiny as the ability of a clam to understand the ocean, of which it is a creature?

63. If a wave is a tiny temporary manifestation of the ocean of which it is a part, does that resemble our relation to God?

64. What is the evidence that free and loving competition may be part of God's method for progress, productivity, prosperity, and spiritual maturity for His children?

65. Are there multiplying evidences of purpose in the universe and in creativity?

66. In the latest one-millionth of time, have humans been created on purpose for purpose? Or for pleasure?

67. What evidence is there that God lives in you and you in Him?

68. Can you be an expression or agent of God in love and creativity?

69. To enhance human comprehension of God, should science research examine benefits of limitless love, purpose, and accelerating creativity?

70. Would we enhance our worship of God by using that word to mean limitless, timeless, total reality instead of merely a separate humanlike superior king as often pictured in ancient scriptures of the chosen tribe of Abraham?

71. Why were we created? Could one purpose be for us to help in God's accelerating creativity? How can we learn to be helpers in God's purposes?

72. How can we discover more about God's purposes? What is the purpose for humans and for human purpose?

73. Always, humans have wondered why they were created. Could a possible purpose be to help accelerate God's creativity, similar in some tiny ways to the ways humans recently created intelligent computers?

74. Is trying to help in God's creativity processes a way to express our worship and thankfulness?

75. How is the search for increasing comprehension of God helped by the New Testament statements, "God is love and he who dwells in love dwells in God and God in him" and "With God were all things made and without Him was not anything made that was made"?

76. Can prayer, worship, and service to others help each of us to discover more of the nature of God?

77. Is it likely that on the planets of over one hundred billion stars in our galaxy and one hundred billion other galaxies there are manifestations of God's creativity not yet imagined by earthlings and maybe more advanced than we?

78. Is it possible to give too much divine love? What English words can separate divine love from hormone love and filial love? How can we distinguish giving too many goods or instructions (which can retard maturity) from divine love, which helps the receiver to gain the joy of giving? If instead of greeting people with the words, "How are you?" we began to say "God loves you and so do I," what could be the benefits?

79. What evidence indicates that heaven on earth can be the result of prayer, worship, usefulness and giving, forgiving and thanksgiving, and unlimited love?

80. What is the evidence that enthusiasm for worship can increase as we learn more of the timeless, limitless, omnipresent God?

81. How large is your God? Is he only a wise Father? Is he God of a single tribe or race or planet? Is he somehow separate from reality, or is he the only reality? Besides searching for intelligences in the vast cosmos, should we search for intelligences around us and within us not yet comprehensible by us?

82. Could even atheists, who deny the reality of a personal God, begin to worship fundamental reality or unlimited mind or unlimited love?

83. If dinosaurs were egotistical, could they have thought of themselves as the ultimate purpose of the universe?

84. If the first microbes on earth more than a billion years ago were egotistical, could they have thought of themselves as the ultimate purpose of the universe? If one of the more than four hundred varieties of microbes, which help us digest our food, were egotistical, could they now think of themselves as the ultimate purpose of the universe because they are unable to comprehend more complex or intelligent creatures?

85. In what ways can free competition of diverse spiritual concepts accelerate progress in religion, ideas, and human welfare?

86. Can new information from science research reduce conflict between religions?

87. Have all wars that were called religious really been manifestations of egotism where one tribe or bureaucracy imagined itself to possess the total truth and, therefore, should either convert or kill any persons suggesting a different concept?

88. Could religious wars vanish if 90 percent of spiritual information came from science research, which is verifiable, worldwide? Can the motto of religions become "How little we yet know, how eager to search"?

89. Should universities and schools that teach sciences of visible materials also teach sciences of unlimited love and purpose and ethics? By statistics and questionnaires, can scientists research realities such as love and purpose and worship?

90. Can some universities encourage and train some students to choose careers in humility theology research?

91. Is agape love a product of the human mind, or can human minds be a product of pure, limitless, timeless love, which some call God?

92. Are multiplying mysteries even more awesome and worshipful than a king above the sky of one planet? Although most of the world's religious people will now say, if asked, that their God is limitless, do most atheists think that word means some concept smaller or separate?

Notes

Notes to the Introduction

1. The Templeton Prize for Progress in Religion was renamed the Templeton Prize for Progress toward Research or Discoveries about Spiritual Realities (including research in love, creativity, purpose, infinity, intelligence, thanksgiving, and prayer). It is often referred to simply as the Templeton Prize.

2. John Marks Templeton, *Possibilities for Over One Hundredfold More Spiritual Information: The Humble Approach in Theology and Science* (Philadelphia, PA: Templeton Foundation Press, 2000), vii.

3. John Marks Templeton, *Wisdom from World Religions: Pathways toward Heaven on Earth* (Philadelphia, PA: Templeton Foundation Press, 2002).

4. John Marks Templeton with Rebekah Alezander Dunlap, *Why Are We Created? Increasing Our Understanding of Humanity's Purpose on Earth* (Philadelphia, PA: Templeton Foundation Press, 2003).

Notes to Chapter 1

1. John Marks Templeton and Robert L. Herrmann, *The God Who Would Be Known* (Phidadelphia, PA: Templeton Foundation Press, 1986), 5.

2. Timothy Ferris, *Coming of Age in the Milky Way* (New York: William Morrow, 1988), 383.

3. John Marks Templeton, *The Humble Approach* (Phidadelphia, PA: Templeton Foundation Press, 1995), 18–20.

4. Ibid., 34–46.

5. Ronald S. Cole-Turner, *An Unavoidable Challenge: Our Church in an Age of Science and Technology* (Cleveland: United Church Board for Homeland Ministries, 1992), 20.

6. Templeton, *The Humble Approach*, 39–41.

NOTES TO CHAPTER 2

1. John Marks Templeton, *The Humble Approach* (Phidadelphia, PA: Templeton Foundation Press, 1995), 118–21.

2. Ibid., 121–22.

3. William Proctor, *The Templeton Prizes* (New York: Doubleday, 1983), 2.

4. Templeton, *The Humble Approach*, 122.

5. Ibid., 125–26.

6. Ibid., 122.

7. Ibid., 123.

8. Ibid.

9. Ibid.

10. John Marks Templeton to Father Robert Sirico, the Acton Institute for the Study of Religion and Liberty, Grand Rapids, Michigan, July 5, 1991.

11. Templeton, *The Humble Approach*, 123.

12. Ibid.

13. John Marks Templeton, "The Laws of Life," *Plus* 40, no. 3 (April 1989).

14. John Marks Templeton, *Discovering the Laws of Life* (Phidadelphia, PA: Templeton Foundation Press, 1994), 3–7.

15. A Russian-language version of *Discovering the Laws of Life* for schools has been produced already. The two hundred laws of life in this version are coupled with quotations from the writings of famed Russian author Leo Tolstoy. There is also a British school edition adapted for classroom use under the direction of Templeton Foundation trustee Dr. Russell Stannard of the Open University and Reverend Stephen Orchard of the Christian Education Movement in the United Kingdom. This book, called *Looking Inward/Looking Outwards*, is produced for students of religious education (aged thirteen and up) in the British secondary schools to help them meet their legal requirement of 5 percent of religious education instruction in their daily coursework through the twelfth school year. The British version includes an appendix with information for teachers and a series of work assignments for students. In addition, *Worldwide Laws of Life* has also been published in Croatian, Slovenian, Italian, Bulgarian, Chinese, and Lithuanian.

NOTES TO CHAPTER 3

1. Quoted in John Marks Templeton, *Evidence of Purpose* (Phidadelphia, PA: Templeton Foundation Press, 1994), 7–9.

2. Paul C. Davies, *The Mind of God* (New York: Simon & Schuster, 1992), 226–27.

3. David Wilcox, "How Blind the Watchmaker?" in *Evidence of Purpose*, ed. John Marks Templeton (Philadelphia, PA: Templeton Foundation Press, 1994), 176–77.

4. Fred Hoyle, "The Universe: Past and Present Reflections," in *University of Cardiff Report 70* (1981): 43.

5. Davies, *The Mind of God*, 229.

6. Ibid., 232.

7. Russell Stannard, *Grounds for Reasonable Belief* (Edinburgh: Scottish Academic Press, 1989), 169.

Note to Chapter 4

1. In that same vein, in 2003 *Newsweek* reported results of NIH-commissioned papers showing clear evidence that churchgoers live longer than others and that churchgoing promotes healthy habits. The article continues, "In an effort to understand the health differences between believers and nonbelievers, scientists are beginning to parse the individual components that compose religious experience.... Even intangibles, such as the impact of forgiveness, may boost health as well."

Note to Chapter 5

1. Since the publication of the first edition of the biography, it has been observed by some readers as well as by some members of the advisory board that the term "humility theology" may convey the idea that Sir John is proposing a new theology, one which supercedes or even nullifies traditional views of God and the sacred writings about God. But Sir John has been quick to point out that this is not at all the intent of humility theology. Rather, the emphasis is on openness to new ideas about God and an eagerness to learn, humbly accepting that even with all our study and revelation we know almost nothing about the awesome infinite Creator of the vast universe.

See Appendixes I, K, and L for more information.

Notes to Chapter 7

1. John Marks Templeton, *The Humble Approach* (Philadelphia, PA: Templeton Foundation Press, 1995), 1–2.

2. Ibid., 32–33.

3. Robert Sollod, "A Hollow Curriculum," *The Chronicle of Higher Education* 38, no. 2 (March 18, 1992): A60.

4. Stephen Cain, "U-M Studies Ways to Instill Values," *The Ann Arbor News*, October 27, 1994.

5. Margaret Wertheim, *Zygon* 30, no. 3 (September 1995): 491–500.

NOTES TO CHAPTER 11

1. William Proctor, *The Templeton Prizes* (New York: Doubleday, 1983), 62–63.

2. "The Principle of Maximum Pessimism," *Forbes*, January 16, 1995, 68.

3. Gary Moore, *Ten Golden Rules for Financial Success* (Grand Rapids: Zondervan, 1996), 19.

4. Burton D. Morgan, "How Sir John Saved My Life," John Templeton 80th Birthday Memory Book, 1992.

NOTES TO CHAPTER 12

1. The complete list of winners is included in Appendix D.

2. This account and much of information in this and the next if chapter has been reprinted from articles I wrote during the 1990s for *Progress in Theology*, a Templeton Foundation newsletter. Used with permission.

NOTE TO CHAPTER 13

1. Advisory board members from 2000 to 2003 are listed in Appendix B.

NOTES TO CHAPTER 15

1. Advisory board members from 2000 to 2003 are listed in Appendix B.

2. Robert L. Herrmann, "How Large Is God? How Deep Is Reality?" in *How Large Is God? The Voices of Scientists and Theologians*, ed. John Marks Templeton (Philadelphia, PA: Templeton Foundation Press, 1997).

3. Information about the Institute for Research on Unlimited Love was taken from a news release prepared by Nolan/Lehr Public Relations Group.

4. W. Mark Richardson, Robert John Russell, Philip Clayton, and Kirk Wegter-McNelly, eds., *Science and the Spiritual Quest: New Essays by Leading Scientists* (London: Routledge, 2002).

5. See Appendix F for a list and brief description of subsequent symposia.

Index

The initials, JMT, are used for Sir John Marks Templeton